James Francis Hogan

The Gladstone Colony

An unwritten chapter of Australian history

James Francis Hogan

The Gladstone Colony
An unwritten chapter of Australian history

ISBN/EAN: 9783337319298

Printed in Europe, USA, Canada, Australia, Japan

Cover: Foto ©ninafisch / pixelio.de

More available books at **www.hansebooks.com**

THE
GLADSTONE COLONY

An Unwritten Chapter of Australian History

BY

JAMES FRANCIS HOGAN, M.P.

AUTHOR OF "THE IRISH IN AUSTRALIA," "THE AUSTRALIAN IN LONDON,"
"ROBERT LOWE, VISCOUNT SHERBROOKE," ETC.

LONDON
T. FISHER UNWIN
PATERNOSTER SQUARE
1898

PREFATORY NOTE

By Mr GLADSTONE

HAWARDEN, *April* 20, 1897.

DEAR MR HOGAN,

My recollections of Gladstone were most copious, and are now nearly half-a-century old.

The period, December 1845, when I became Colonial Secretary, was one when the British Government had begun to feel nonplussed by the question of Transportation. Under the pressure of this difficulty, Lord Stanley, or the Colonial Office of his day, framed a plan for the establishment, as an experiment, of a *pure* penal colony without free settlers (at least at the outset).

When I came in, the plan might have been arrested in the event of disapproval, but the Government were, I think, committed, and I had only to put the last hand to the scheme.

So it went on towards execution.

In July 1846 the Government was changed, and Lord Grey succeeded me. He said he would make none but necessary changes in pending measures. He, however, annihilated this scheme. For that I do not know that he is to be severely blamed. But he went on and dealt with the question in such a way as to produce a mess—I think more than one—far worse than any that he found. The result was the total and rather violent and summary extinction of the entire system.

Here I lost sight of the fate of "Gladstone." It has my good wishes, but I have nothing else to give.

Yours very faithful,

W. E. GLADSTONE.

CONTENTS

CHAP.		PAGE
	PREFATORY NOTE BY MR GLADSTONE	v
	INTRODUCTION	1
I.	THE GENESIS OF THE GLADSTONE COLONY	5
II.	THE CONSTITUTION OF THE NEW COLONY	22
III.	MR GLADSTONE ENUNCIATES HIS LAND POLICY	29
IV.	THE FOUNDING OF THE COLONY	37
V.	THE VETO OF EARL GREY	51
VI.	THE VINDICATION OF COLONEL BARNEY	65
VII.	THE GROWTH AND DEVELOPMENT OF GLADSTONE	71
VIII.	THE EXPERIENCES OF A PIONEER SQUATTER	85
IX.	THE GREAT GOLD RUSH	93
X.	A MARVELLOUS WILD-GOOSE CHASE	105
XI.	THE HOST OF DISAPPOINTED DIGGERS	116
XII.	THE CORRESPONDENCE OF SIR MAURICE O'CONNELL	135
XIII.	A GRIEVOUS ERROR OF MR GLADSTONE'S	150
XIV.	MAJOR DE WINTON: OLDEST LIVING GLADSTONIAN	175
XV.	THE GLADSTONE OF TO-DAY	188
XVI.	MR GLADSTONE'S TRUE PRINCIPLES OF COLONISATION	205
XVII.	MR GLADSTONE AND THE COLONIES	223
XVIII.	A COUPLE OF COLONIAL LECTURES	255
	INDEX	271

INTRODUCTION

LORD ROSEBERY, in that spirit of *persiflage* combined with shrewd common-sense which is the special characteristic of his speeches, told Mr Gladstone on one occasion that, when the time came to write his life in full, the work would have to be undertaken by, and distributed amongst, a limited liability company. As the proverb reminds us, there is many a true word said in a joke, and this is certainly a case in point, for it is obvious that no single-handed biographer, within the limits of an ordinary book, could possibly do adequate justice to the marvellous and many-sided career of Mr Gladstone. Statesman, orator, Colonial Administrator, theologian, essayist, controversialist, philanthropist, Homeric student—an interesting and instructive volume might be written on Mr Gladstone in each of these capacities. I have ventured to constitute myself the Colonial member of Lord Rosebery's Gladstonian biographical syndicate. It will probably be a surprise to many of the present generation to learn how close and intimate were the relations that subsisted for many years between Mr Gladstone and our Colonial Empire. The surprise will be shared by most of those who have already written what profess to be biographies of Mr Gladstone, and who have either entirely ignored, or dismissed in a few lines, his career as a Colonial Administrator and as the searching critic of the Colonial policy of his opponents when they were in power. Mr Gladstone has for so long been chiefly concerned with problems of domestic statesmanship that it is necessary to recall, for the information of not a few, the fact that from 1832 until 1852—for the first two decades of his unparalleled career in the House of Commons—Mr Gladstone's political talents and activities were mainly devoted to Colonial affairs. As far back as January 1835 we find him Under-Secretary for the Colonies, but it was not until ten years later, when he became Secretary of State for the Colonies in the Ministry of Sir Robert Peel, that he had the opportunity of giving full effect to his ideas on Colonial policy and Imperial administration. The circumstance that his father was a Liverpool merchant, having large commercial interests and intercourse with the Colonies, was probably not without its influence in directing the early political energies, tastes, and studies of the young and promising statesman into this particular groove.

In this book, then, I have endeavoured to present a complete and comprehensive survey of Mr Gladstone's political connection with the Colonies. For the first time a full and detailed account is given of Mr Gladstone's most interesting experiment as Colonial Secretary, namely, his attempted establishment, just fifty years ago, of a new colony to be called North Australia. That colony did not succeed in securing a permanent place on the map, but its intended metropolis—the site on which Mr Gladstone's pioneer settlers encamped—was successfully established and continues to bear Mr Gladstone's name to this day. This beautifully-situated town, with its capacious harbour—next to that of Sydney the finest on the coast of Australia—has had a singularly interesting and chequered history, and the time is opportune for writing and publishing it. In a few months Gladstone will be the terminus of the Australian transcontinental railway system. It will occupy a position on the Australian side of the Pacific analogous to that of Vancouver and San Francisco on the American side, and it does not need much of the gift of prophecy to perceive that it is destined in the not distant future to develop an importance and prosperity such as, under similar circumstances, the terminal ports of the American transcontinental railway systems have securely attained.

In addition to a full and authentic narrative of the incidents and circumstances connected with Mr Gladstone's effort to found the new colony of North Australia, and an historical sketch of the consequential rise, progress, and vicissitudes of the town of Gladstone, I have devoted some space to Mr Gladstone's ideas on the problem of the treatment and reformation of the prisoners transported from the British

Isles to the penal Colonies—a subject in which, as Colonial Secretary, he took the deepest interest, and which was the main impulse and inspiring motive of the new colony that he endeavoured to establish. As an appropriate supplement, and with a view to showing the gradual development of Mr Gladstone's views and ideas in relation to the Greater Britain beyond the seas, his principal and permanently-interesting pronouncements on Colonial and Imperial policy are given in chronological order and regular sequence. The book, I trust, will thus be found to present a complete and comprehensive, luminous and accurate account of the Colonial side of the career of the greatest English statesman of the century. It will also, I venture to hope, be deemed not unworthy of perusal as a striking and suggestive object lesson in the art of colonisation—a concrete example of pioneering work within a limited compass. There are many books dealing with colonisation in general, and covering large areas of colonising activity; here, in the Gladstone Colony, we have a study of a single colonising experiment, within the confines of a comparatively small district, conducted for half a century under diverse conditions and with varying fortunes until now, when we see the metropolis, of which Mr Gladstone laid the foundation-stone just fifty years ago, springing at last into power and prominence, asserting itself as a leading Australian centre, and giving every promise of becoming one of the most prosperous and progressive of the ports of the Pacific.

[In his recently published "History of the Catholic Church in Australasia," Cardinal Moran, Archbishop of Sydney, identifies Port Curtis—the harbour of Gladstone—as the spot on which the famous Spanish navigator, De Quiros, landed in 1606. "The trend of the land from east to west, the row of islands in front of the harbour, the large Curtis Island at the distance of a few miles, all correspond to the 'Harbour of the Holy Cross' in which De Quiros cast anchor." The Cardinal is convinced that it was on the shores of Port Curtis the first celebration of Mass on the Australian continent took place. It also appears from the same valuable work that Archbishop Polding, the first Catholic Primate of Australia, suggested Gladstone as the seat of a new bishopric in 1858].

CHAPTER I

THE GENESIS OF THE GLADSTONE COLONY

TAKE up the map of Australia and run your finger along the Tropic of Capricorn until you come to the point where the tropic intersects the eastern coast of the Australian continent. Directly underneath you will see the town of Gladstone at the head of Port Curtis. That town has a strange and eventful history which it is the purpose of these pages to unfold and narrate.

When the Right Hon. W. E. Gladstone came into office in December, 1845, as Secretary of State for the Colonies, he found himself confronted with a problem of considerable complexity and unavoidable urgency. Six years previously the transportation of British convicts to New South Wales had ceased, partly as the result of the shocking revelations elicited by a House of Commons Committee of Enquiry, and partly owing to the strong remonstrances of the large numbers of free and crimeless British emigrants who had become permanent settlers in the Colony. The extensive territory that, for more than half-a-century, had been utilised as the principal penal settlement of the British Isles, being now no longer available for the absorption of prisoners, the full stream of convictism had to be diverted to the only remaining penal colony of Australasia, the comparatively small island then known as Van Diemen's Land, now the self-governing Colony of Tasmania. Strange as it may sound in our latter-day ears, the fact is unimpeachable that, during the first half of the nineteenth century, nobody in authority considered it the duty of England to keep her criminals within her own shores. The general conception of a colony in official circles was — a convenient receptacle for British convicts. The natural and inevitable consequence of the cessation of transportation to New South Wales was to flood Van Diemen's Land with the convict element. Transported prisoners were poured in at the rate of five thousand a year. The aggregation of so much vice and criminality on a small island resulted in a repetition and a re-enacting of the hideous horrors that had appalled the nation a few years before. The labour market became disorganised by a chronic redundancy of hands; there was no security for life or property, and large numbers of time-expired convicts were roaming about the colony unable to find work, a standing menace to public order and a constant terror to peaceable settlers.

This was the disagreeable and dangerous situation that Mr Gladstone had to face on assuming office as Colonial Secretary in the Ministry of Sir Robert Peel. His predecessor in Downing Street, Lord Stanley, had also pondered over the perplexing problem, and had a hazy idea of a solution in the shape of a new penal colony in the uninhabited northern regions of Australia. What is now the great Colony of Queensland was then nominally attached to New South Wales, and was known as the "northern district." But the district, or any portion of it, could, at any time, be detached by the Imperial Government, and erected into a new colony by an order of the Queen-in-Council. The project, however, was only in a nebulous and embryonic condition when Lord Stanley retired from office. It was Mr Gladstone who gave it form and substance, and who took all the official steps necessary to convert suggestion into action.

The germ of the Gladstone Colony, the first formulation of the ideas that eventually found expression in this novel experiment, is to be found in a despatch dated Downing Street, April 30, 1846, and addressed by Mr Gladstone to Sir Charles Fitzroy, the newly-appointed Governor of New South Wales. Mr Gladstone began by intimating his desire that Sir Charles should, at the commencement of his administrative duties, be placed in full and definite possession of the views of Her Majesty's Government with regard to the introduction of convicts. The new Governor is reminded that the practice of sending transported convicts to New South Wales had ceased for some years, and that this cessation was commonly reported to rest upon a promise to that effect made by the Imperial Government in or about the year 1839. Then comes a delightfully Gladstonian passage. The fact of this promise having been made could not be denied, inasmuch as it was a matter of general notoriety and even of official record on the minutes of the Queen-in-Council, and therefore Mr Gladstone skates over the thinnest of ice in this consummate fashion :—" I do not think it necessary to examine the origin, or to question the accuracy of, this opinion, for, taking together the subject matter to which it refers, and the extent to which it prevails, I am inclined to believe that the practical mischief of exciting jealousies by controverting it would be greater than any that can arise from acquiescence in the assumption of its correctness." Even at this comparatively early period of his political career, Mr Gladstone seems to have been a past master in the art of distracting attention from an awkward point by surrounding it with a cloud of rhetorical dust.

Mr Gladstone proceeds to assure Sir Charles Fitzroy that Her Majesty's Government has no intention of resuming the transportation of convicts to New South Wales without the general approval of the colony. At the same time, they are desirous to lessen the number of convicts annually sent to Van Diemen's Land, and they therefore suggest whether it might not be a measure favourable to the material fortunes of New South Wales, and unattended with injury to its higher interests, to introduce, either directly from England at the commencement of their sentences, or from Van Diemen's Land during their course, a number of prisoners, small in comparison with the numbers carried to the colony under the former system of transportation, and smaller still, relatively, to the augmented population among whom they would now be dispersed. Those prisoners would be employed upon a system different to that of former times, under which the abuses then complained of were generated. Mr Gladstone emphasised his suggestion by indicating the probability of the time being at hand, if it had not already arrived, when the supply of free labour in Australia would be unequal to the demand. In the district around Melbourne, he said, the unequivocal signs of a scarcity of free labour had already begun to appear, and had taken a direction not unnatural, namely, a desire for the introduction of prisoners passing through the late stages of their sentences in Van Diemen's Land. Such emancipated labourers would be thinly dispersed amongst the general population, would form a scarcely perceptible element in the composition of society, and would enjoy those favourable opportunities of improving habits and character which transportation, according to its original theory, was designed to afford. Mr Gladstone concluded with an intimation to Sir Charles Fitzroy to ascertain the sentiments of the colonists on two questions:—first, as to the advisability of introducing into New South Wales, either under engagement or as candidates for private employment, persons who had passed through their periods of probation in Van Diemen's Land; and secondly, as to the willingness of the colonists to receive regularly a limited number of convicts from England to be employed on such works as the making and repairing of the public roads, "always presuming that such occupations are neither destructive to health nor essentially liable to moral objections, and therefore at variance with the reformatory principles on which it is the earnest desire of Her Majesty's Government to regulate the system of transportation."

Mr Gladstone had marked this despatch "Private and Confidential," but in a postscript he left it to the discretion of Sir Charles Fitzroy to communicate its contents to the public if the Governor considered that course the more desirable. In the exercise of this discretion Sir Charles did publish the despatch a few days after its receipt, and the result was an immediate and formidable agitation against the re-introduction of convictism in any shape or form. This agitation was headed by the *Sydney Morning Herald* in the press, and by the Hon. Robert Lowe in the legislature and on the platform. Mr Lowe, who was destined in after years to became in turn Mr Gladstone's keenest critic on the floor of the House of Commons and his distinguished colleague on the Treasury bench, was, at this time, a leading Australian barrister, the writer of stinging articles in the *Atlas*, and the member for the combined counties of Auckland and St

Vincent in the one rudimentary legislative chamber that then existed in the whole of Australia and deliberated in Sydney. By his vehement and eloquent denunciations of the attempted revival of the transportation system, Lowe attained the highest pinnacle of popularity in the southern hemisphere. Not only was he triumphantly returned for the city of Sydney at the first opportunity; not only did he harangue vast and excited crowds from the roofs of omnibuses and the stages of theatres, but on more than one occasion his carriage was unhorsed and he was drawn to his residence by an admiring and vociferous populace. What a strange and dramatic contrast to the after-years in the northern hemisphere, when he was mobbed and hooted in Whitehall, and when he became the object of the utmost dislike and detestation by the British democracy!

Mr Gladstone's proposals for the revival of transportation in a guarded and modified form, although approved by the Committee of the Legislative Council, to whom they were referred for consideration and report, were rendered abortive by the strength and unanimity of the popular opposition, fanned and headed by Lowe and the other leaders of the anti-transportation movement. Mr Gladstone therefore proceeded with his plans for carving out a new colony in the north as the theatre and testing-ground of his transportation policy. He selected as the adminstrative head of the new settlement a distinguished officer of the Royal Engineers, Lieutenant-Colonel George Barney, who was, at the time, in command at Woolwich, but who had previously served with his regiment in Australia, and, while there, had practical experience of the management and discipline of convicts. Colonel Barney proceeded to Sydney as soon as practicable, and having presented his credentials to Sir Charles Fitzroy, voyaged northwards along the coast to discover and decide upon the most suitable site for the first settlement and landing-place. It might easily have been predicted that his choice would fall upon the shores of Port Curtis, for not only was that the finest and most spacious harbour—that of Sydney alone excepted—on the whole eastern coast of Australia, but it was sufficiently near to Sydney to avert the danger of being cut off from the only available base of supplies, and at the same time sufficiently remote to leave no reasonable ground of objection to the sensitive Sydney people that Mr Gladstone was starting a new penal colony at their doors, although the *Sydney Morning Herald* did describe it in a somewhat exaggerated style as "a monster prowling along our northern frontier."

Port Curtis was discovered * by Captain Matthew Flinders on August 4, 1802, when voyaging northwards along the coast from Sydney. His famous predecessor in the work of discovery, Captain Cook, had sailed by in the night, and missed seeing the entrance to this particular harbour. "In honour of Admiral Sir Roger Curtis, who had commanded at the Cape of Good Hope, and been so attentive to our wants, I gave to it the name of Port Curtis," Flinders records at page 19 of the second volume of his "Voyage to Terra Australis." A number of blacks gathered on the shore and protested against the landing of the white men by volleys of stones, but they soon disappeared when two or three muskets were fired over their heads. Seven bark canoes were found lying on the shore, and near them, hanging upon a tree, were some parts of a turtle and a few scoop nets. Taking provisions for two days, Flinders set out in the whale boat to make a systematic examination of the port, which he describes with characteristic care and minuteness. He found the contiguous country covered with grass. The soil, being either sandy or covered with loose stones, he considered generally incapable of cultivation. The shores and low islands were overspread with mangroves. Traces of inhabitants were found wherever Flinders and his companions landed, but the blacks kept out of sight, being evidently frightened by the reports of the guns on the first day that they saw and attacked the white men. These blacks lived luxuriously on turtle. Flinders himself saw three turtles lying on the water, and he laments his ill-luck in not being able to secure a supply of the aldermanic dainty. Fish seemed to be plentiful, but the white men's efforts to catch them were also unsuccessful. The shores abounded with oysters, amongst them the species producing pearls, but being small and discoloured, the Port Curtis pearls were of

---

* See Note, p. 3.

no value. Fresh water was found in small pools on both sides of the northern entrance to the port. Captain Flinders concluded his stay in Port Curtis at daylight on the morning of August 9. He had a misadventure on leaving, which seems to show that "scamping" work was as common at the beginning as it is at the end of the nineteenth century. "On getting under way at daylight of the 9th," he writes, "to prosecute the examination of the coast, the anchor came up with an arm broken off, in consequence of a flaw extending two-thirds through the iron. The negligence with which this anchor had been made might, in some cases, have caused the loss of the ship."

Twenty years afterwards Port Curtis was visited by Mr John Oxley, the then Surveyor-General of New South Wales.

He left Sydney on October 23, 1823, in His Majesty's cutter, the *Mermaid*, for a cruise to the northward in search of a suitable site for a new convict settlement. The *Mermaid* anchored in Port Curtis on November 5, and Mr Oxley proceeded to explore the harbour and the surrounding country. The impressions he formed were not favourable. He thus summarised them in his official report:—" Having viewed and examined, with the most anxious attention, every point that afforded the least promise of being eligible for the site of a settlement, I respectfully submit it as my opinion that Port Curtis and its vicinity do not afford such a site; and I do not think that any convict establishment could be formed there that would return, either from the natural productions of the country, or as arising from agricultural labour, any portion of the great expense which would necessarily attend its first formation. In short, it did not appear to me that the country, taking it in an extended sense, could either afford subsistence, or supply the means of profitable labour for a large establishment; and even in one on the smallest scale the greatest difficulties would arise from the scarcity of timber for building, and of bark and shingles for covering."

Mr John Uniacke, a member of Oxley's Expedition, published a graphic and interesting narrative of the proceedings of the party. He says that throughout the whole of their first night at Port Curtis they were persecuted by mosquitoes and sand-flies. At six o'clock next morning they started to survey the country, leaving a corporal and three men in charge of the tents. They saw several kangaroos, but could not get near enough to shoot them. They did not descry a single blackfellow, although they came across a grave at the foot of a large tree, the wood of which was deeply engraved with a variety of rude symbols, from which they judged that it was the resting-place of a mighty hunter. Mr Uniacke appears to have been more favourably impressed with the productive possibilities of the country than Mr Oxley, for at one stage of the journey he records :—" The soil here was of the richest description, and calculated to grow cotton, sugar, indigo, and all other Indian productions." Time and experience have shown this opinion to be well-founded, for the vicinity of Port Curtis is one of the chief centres of the sugar-growing industry. What struck and alarmed the party most was the evidence of tremendous floods they observed in their travels. Mr Uniacke says he saw in many of the trees, at least sixty feet above the level of the water, the wreck which had been deposited by successive inundations. On the banks of a river flowing into Port Curtis, which they christened the Boyne, they saw three or four different kinds of timber, but the quantity was comparatively small. The river was covered with multitudes of teals, widgeons, and wild ducks. Mr Uniacke's account of their last excursion into the Port Curtis country would seem to indicate that Mr Oxley was unduly pessimistic in his conclusions:—" The country through which we passed this day was similar to what we had seen the day before. The timber was, however, becoming larger and more plentiful. In many places the right bank of the river was composed of a remarkably fine slate, while the left was a hard, close-grained grey granite, and the soil everywhere rich and fertile. Before we returned we ascended a high hill on the left, from which we had a beautiful and extensive view of the river for many miles through a rich brush country, the banks, in many parts, well-clothed with timber. A very lofty range of hills formed a fine termination to the scene. On our return we were fortunate enough to shoot a brace of wild ducks, and catch a good deal of perch, with which, and many other descriptions of fish, the beautiful river abounds." Mr Uniacke concluded by expressing a fear that this splendid river—the Boyne—could never be turned to practical account for the purposes of colonisation in consequence of the excessive floods to which it was evidently subject, but the prophecy has been completely falsified by the events of subsequent years.

The waters around Port Curtis were not at that time ideally suitable for bathing, nevertheless several members of the expedition, tortured by the intensity of the heat, ventured in. Mr Uniacke mentions that "in all parts of the harbour we saw a great many green and black snakes playing about in the water, while the number and boldness of the sharks exceeded credibility. They were continually striking at the oars, and one large one very nearly succeeded in pulling the steer-oar out of Mr Penson's hands."

An interesting incident of the Oxley Expedition was the rescue of a couple of shipwrecked sailors who had been living with the blacks for seven months. When the *Mermaid* cast anchor in the Pumice-stone River, a number of natives were seen approaching. Mr Uniacke scrutinised them with a glass from the masthead, and his attention was arrested by one who appeared much taller than the others, and of a lighter colour. This man hailed the ship in English from the shore. A boat was immediately launched, and Mr Oxley, Mr Stirling, and Mr Uniacke hastened ashore. As the boat advanced to the beach, the blacks indulged in demonstrations of joy, danced, and embraced the white man. He turned out to be Thomas Pamphlet. He was one of a crew of four on a small vessel that left Sydney in quest of a cargo of cedar, but which was blown out of her course and wrecked on this part of the Australian coast. They were twenty-one days without water, and one perished of thirst. Pamphlet and his two surviving companions, Richard Parsons and John Finnegan, endeavoured to walk along the coast to Sydney, but Pamphlet, after having accomplished fifty miles, broke down and returned to the blacks, who treated him with much kindness. Finnegan also abandoned the project and cast in his lot with the blacks. Parsons probably perished in the attempt.

As far back as 1822 Mr J. T. Bigge, the Commissioner appointed by the Imperial Government to enquire into the condition of the Colony of New South Wales, recommended the formation of a convict settlement at Port Curtis, on the shores of which, a quarter of a century afterwards, the actual experiment was attempted at the instance of Mr Gladstone. Mr Bigge contemplated the employment of the convicts in the cultivation of maize, vegetables, flax, and tobacco, and the collection and preparation of bark. He estimated the total annual expenses of his proposed new settlement at Port Curtis, on the assumption that three thousand convicts would be sent there, at £82,304, 17s. 2d., with a supplementary estimate of £6400 for Government buildings. But the Home Government at the time was not disposed to incur this heavy annual expenditure, and so the Imperial Commissioner's recommendation was duly pigeon-holed and forgotten.

Early in 1839 the project was revived. On the second day of January in that year, Lord John Russell published what he described as a "Note on Transportation and Secondary Punishment," which, from its length and elaborate treatment, would have been more accurately termed a treatise or essay. In this production he developed a theory of probationary punishment for transported convicts, which was to be partially carried into effect either in Norfolk Island, or Tasmania, "or in a new colony in Australia." Later on, his Lordship says, if his plan would be adopted, "it would be advisable to send instructions to New South Wales and Van Diemen's Land to make preparations for the change. A new settlement on the northern coast of New Holland would, of course, require extensive arrangements."

In reply to an invitation from Lord John Russell, Sir Richard Bourke, the late Governor of New South Wales, stated his views on the subject, and endorsed the suggestion of creating a new penal colony in Northern Australia. Under date December 26, 1838, Sir Richard wrote:—"If transportation to New South Wales be discontinued, some other vent must be found for criminals sentenced to that punishment, or some other punishment must be substituted. I will venture to express my apprehension of the success of penitentiaries upon a scale of such magnitude as to contain the whole number of offenders now sentenced to transportation. The expense of such a measure would be immense, and in countries fully peopled, as Great Britain and Ireland, it would be a hazardous experiment to return to the population the numbers who would annually be discharged from these prisons as sentences expired. To obviate this inconvenience, the Committee, in the Report to which I have referred, recommend a course which would be grievously expensive to England, and, upon the view they take of convictism, hardly less objectionable as to the Colonies, than transportation as now conducted. Better far, in my opinion, to lay the foundation of a new colony on the northern coast of New Holland, under management improved by the experience derived from New South Wales and Van Diemen's Land."

Lord Stanley, writing to Sir Eardley Wilmot, Governor of Van Diemen's Land, in September, 1845, emphasised the wisdom and the propriety of providing a certain and regular outlet for the liberated convicts who threw themselves on the Government of Van Diemen's Land for support, on the allegation frequently made, and probably well-founded, that they were unable to obtain employment and wages either there or in the adjacent Colonies. In order to provide such a resource, it was proposed to establish a new colony in North Australia, to which would be conveyed all such liberated convicts as might solicit support from State funds. The certainty of being able to obtain the labour of these men would probably invite capitalists to settle in the new colony, but even on the opposite supposition, Lord Stanley thought the liberated convicts arriving there would, with comparatively little aid from the Government, be able to maintain themselves by the cultivation of lands to be assigned to them for that purpose.

Lord Stanley then proceeded to state and answer the objections that might be raised to the creation of the new colony. The first was that North Australia was too tropical a region to be cultivated by European labourers. To this Lord Stanley replied that the laws, both meteorological and sanatory, which prevailed in other quarters of the globe were so modified in Australia that little or no reliance could, in this particular case, be placed on the supposed influence of tropical climates in general on the European constitution. At Moreton Bay, which was only one degree and a half more distant from the Equator than the site of the proposed new colony of North Australia, convicts and free settlers had, for many years, laboured in the open air with no inconvenience and without prejudice to their health.

Secondly, it might be objected that there was no evidence of the practicability of the scheme. To this the answer was that the occupation of North Australia as a convict settlement had been recommended by such an able and experienced Governor of New South Wales as Sir Richard Bourke, and by such a practical and well-informed colonist as the Rev. Dr. Lang in his evidence before the House of Commons Committee in 1837. Other witnesses before the same Committee had repeatedly referred to it as a practicable scheme. In Lord Stanley's judgment, the facility, so often proved, of making settlements along the eastern shores of Australia excluded any reasonable doubt under this head.

Thirdly, the expense of settling such a colony might be represented as an almost conclusive objection. Lord Stanley's answer was, that if, eventually, it should expand into a wealthy and populous settlement, the inhabitants would be able and willing to defray the charge of their own government. This, however, was a result not to be expected for a long time to come. Perhaps it was not to be desired. While maintained exclusively or chiefly as a receptacle and place of refuge for liberated convicts, the local government and all its institutions would be managed on a scale so humble, moderate, and frugal, as not to exceed the charge for the government of Norfolk Island—another penal dependency of New South Wales—without the burden of the responsibility encountered there for the maintenance of the inhabitants. In such a climate, with such a soil, and with some preliminary aid, the first settlers in North Australia would certainly be able, and might reasonably be required, to maintain themselves.

The last, and what Lord Stanley considered the most serious objection was, that the community of the proposed new colony would be composed of males only—an objection that would be conclusive, unless admitting of some satisfactory answer. Lord Stanley answered it by saying that it was contemplated to send to North Australia for the future, if not the whole, at least a large portion of the female convicts from England, and a similar course might be pursued with regard to those transported to Van Diemen's Land, who might be considered the most deserving, and who were in need of employment. Most of the transported female convicts were unmarried women, with whom the emancipated male convicts might therefore form legitimate unions. But the transportation of married men was no infrequent occurrence. After a convict of that class had regained his freedom, the sending of his wife and children to join him in North Australia would often be a measure, which, in Lord Stanley's belief, parishes and British poor-law unions would be disposed to undertake on the ground of economy. It was probable, also, that the female population of the colony would be increased by migration of families from New South Wales. But if, after all, there should still be no due proportion of females in North Australia, the deficiency could be supplied by emigration from the Mother Country. A larger proportion of female emigrants than had been customary could be despatched, and Lord Stanley did not anticipate that Parliament would withhold the funds that would be necessary to provide for such an object.

Sir James Graham, as Home Secretary, wrote on September 10, 1845, that he entirely approved of the plan for establishing a new colony in North Australia, and was most anxious to see it carried into immediate execution. It also appeared to him that the course of proceedings indicated by Lord Stanley was very judicious, and that the reasons in support of it were sound and stated with great ability.

On the following November 21, 1845, Lord Stanley approached the Lords Commissioners of the Treasury on the subject of the creation of his proposed new colony, pointing out that the convict population in Van Diemen's Land far exceeded any effective demand which existed for their labour in that island, and that thus the evil of a great population living, not by a healthy competition for employment, but by an habitual and listless dependence on the public purse, had reached a grave and formidable height. Such a state of things induced habits of indolence and apathy, most injurious to the growth of those social and personal virtues that were peculiarly requisite in a society composed of such elements. It also impaired, even where it did not entirely destroy, the efficacy of pardons or of relaxations of punishment, considered as stimulants to activity and good conduct. For when the condition of those who possessed such rewards was palpably and notoriously as much depressed, dependent and uninviting as was the condition of those who did not possess them, it followed, as a matter of course, that no strenuous effort would be made to secure so equivocal an advantage. To this was to be added the consideration that the effect of their inability to earn a decent maintenance by independent labour, threw together, on the hands of the local government, a great mass of persons who, though differing in character, capacity, and good or ill desert, were all, of necessity, reduced to the same general level, and compelled to associate together as fellow-workmen in the same pursuits—an association inducing among the whole body the same low tone of moral feeling, and the same degrading and lamentable habits. The migration of pardoned convicts to neighbouring colonies would always be liable to be checked by fluctuations in the demand for labour there, and would probably be resisted by a popular feeling with which it might be found useless to struggle. In Lord Stanley's opinion, the difficulties of the situation could only be adequately met by founding a new colony in North Australia, to be settled partly by pardoned convicts from Van Diemen's Land, and partly by that class of prisoners who had recently been sent from the Mother Country under the designation of exiles. Contemplating the proposed new colony only as a receptacle for these classes, and not anticipating that they would resort thither in any large numbers for some years to come, Lord Stanley expressed his belief that the establishments, official salaries, and public works undertaken there should be on the lowest and most moderate scale. In that, as in every other society, provision would have to be made for the enactment and execution of laws for the maintenance of the public peace, the collection of the public revenue, and the care of public property; but high-salaried and elaborately-titled functionaries were not necessary for the performance of these functions in an infant colony with scanty resources. In Lord Stanley's opinion, the formation of the new colony would necessarily be gradual, and probably slow, but it would supply a resource of which men of energetic minds and habits would gladly avail themselves. It would give to pardons a palpable and immediate advantage, and would stimulate the candidates for them to self-denying, industrious, and virtuous habits. It would also supply an effectual check to the spirit of listless dependence on the Government, into which the pardoned convicts of Van Diemen's Land so readily, and perhaps unavoidably, fell, because to every such person would then be tendered the alternative of finding an honest maintenance for himself elsewhere, or of becoming a settler in the new colony, where such a maintenance would be within his reach. On the last point, Lord Stanley declared that he did not entertain the shadow of a doubt. The history of British colonisation in every part of the world, and especially in Australia, appeared to him to justify the belief that a body of natives of the British Isles, thrown on their own resources, on a productive soil and in a favourable climate, and placed under the guidance of an intelligent and active leader, would rapidly secure for themselves all the necessaries and many of the comforts of life. They would require no other aid than an adequate supply of such provisions as might be necessary during the first year of their settlement—cattle, seed-corn, tools, a stock of plain but strong clothing, and sufficient bedding to last for twelve months. Thus equipped, the earliest body of settlers in North Australia would, as in Western Australia, South Australia, and Port Phillip, prepare within two or three years, under proper guidance, everything requisite for the reception of their successors, and in a very short space of time such a settlement might be able to defray the charge of its own government.

Lord Stanley concluded with a series of recommendations

to the Lords Commissioners of the Treasury, of which the following may be mentioned:—

That the expense of founding the new colony should be defrayed from the funds appropriated by Parliament for convict services.

That, with the concurrence of the Home Secretary, all exiles—that is, convicts transported with pardons to take effect immediately on their landing—should, for the future, be conveyed to North Australia.

That all pardoned convicts in Van Diemen's Land, unable or unwilling to earn an independent subsistence, should also be removed to North Australia.

That, for the next three years, all pardoned convicts arriving in North Australia should, during one year after their arrival, and no longer, be provided with rations, clothing, tools, seats, bedding, and tents for immediate shelter, except in cases of wilful indolence or other misconduct which might justify the withholding of such allowances in any particular case; and that at the end of three years from the foundation of the colony no such allowance should be made to any settler, except on proof that there were no means open to him of obtaining a maintenance by his own labour.

That all settlers receiving rations and other allowances should be bound to work, not only at preparing huts for their own residence, and ground for their own subsistence, but also in effecting such indispensable public works as might be approved by the Governor of New South Wales, who should also be armed with all necessary powers for investigating, and, as far as possible, correcting any errors that might be brought to light.

The Lords Commissioners of the Treasury did not reply to this communication until February 2, 1846, and in the interim Mr Gladstone had succeeded Lord Stanley as Secretary of State for the Colonies. Their Lordships informed Mr Gladstone that the state of society in Van Diemen's Land, as depicted in the various documents which had been brought under their notice, had been to them a source of the most painful consideration. They could not conceal from themselves the necessity of providing some outlet for that portion of the population who, having expiated their crimes, had attained a condition of limited or absolute freedom from restraint. Having regard to the manner in which such persons, for the most part, appeared to be then living in Van Diemen's Land, their Lordships entertained serious doubts whether there would be any disposition on their part to adventure a change which, whatever might be the advantages of North Australia in regard to soil and climate, must necessarily be, for a time at least, attended by great labour and much anxiety. Their Lordships therefore asked Mr Gladstone to consider whether it would not be expedient to hold out to such persons, on their removal to North Australia, some additional inducement, either by grant of land to a limited extent, or by the promise of other advantages. But the necessity of affording relief to Van Diemen's Land was so urgent, and the obligation upon the Government of finding for the better class of exiles, who had made some progress in reform, a refuge from the contamination to which they were then exposed, was so imperative, that their Lordships did not feel justified in refusing their acquiescence in the formation of the proposed new colony, approved, as it had also been, by the Secretary of State for the Home Department. They would therefore give directions for including this charge, as estimated by Lord Stanley, in the vote for convict expenditure for the ensuing year, but they would request Mr Gladstone to take measures for ascertaining, at the earliest possible period, what would be the amount of additional expenditure it might be necessary to incur. They also asked Mr Gladstone particularly to inculcate upon the Governor of New South Wales, to whom the foundation of the new colony was to be entrusted, the extreme importance of so framing his estimate as to confine the expense to what might be absolutely indispensable, and of selecting parties to fill the proposed new appointments as far as possible from those persons whose previous employment in the convict departments and service might have given them claims to consideration and compensation, the colony being, in the first instance, to be considered rather as an experiment than as a settled and permanent establishment.

CHAPTER II

THE CONSTITUTION OF THE NEW COLONY

THE consent of the Treasury having been thus obtained, Mr Gladstone lost no time in translating the theory of North Australia into actual fact. As Mr W. H. Traill truly observes in his "Historical Sketch of Queensland:"—The idea of thus combining a colonisation of territory with a humanitarian scheme for affording opportunities to offenders to retrieve the past and co-operate in mutual reformation, appears to have had a peculiar fascination for the mind of Mr Gladstone, who threw himself heart and soul into the task of its accomplishment. Beaten on the anvil of his powerful and imaginative mind the project expanded, and took definite and even attractive form. Having observed the formation in New South Wales of a regular and law-abiding community, evolved out of a revolting chaos of elements, chiefly evil, and despite the absence of all sorts of encouragement, and, in fact, despite every disadvantage which ignorant and careless misgovernment could interpose, he might naturally contemplate with sanguine expectancy the operations and possible results of a scheme, thoughtfully defined and conducted with a prudent mingling of paternal authority and solicitous affection for the welfare of the participants. He entered into a copious correspondence with his colleagues and with the Governor of New South Wales. He was at pains to secure the assent of the Treasury, ever apt to veto projects which would require for their realisation disbursements previously unprecedented. As it was hopeless to expect any reformation in a community from which the softening and refining influence of domestic life should be withheld, he made arrangements for the conveyance in advance to North Australia of the families of the happy exiles. From the prisons and the workhouses he looked to procure female emigrants. Expiree offenders were also to be encouraged to proceed thither. In March, 1846, he formally offered Colonel Barney the charge of the proposed new colony, impressing upon him at the same time the importance of the trust, and the necessity for "the promotion, by all means in your power, of a healthy moral tone in the community whose foundations you are about to lay." Mr Traill adds a statement that Mr Gladstone's scheme for the establishment of a North Australian colony was accepted with considerable favour by the pastoralists of Moreton Bay and all the surrounding districts. In consequence of the cessation of transportation, the ordinary supply of labour had already begun to fail, and the squatters looked hopefully to the new colony as likely to meet their requirements in that particular.

On May 7, 1846, in a lengthy communication addressed to Sir Charles Fitzroy at Sydney, Mr Gladstone laid down what may be called the ground plan or general constitution of the new colony. He commenced by citing a series of Parliamentary papers from which, he said, Sir Charles Fitzroy would learn, with all necessary precision and copiousness, the motives by which Her Majesty had been induced to erect into a separate colony, to be called North Australia, such of the territories comprised within the Colony of New South Wales as lay to the northward of the twenty-sixth degree of south latitude. The letters patent constituting Sir Charles the first Governor of the new colony were then quoted, and Mr Gladstone proceeded to inform the Governor that he would gather from the documents referred to, that the new colony had been founded as a receptacle for convicts who, by pardon or by lapse of time, had regained their freedom, but who might be unable to find elsewhere an effective demand for their services. If the principles on which the settlement of new countries ought to be effected were alone to be considered, to the exclusion of the actual state of affairs then existing in the Australian Colonies, the foundation of the proposed colony, with settlers such as he had mentioned, could not, Mr Gladstone admitted, be vindicated, and this, he added, was also the full conviction of his predecessor.

No truths could at once be more familiar, weighty, and indisputable than that the first rudiments of every new colony should be selected from the most virtuous, intelligent, and hardy classes of the colonising state, and should be composed of capitalists and manual labourers bearing a due proportion to each other. Mr Gladstone sincerely and deeply regretted the impossibility of taking those great principles as his guide in the present instance. The obstacles which forbade it were generally these: public opinion had demanded, and Parliament had enacted, the abolition of the punishment of death in almost all cases, except treason, murder, and the infliction of wounds or injuries with a murderous intention. Hence the importance of an effective secondary punishment had become greater than at any former period, and transportation was the only such punishment to which it had been found practicable to resort. For the present, therefore, it formed an indispensable part and adjunct of the penal code in its mitigated form.

But it had been found practically impossible to enforce, to their full extent, sentences of transportation for life or for long terms of years. Excluded from hope, the transported convict would sink into a state of moral and intellectual debasement, and of physical infirmity, which would render him the victim of a premature death, and, in the meantime, a burden to himself and a scourge to the society of which he formed a part. Every year, therefore, necessarily made a considerable addition to the number of the pardoned class. In each year, also, some would be added to the class of those who had attained their freedom by the mere lapse of time and the expiration of their sentences. Another class of persons sentenced to transportation was formed of those who commenced their term of punishment in British penitentiaries. In these establishments their characters were, to a large extent, disclosed and studied, and the best among them received pardons on reaching the place of transportation. These were distinguished by the name of exiles. Thus the free population of the convict colonies was being continually increased by the accession of persons emancipated by pardon, by length of service, or as exiles. After making the necessary deduction for intermediate deaths, Mr Gladstone calculated that between three and four thousand persons were, in this manner, added annually to the free class, and thus became candidates for wages or other means of subsistence.

But it had happened, either by the enactment of positive laws or by pledges said to have been given by the Imperial Government, that no places were left in Australasia for the reception of transported convicts from the United Kingdom except Van Diemen's Land and Norfolk Island. And, practically, owing to the system in force in the latter, the great annual accession of free labourers took place in Van Diemen's Land alone. This, aided by the operation of collateral circumstances, had resulted, according to the reports of Governor Sir Eardley Wilmot, in such an accumulation of free people seeking wages in Van Diemen's Land as effectually to choke up all the avenues to employment. Not only were large bodies of the emancipated class destitute of the means of earning an independent subsistence, but those who had been partially emancipated—holders of tickets-of-leave and probation passes—were deprived, by this competition, of the benefits of those indulgences. The pressure on the free settlers was not less severe or distressing. On the whole, it was imperative that either some vent must be found for the redundant population, or the United Kingdom must be deprived of the only effective secondary punishment, in reliance on which the punishment of death had been discontinued. It was to afford this relief that the plan of establishing the new colony of North Australia, as a distinct settlement for the reception of persons, collectively distinguished as emancipists, had been adopted.

At the same time, Mr Gladstone declared that it was entirely remote from his purpose to form in North Australia a government on a large or expensive scale. It was a fundamental and essential part of his design that the local establishments should be maintained on a low and moderate scale in the matters of emolument, rank, and the titular distinctions to be enjoyed by the various officers employed there. Thus the actual administrator of the Government would bear the title of Superintendent, and the chief judge would be designated as Chairman of Quarter Sessions. The

Superintendent was to be implicitly guided by instructions from the Governor of New South Wales, who was empowered to visit the new colony at any time, and assume in person its temporary administration. It would not be competent for the Superintendent to assent to any law, create any new office, or sanction any expenditure of public money, without the previous authority, either special or general, of the Governor of New South Wales. At the same time, North Australia would be a perfectly distinct colony, under a perfectly distinct government, although the authority which the Secretary of State for the Colonies would otherwise exercise, had been deputed, in the first instance, to the Governor of New South Wales. The object of thus delegating his control, Mr Gladstone explained, was to secure for the proceedings of the new colony—and especially for its earlier proceedings—a supervision more prompt, more effective, and motived by an earlier and more complete intelligence than could characterise any supervision emanating from Downing Street.

North Australia would at first be destitute of any local laws adapted to the wants of the inhabitants. But the law of England was a code which, without some adaptation to local circumstances, would inevitably raise perplexing and even insuperable difficulties, and therefore Mr Gladstone thought it would be convenient that the first act of the legislature of the new colony should be the adoption of the modification of English law in force in New South Wales. Commencing thus, the legislature of North Australia might gradually, and at leisure, adapt the other parts of English or Colonial law to the exigencies of the new society.

In the selection of the public officers of North Australia Mr Gladstone confined himself to the choice of the Superintendent, Colonel Barney, and the Chairman of Quarter Sessions, W. W. Billyard, Esq., although, he added, it was probable that a chaplain also would be appointed from England. Mr Gladstone preferred to leave to Colonel Barney the selection, in New South Wales, of all the other original officers of the Government. They would be few in number, and their emoluments would be of small amount, yet not, Mr Gladstone hoped, so small as would be insufficient to induce competent persons in New South Wales to accept the offices in question.

With respect to the removal of emancipists from Van Diemen's Land to North Australia, Mr Gladstone pointed out that the transference would not be practicable until after the lapse of a few months from the first foundation of the settlement. The earliest settlers would be exiles sent from England, whose arrival might be expected about the beginning of 1847. With their assistance, and the aid of such other persons as might be at his disposal, the Superintendent would make preparations for the reception of the emancipists. He would from time to time report to the Governor of New South Wales the progress of these preparations, and what number of new settlers could properly and safely be admitted into North Australia. It would be in the power of the major-general commanding the Imperial troops in New South Wales to detach to North Australia any military force whose presence might be required by the exigencies of the public service in the new colony, but Mr Gladstone trusted that no such exigencies would arise. If they did, the expense and other inconveniences of increasing the number of detachments into which the Australian garrison was already broken up, should be minimised as much as possible.

In conclusion, Mr Gladstone considered it his duty to advert to a difficulty, possible, but doubtless improbable, with which Sir Charles Fitzroy might have to contend, viz. the dissatisfaction with which the Legislature and the colonists of New South Wales might contemplate the creation of the new colony. He would much lament the manifestation or existence of such a feeling. It would be with sincere regret that he would learn that so important a body of Her Majesty's subjects were inclined to oppose themselves to the measures he had attempted to explain. Any such opposition would have to be encountered by reminding those from whom it proceeded, in terms alike respectful and decided, that it would be impossible that Her Majesty should be advised to surrender what appeared to be one of the vital interests of the British Empire at large, and one of the chief benefits which the British Empire derived from dominion over the

vast territories of the Crown in Australia. By establishing
and maintaining such a colony as North Australia as a depôt
of labour available to meet the wants of the older colony, or
to find employment for the capital accumulated there, Mr
Gladstone hoped to promote, rather than impede, the
development of the resources of New South Wales. But
even if that hope were disappointed, he would not, therefore,
be able to admit that the United Kingdom was making an
unjust or unreasonable exercise of the right of sovereignty
over those vast regions of the earth in thus devoting a part
of them to the relief of Van Diemen's Land. The Mother
Country having practically relieved New South Wales, at no
small inconvenience to itself, of the burden—as soon as it
became a burden—of receiving convicts from the British Isles,
the Imperial Government was acquitted of any obligations in
that respect which any colonist, the most jealous for the
interest of his native or adopted country, could ascribe to the
home authorities. Her Majesty's Government had other
obligations to fulfil towards other parts of the British Empire
in regard to the transportation of convicts and the employment
of exiles and of emancipists. It was in the discharge of those
duties that the plan he had indicated had been projected.

CHAPTER III

MR GLADSTONE ENUNCIATES HIS LAND POLICY

On the following day, May 8, Mr Gladstone formulated, for the information of Sir Charles Fitzroy, his ideas with respect to the disposal and utilisation of the lands within the jurisdiction of the government of the proposed new colony. From the peculiar circumstances of the case, and the novelty of the experiment about to be tried in North Australia, he had thought it desirable to abstain from attempting to embody, in his previous communication, any detailed instructions in regard to the disposal of land, and, indeed, such directions as he was enabled to convey must, of necessity, be very general in their nature, leaving a great deal to the discretion of the Governor in the first instance, and subject to future modification.

The principal objects to be provided for were thus enumerated by Mr Gladstone :—

(1) The selection of the best spot for a harbour, and for the town which might be expected to grow up in that locality.

(2) The immediate reservation there of such water frontage as ought to be open to general use, and of any sites which might appear requisite for public buildings or works of defence.

(3) The prompt distribution of the adjacent country into a sufficient number of lots to meet any probable demands of incoming settlers.

(4) The exception from such lots of any lands likely to be wanted for roads or other public purposes.

(5) The designation of the size of lots for the use of the two principal classes of settlers, and the manner in which the survey of both should proceed.

And finally, the establishment of the distinct principles on which land might be disposed of: first, to persons who had been convicts, and were brought into the colony by the Government in order to enable them to raise their subsistence: and secondly, to any other persons who might come there with a view to establishing themselves as settlers.

As to the selection of a site for the future capital of North Australia, that was a point on which, Mr Gladstone observed, he was obviously unable to convey any definite instruction. Her Majesty's Government had been led to believe that the vicinity of Wide Bay or of Hervey Bay would be best adapted for the purpose, from its geographical position and the relative advantages it possessed by reason of its proximity to the boundary of New South Wales. The advantages of that position would, however, have to be tested by experience, and the point which might at first be selected from its apparent advantages might prove, on more mature consideration, and on a more ample knowledge of the country, to be less desirable than others which might be discovered. Amongst the considerations which would, in a great measure, influence the choice, Mr Gladstone specified the security for shipping and easiness of access from the sea; the facilities of communication with the interior of the country; an abundance of good water; the absence of any marshy grounds calculated to engender disease; the supply of materials for building and the probable productiveness of the surrounding soil.

As soon as the site was finally decided upon, the Government should plainly declare the limits within which lands were to be considered as town lots; the necessary reserves for wharves and public buildings should be proclaimed without delay; and the lines of some streets, at least, should be marked out, in order that dwellings might not be erected where they would interfere with the future plan of the town. Without attempting any positive direction on the subject, Mr Gladstone felt inclined to think that the space set apart for the town should not contain less than 640 acres, or more than 1280. It would be necessary at once to define this space, because the lands within it ought, in conformity with the general usage, and for the benefit of the colony, to be dealt with in a manner different from country lots. By what rules the disposal of town lots should be governed in a colony where it was a matter of importance that the intended town should soon be occupied by industrious persons—and yet the majority, if not the whole, of the early settlers in North Australia must be supposed to arrive without money in their possession—was a question, Mr Gladstone admitted, the consideration of which involved much difficulty, and to it he intended to return at a later stage.

Mr Gladstone directed that the surrounding country should be marked out without delay into a sufficient number of lots, to prevent any accumulation of persons at the landing-place without their being able to get on the land from which it was intended that they should raise their subsistence. The practical experience of Colonel Barney would be serviceable in this connection, and Mr Gladstone also called the Governor's attention to the valuable report of Captain Dawson on surveying in New Zealand and in new colonies generally. Captain Dawson's scheme secured sufficient accuracy for all practical purposes in the division of property, while it avoided unnecessary expense and admitted of far greater expedition than more elaborate modes of survey. With respect to reserves, Mr Gladstone considered it expedient that some of the most desirable lines of roads should be marked out at the beginning, so as not to be included in the lots set out for private occupation, and further, that every grant of land should reserve a right of making any future roads that might be required through the property. Subject to these exceptions, Mr Gladstone thought that reserves in the country should be made as sparingly as possible. With regard to the size of lots, Mr Gladstone declared that three different kinds of allotments would have to be provided for: those of which pardoned convicts should be put in possession without any immediate payment, on the ground of their being in want; allotments of somewhat larger size which, in order to encourage industry, these and other persons of the humble class should be able to acquire on credit; and thirdly, the ordinary lots for the accommodation of settlers who purchase their land for ready money.

In Mr Gladstone's opinion, the first class of lands should

not be less than 5 or more than 10 acres in extent; the second not less than 20 or more than 40; and for all other purposes it would be desirable, in order to avoid the expense of labour and surveying, that the country should not be subdivided into lots of less than 320 acres or half square miles. How far it would be expedient that the two descriptions of lots should be intermingled, and to what degree the surveyor should expedite the preparation of one kind more than the other, were questions to be decided by the Superintendent of North Australia, according to the prospect of a more immediate immigration of one or the other class of settlers, but having regard to what were the principal objects in view in the foundation of the new colony, Mr Gladstone apprehended that, at any rate, in the first instance, the preference would be given to securing a sufficient number of lots for the settlers to be introduced by the Imperial Government. With respect to ordinary purchasers for ready money, Mr Gladstone saw no reason why, in the case of country lots, the same general rules of sale should not be applied as already prevailed in New South Wales; but considering the peculiar constitution of the new settlement, which was founded chiefly with reference to settlers of an humble and even an indigent class, it appeared to him indispensable that there should be the means of acquiring lots of some such size as 20 or 40 acres on easy terms. Even to this limited extent, however, it would probably not be thought expedient to revert to the practice of making absolutely free grants of land, which course had been so much condemned by experience. He thought it better that these allotments of 20 and 40 acres should be allowed to be bought upon credit, subject to the payment of regular and periodical instalments. Until the whole price was paid up no grant should issue, and the settlers should hold no more than permission to occupy their land. This permission was to be given in a formal document to be known as a "location order." It was not to be transferable; it must include a description of the land to which it refers; and it must contain, on its face, the conditions attached to lands of permissive occupancy. The title, however, should be capable of being, at any time, converted into a fee-simple estate upon payment to the Crown of the whole amount of outstanding instalments.

With respect to the class of pardoned convicts who were to be sent to the new colony, and who would arrive with no pecuniary means at all at their command, it would be indispensable to allow of their being put in possession of very small lots without requiring from them any immediate payment. Mr Gladstone thought that such lots as these should not exceed 5 or 10 acres in extent, and that after the lapse of three years they should be paid for by regular instalments. The holders of these small allotments should also receive untransferable location orders. As to the conditions of sale, Mr Gladstone considered that the lowest price of land should be £1 per acre, that all lots should be exposed to auction except those set apart for pardoned convicts, and that all lots of larger size than 40 acres should be paid for in ready money. Purchasers of lots of 20 and of 40 acres should be permitted to make their payments in equal half-yearly instalments, to be distributed over a period of ten years, provided that they remained in continuous occupation of the land. Otherwise, their right would be forfeited, and in no respect would the land be transferable until the whole of their instalments had been paid up. Holders of conditional pardons and exiles, sent to North Australia by the Government, were to be put in occupation, without auction, of not less than 5 acres or more than 10, but any holder of a pardon, who was accompanied or joined by his wife, should receive double the allotment to which he would otherwise have been entitled. Nothing in the rules respecting the terms on which holders of conditional pardons were to be put in possession of lots without payment was to prevent them from purchasing additional lots, if they acquired the means, in the same manner as other settlers in the colony. As to the manner in which persons should be allowed to appropriate to themselves sites in the intended capital of North Australia, considering the value which in all parts of the world lands situated in the first established town and port of a new colony were found to possess, Mr Gladstone was certainly of opinion that there was no description of allotments for which it would seem more reasonable to insist on payment of a fair price. On general grounds it was obviously to be wished that such property should fall into the hands of persons who, by the amount which they paid for it, gave a substantial earnest that they were possessed of the means which would enable them to develop with quickness the resources of the place. On the other hand, as it was expected that North Australia would be colonised, in the first instance, by persons who had found a difficulty in supporting themselves elsewhere, there was the objection that, if the rules as to price were such as to prevent them from acquiring any part of the proposed town, it might at the outset remain unoccupied, to the detriment of the prosperity of the settlement. Nevertheless, Mr Gladstone apprehended that a certain number of temporary buildings would have to be erected immediately to provide for the pioneer settlers, and to that extent the town would be at once inhabited. Beyond this first provision for their accommodation, Mr Gladstone thought it was on many grounds undesirable to keep this class of settlers necessarily collected at the port. Besides, Government establishments, however limited, could not be set on foot without very shortly leading to an immigration of some persons possessed of capital of their own. On the whole, therefore, Mr Gladstone was not disposed to think that the settlers introduced at the Government expense should have any means held out to them of obtaining a free grant of any ground situated in the town. In the case of ordinary immigrant settlers, town allotments were to be disposed of to them by public auction in the same manner as in the other Australian colonies—either to be sold absolutely or disposed of on lease, as might from local circumstances be deemed most expedient. In the latter case, the subject of competition should be the annual rent to be paid, and not a premium on a fixed rent, as Mr Gladstone was of opinion that the former method was the more advantageous to the public. Finally, Mr Gladstone was disposed to think that it would be desirable to allot a moderate portion of land as a glebe to the chaplain. But he was sensible that there might be objections to such a proceeding, and not feeling himself to be in a position to judge of the weight to be attached to such objections in this particular case, he preferred to leave the point to the judgment of the Superintendent. If Colonel Barney should consider such a measure desirable, he would be at liberty to assign an allotment of land for that purpose to an extent not exceeding 40 acres.

The Rev Dr John Dunmore Lang, a Presbyterian divine, a vigorous controversialist, an active member of the New South Wales Legislature, and a prolific author on colonial subjects, energetically protested against Mr Gladstone's new colony being styled North Australia. "North Australia, forsooth! Why, I have no doubt that in a very few years hence there will be three or four British colonies along the northern coast, all equally entitled to the same general designation." His suggestion was that the proposed Gladstonian colony of North Australia should be christened "Cooksland," in honour of Captain Cook, the Columbus of the Australian seas, "to whose memory," added the bellicose doctor, "it will universally be allowed there has hitherto been no monument erected by his country at all worthy of his high deserts, of his imperishable fame. With your permission, therefore" (he is addressing the people of Great Britain and Ireland), "I shall not hesitate to perform this tardy act of national justice to our illustrious circumnavigator by designating what is now the northern division of the great colony of New South Wales, Cooksland."

But in the decrees of fate, neither Cooksland nor North Australia was destined to be the permanent name of the new colony created in that quarter of the Australian continent. Queensland it was called at its inception, and Queensland it has remained to this day.

Dr Lang volunteered no small amount of advice and suggestions to Mr Gladstone on the subject of the new colony, which, he earnestly hoped, "would eventually become a free colony, the seat of commerce and manufactures, and the chosen abode of an industrious and virtuous people." This ultimate destiny, he urged, should be kept steadily in view from the formation of the first settlement within its territory. The boundaries should be permanently fixed, the entire coast-line accurately surveyed, and the capabilities of the country thoroughly ascertained. The labour of the pioneer convict settlers should be expended, not in attempting to raise supplies of food that could be more economically obtained from the neighbouring colonies, but in the formation of quays and wharves, the making of roads and streets, the construction of tanks and reservoirs, and the erection of public buildings. In this way much valuable property would be created in the shape of building allotments, etc., the subsequent sale of which to free settlers would reimburse the Government the expenditure incurred, besides adding to the comfort of the colonists and the advancement of the colony. Recent explorations had established the fact that there was a large extent of pastoral country of the first quality within the limits of North Australia, and in view of the comparative mildness of its climate, its adaptation to the agricultural productions of the East and West Indies, and its command of the Pacific on the one hand and the Gulf of Carpentaria on the other, its prospects as a new British colony were unquestionably peculiarly favourable.

CHAPTER IV

THE FOUNDING OF THE COLONY

COLONEL BARNEY, who was selected by Mr Gladstone as the first Superintendent or Lieutenant-Governor of North Australia, was born in London on May 19, 1792, and entered the Army when he was only slightly over the age of sixteen. He took part in the defence of Tariffa in the years 1811-12, and in the capture of the islands of Mariegalante and Guadaloupe in 1815. From July 1835 to April 1844, he was engaged as an officer of the Royal Engineers in Australia, and no doubt it was the knowledge and experience of Australian life and character he thus acquired that specially recommended him to Mr Gladstone as a suitable, trustworthy, and well-informed gentleman to preside over the formation and guide the early development of the new colony.

Colonel Barney's appointment was officially notified in the *London Gazette* of May 8, 1846, in these terms :—" The Queen has been pleased to appoint George Barney, Esq., Lieutenant-Colonel in the corps of Royal Engineers, to be Lieutenant-Governor of North Australia, and to administer the Government of that colony under the style and title of Superintendent thereof." Mr W. W. Billyard was simultaneously gazetted as " Chairman of the Quarter Sessions of North Australia," with power to act both as civil and criminal Judge. Colonel Barney and Mr Billyard, accompanied by their wives and families, arrived in Sydney on September 15, 1846, as passengers on board the barque *William Hyde*, after a voyage of four months from London.

Colonel Barney, after a stay of a few days in Sydney, set out in a small steamer of ninety-four tons, called the *Cornubia*, on a preliminary cruise along the coast of the proposed new colony, with a view to discovering and determining the best site for the first settlement. The steamer put into Bustard Bay, but as there was no shelter for shipping, that locality was not considered good enough. Rodd's Bay was then surveyed—a very fine harbour, and easy of access, but no fresh water in the vicinity. Port Curtis was next visited, and it at once secured the suffrages of Colonel Barney. He described it as one of the finest harbours on the Australian coast, with room enough for the British Fleet to manœuvre. A large number of the native blacks appeared to greet the newcomers. One asked for flour, and their knowledge of a few common English words showed that they had been in communication with white people before. In all probability, some of the numerous whaling ships that were then employed in Australian waters occasionally called in at Port Curtis for spars. Numerous pieces of timber were found strewn along the beach in the harbour, apparently portions of wrecks which had drifted in with the tide.

Returning to Sydney, Colonel Barney set about the work of organising the first band of pioneers to settle on the shores of Port Curtis, and making all the necessary preparations for the founding of the new colony. He chartered a barque called the *Lord Auckland*, and early in the new year he was ready to start for the selected site of the metropolis of North Australia.

Before leaving Sydney to carry out the instructions of Mr Gladstone, Colonel Barney was examined as a witness by the Select Committee appointed by the Legislative Council to consider and report on Mr Gladstone's despatch, suggesting the revival of transportation. In answer to questions, the Colonel said that the pioneer party to colonise North Australia would be sent from Pentonville, and these would be followed by a contingent of well-conducted probationers from Van Diemen's Land. In his opinion, the men from Pentonville would be likely to make a very useful class of colonists. During his previous experience as a squatter and resident in New South Wales, he had found the assigned prisoners generally quite as useful as the ordinary class of free immigrants. Indeed, he would not hesitate to say that of the two classes of labour he preferred the Pentonville prisoners, because they had all been taught some trade, and were not criminals in the ordinary sense at all, their offences being of a light character, and, as a rule, the direct outcome of poverty and distress. Asked what arrangements had been made with respect to sending out the wives and families of the first colonists of North Australia, the Colonel replied that he understood the Imperial Government and the parishes concerned would co-operate in the matter. The men, upon landing at Port Curtis, would be placed in tents until such time as permanent huts were erected, and for the first year they would be supplied out of the Government stores with tools, provisions, clothing, seed, and stock. He was not aware that any restriction could be placed upon them. In fact, he regarded North Australia, in the first instance, principally in the light of a labour depôt for New South Wales. If the settlement prospered and proved successful, no doubt its status would be raised and improved, and the salaries of its officials would be correspondingly increased. Personally, he thought this settlement on the shores of Port Curtis would be sure to develop into an important place, with a considerable population. He had already had many applications from parties in Sydney, anxious to be allowed to go and settle there. Some of them wished to become store-keepers, and others to engage in the cultivation of sugar, cocoa, coffee, rice, etc. In reply to Sir Maurice O'Connell, Colonel Barney stated he had reason to believe that there would be a very appreciable emigration of capitalists to North Australia from England.

On January 8, 1847, the *Lord Auckland*, under the command of Captain Brown, sailed out of Sydney Harbour, having on board the founders and pioneers of Mr Gladstone's new colony, viz. His Honour Lieutenant-Colonel Barney, Superintendent, Mrs Barney, and family; W. W. Billyard, Esq., Chairman of Quarter Sessions; J. S. Dowling, Esq., Crown Prosecutor; E. C. Merewether, Esq., Colonial Secretary; Mr G. H. Barney, Clerk; Assistant Commissary-General Darling; Captain Day, of the 99th Regiment, Mrs Day, and family; Mr W. A. Brown, Deputy-Sheriff; Mr Robertson, Surgeon; Mr G. O. Allen; Mr W. K. Macnish, wife, and family; Miss Stokes, Mr and Mrs Vellier, Messrs W. Thew, W. Carney, A. Cook, T. Shaddock, J. Rutter, C. Jones, W.

Rowell, C. Smith, J. Harrison, twenty-two soldiers of the 99th Regiment, seven women, and twelve children.

The *Lord Auckland* was followed on February 26 by the barque *Thomas Lowry*, under the command of Captain Graham. In addition to all the stores and requisites for the founding of the new colony, she had as passengers from Sydney to North Australia Mr and Mrs Connell and family, Colonel Grey and son, Lieutenant de Winton, Mr Loundys, Mr Bates and family, and fifty soldiers.

The *Lord Auckland* had a very unpleasant passage from Sydney to Port Curtis, the rough seas inundating the passengers' cabins, and making matters exceedingly uncomfortable for the officials and pioneers of North Australia. But after eighteen days they came at last within view of the site of the projected capital of the new colony, and Colonel Barney and his chief officers attired themselves in their most gorgeous uniforms, and made preparations for landing with all the ceremonies befitting the birth of a new dependency of the British Crown. Guns were to be fired, flags displayed in profusion, and Colonel Barney was to land officially, amidst all the available pomp and circumstance of Vice-Regal display. But, alas! an untoward and unforeseen incident rudely interposed, and effectually prevented the carrying out of this carefully-planned ceremonial programme. On the afternoon of January 25, while abreast of Facing Island at the entrance to Port Curtis, the *Lord Auckland* grounded on a shoal, and her position soon began to look so critical that Colonel Barney considered it prudent to go ashore with his wife and family in the first boat, and postpone all considerations of ceremony and official etiquette until circumstances became more propitious. It was not until the 31st —all hands labouring incessantly in the meantime to lighten her, and bring her stores to land—that the *Lord Auckland* floated off into deep water. An eye-witness states that she was scarcely off one bank when she grounded upon another, and she continued to strike the ground so violently that he expected every minute to see the masts go overboard. Had she not been a remarkably strong ship, she must have gone to pieces. Notwithstanding continual pumping, she had five feet of water in the hold, and large patches of sheathing were every now and then tearing off her bottom. There were general fears that the vessel would become a total wreck, and the captain had all his portable property packed up in readiness for removal at a moment's notice.

On the day after the vessel struck, the rest of the officers and passengers were landed. The celerity with which Colonel Barney transferred himself and his family from the ship at the first symptoms of danger seems to have attracted unfavourable notice. A diary of one of the passengers is still extant, and the entry on January 26 concludes with a sarcastic comment at the expense of the head of the new colony :—

"Endeavoured to get into deep water. Ship striking violently. Again settled down in the sand. All hands at work nearly all night. Ship making water. Many of the passengers sent ashore, and all the females and children. Determined to discharge cargo. Came ashore in charge of stores. Boats discharging during the day. Finding that the vessel had not gone to pieces, Colonel Barney ventured on board this morning."

It was not until January 30, that the interrupted ceremony of swearing-in Colonel Barney and the other officials of North Australia was proceeded with. The function was shorn of most of the picturesque accessaries that were originally contemplated; indeed one depressed onlooker has summed up his impressions of the scene in the word "forlorn." Still all the prescribed formalities were complied with, and the first *Government Gazette* of North Australia was issued the same day in manuscript. It contained a Proclamation from His Honour the Superintendent, Colonel Barney, that all the land lying to the north of the 26° of south latitude, should thereafter be called and known as North Australia, and that he had taken the prescribed oaths and assumed the administration of the colony as Her Majesty's duly appointed representative. An Executive Council and a Legislative Council were simultaneously proclaimed, the former to consist of the Lieutenant-Governor, the Colonial Secretary, the Colonial Treasurer, and the Attorney-General, and the latter to comprise these same officials with the addition of the first three justices of the peace in a list of magistrates to be appointed by the Lieutenant-Governor. Captain Day was proclaimed Police Magistrate, and the first *Government Gazette* concluded with a caution against allowing the blacks to enter the tents, and a reminder that any outrage upon those aboriginal inhabitants of the soil would be taken cognizance of in the same manner as if committed upon any other of Her Majesty's subjects.

This caution to be circumspect in dealing with the natives was speedily justified by events. A few days after the warning was issued, a party of the pioneer settlers, consisting of three well-sinkers and a mason, came into collision with the blacks. While the men were engaged at their work, a party of eight blacks approached, and remained looking on in a friendly manner for an hour or two. But on departing, they gave rein to their predatory instincts to the extent of seizing and carrying off an axe. They then ran with all their speed into the bush, and were pursued by the whites, who, however, were soon compelled to retreat under a volley of stones thrown from slings. Next day the blacks reappeared with more formidable weapons—their spears—to the number of two hundred, but by this time the whites had been reinforced by a detachment of five soldiers, who fired over the heads of the natives to frighten them off. The firing had the desired result for the moment, but the blacks gradually regained their courage, returned, and threw a number of spears at the little band of whites. No lives were lost, but there were some narrow escapes. As the blacks were thus developing unmistakable evidences of hostility, thirty-two more soldiers of the 99th Regiment were told off to disperse them.

Pioneer settlers in every part of the globe must be prepared for privations, difficulties, and annoyances, and the people sent to start the Gladstone Colony in North Australia had certainly more than the average share of such troubles and misfortunes. A letter from one of them thus graphically depicts the drawbacks and inconveniences of the situation:—

" We have three great evils to contend with here—excessive heat, heavy rains, and mosquitoes in millions, particularly after wet weather. We are thus in constant misery. After enduring a day of overpowering heat, and when we would fondly welcome the cool of the evening, we are literally tortured by these vagabond insects. We have no retreat either from the heat or the rain. On a warm day the atmosphere in the tents is suffocating, the thermometer ranging for days together at 110°. I can compare it to nothing but an oven, the heat appearing all to concentrate in these delightful habitations. In wet weather (and we have experienced very heavy rains) the tents are of very little service. We have already undergone four weeks of these miseries, and from what we have suffered, I believe I am correct when I say that there is scarcely one amongst us who does not regret coming on this mad expedition, which, I fear, must ultimately be a failure, or be supported at great expense by the Government, as, so far as I can judge, the place can never support itself.

"Our regular scale of rations is very limited. For example, a man has only fourteen ounces of biscuit, twelve ounces of pork, and four ounces of rice daily; his wife, one-half that allowance; a child under seven years, one-fourth; one seven and under fourteen, one-third. The only exception is in tea and sugar, of which a woman gets the same as a man, viz. a quarter of an ounce of tea and two ounces of sugar. But only imagine three and a half ounces of bread daily for an urchin seven years old, and less than five ounces for a boy up to fourteen. Zounds! a two-pound loaf would be liker the thing. At that age every one knows a child eats four times the bread that a man does. We have had fresh meat only twice since we landed."

The catering arrangements of the new colony evidently left much to be desired, but unsatisfactory and disappointing as was the state of things revealed in the above letter, the condition of the cooking department soon became decidedly worse and more disagreeable. The arrival of the *Thomas Lowry* from Sydney, with the main supply of stores and provisions, was delayed for some weeks, during which the pioneer settlers of North Australia were threatened with downright famine. Six sheep in a very attenuated condition constituted the sole available live stock; vegetables were nowhere to be found, and the whole colony was reduced to keeping body and soul together on biscuit and salt junk. At this crisis a couple of small coasting vessels—the *Harriet* and the *Secret*—fortunately called in at Port Curtis, and saved the Gladstone Colony from threatened extinction by starvation. The *Thomas Lowry* hove in sight shortly afterwards, and there were no further alarms and excursions in the Commissariat department.

Colonel Barney appears to have been in no hurry to set

about establishing a permanent settlement, and this dilatory and inconsiderate conduct of the Queen's, or Mr Gladstone's, representative, is the burden of complaint in all the letters of the pioneers to their friends and relatives in Sydney. One of them, writing under date March 1, 1847, says :—

"Although we have been here five weeks, we have done absolutely nothing. We are at a loss to know what the intentions of His Honour the Superintendent are. Not a move has been made. The rain during several days has been very heavy, and the wind so high that the *Lord Auckland* drifted about three miles, and several tents were blown down during the night, leaving the unfortunate inmates—men, women, and children—exposed in their beds to all the fury of the weather. We should all be happy to return to the shelter of the ship; and I am utterly at a loss to conjecture why we are detained here, subject to such dangerous exposures, and the vessel so close at hand."

A letter from one of the pioneers, dated March 30, gives particulars of the first offences committed in the embryonic colony:—

"We are still in precisely the same condition as on the day we landed, living in a state of primitive, but uncomfortable, simplicity in our tents. I believe Colonel Barney is awaiting the arrival of definite instructions as to his future movements. The newly-appointed magistrates are about to have two opportunities of exercising their judicial functions. The first is a case of assault committed by a servant upon one of the officers of the Commissariat. The second is a case of a graver character. A sailor belonging to the *Harriet* discovered a soldier drowning, and rescued him from the perils of the sea to suffer one of the many on land. A cask of wine belonging to Colonel Grey had been stolen and broached, and was found near the spot almost empty. It is supposed that the unfortunate man had partaken largely of it, and staggered into the sea unconscious of his danger. On further inquiry, it was discovered that several of the military had been drunk during the night. A number of them, together with a civilian, are in custody. This is another of the many thousand instances of evil arising from the presence of intoxicating liquors. Hitherto, we have been without it altogether, and although nine weeks here, save the assault above-mentioned, there has not been the slightest disturbance.

"The passengers by the *Thomas Lowry* are all landed. May God send the steamer soon. You may conceive that we are most uncomfortably situated. We have not been blessed with a candle or a drop of oil since landing. The only light we have at night is the moon (when it shines), and our bush fires."

One of the earliest reports on the site of the new settlement was that of Mr Thomas Robertson, the Assistant-Surveyor of North Australia. He describes Port Curtis as an inlet of considerable size, twenty-five miles in length, and varying in breadth from two miles to fifteen. It is easy of access, well sheltered, and with good holding ground. Several small and highly picturesque islands rise in bold and graceful outlines from the surface. On these the soil is moderately good, thickly grassed, and timbered with green, stringy-bark, mangrove, and some beautiful tropical acacias unknown in New South Wales. The rocks are of quartz, trap, and iron-stone; and on the surface are lumps of metallic scoria. The shores of the mainland are lined with a narrow belt of mangroves, behind which lies an open forest country. To the west a narrow ridge of land juts into the port, and forms a small bay. Here Colonel Barney proposed to form a town. Owing to copious rains and an almost vertical sun, the lands around the port are now thickly clothed with grass—a striking proof of what the combined forces of heat and moisture may effect. Mr Robertson concludes his report with the remark :—

"We felt the heat on first landing very oppressive, but have now become assimilated to the climate, and do not experience the slightest inconvenience from the heat. The climate is exceedingly healthy ; no disease has taken place amongst us, and all seem to enjoy the best of health."

The *Sydney Morning Herald* strongly opposed the creation of the new colony, and coined a new phrase in order to emphasise its objections. It charged the Imperial Government with "felonising," instead of colonising North Australia.

"The vicinity of the new settlement to our own borders would necessarily reflect upon us, in the estimation of the people of England, no small portion of its contamination and evil repute. And that vicinity would, moreover, afford such facilities of escape as it would be madness to suppose the free convicts would not frequently embrace. The northern Egypt would pour upon our southern Goshen its hordes of marauding and blood-thirsty reprobates. Our graziers in the far districts of the north-west would be exposed to irruptions more fearful and desolating than those of the swarthy barbarians."

Mr Gideon S. Lang pointed out in the *Herald* that there were no capitalists in North Australia to employ the prisoners, and that the Imperial Government would have to form agricultural establishments, or sugar and coffee plantations, the expense of which would be enormous, and would make every prisoner an encumbrance on the home Government every day that he remained in the settlement. The principal object of the authorities would, therefore, be to get rid of the prisoners. They would not labour hard upon their 10 acres each, allotted to them by Mr Gladstone, for the bare necessaries of life, when they could receive good wages for little work in New South Wales, and the people of New South Wales would, therefore, have to receive these men ultimately either as expirees, bolters, or ticket-of-leave holders.

When the first accounts of the curious and somewhat unfortunate circumstances under which Colonel Barney landed at Port Curtis arrived in Sydney, there was naturally a considerable amount of unfavourable comment, scoffing allusion, and acrimonious criticism on the part of the numerous, active, and influential opponents of the revival of transportation. The *Sydney Morning Herald* put the worst possible construction on the actions of the Colonel—a construction that is entirely at variance with the known character of the man and his high and honourable record as a British officer. The *Herald* asked in its leading columns:—

"How is this abrupt debarkation of the Superintendent and his friends to be reconciled with that spirit of kindness and magnanimity by which British officers, especially the chief in command, are in such emergencies usually distinguished? It has ever been their professional pride to be the last to flee from the post of danger, the first to see that no precaution was wanting for the safety of others. Danger or no danger, we know not how the abandonment of so many of his dependents, consisting in part of women and children, if faithfully represented, is to be justified. If the Superintendent landed because he believed the lives of all on board to be in jeopardy, it was plainly his duty, by remaining until the whole of his own people had been rescued, to show that he cared for their lives as well as for his own. If, on the other hand, he thought there would be no danger in passing the night on board, he ought to have stayed there for the purpose of keeping up the spirits of all, particularly those of the females and children.

"The next very painful circumstance is the Superintendent's dilatoriness on shore. For the long period of five weeks, His Honour appears to have been as inactive as though he had been fast asleep. Not a single step taken; not a single movement made; not a single word uttered beyond the cords of his own tent with respect to the final dwelling-place of his suffering people. Five weeks of inaction would have been tedious under the most favourable circumstances; but here they were weeks of accumulated misery."

Here is another contemporary journalistic comment on the proceedings of Colonel Barney at Port Curtis:—

"With all proper respect for Colonel Barney as a resident for several years in this colony, and as an officer to whom Her Majesty had confided the important task of founding a new settlement upon our shores, a sense of public duty constrains us to express the feelings, the painful feelings, with which we have noticed his proceedings in North Australia. The facilities placed at his disposal at the outset for the selection of an eligible site appear to have been all that he could have desired. A commodious steam vessel, a military guard, a staff of surveyors under the able and experienced guidance of our Deputy-Surveyor-General, supplied him with ample means for accomplishing this primary object. And when he returned from his expedition to headquarters and commenced preparations for finally removing his establishment to Port Curtis, no one doubted, no one could think of doubting, that, wisely or unwisely, for better or for worse, he had at least made up his mind as to the spot upon which the nucleus of his future colony should be fixed. He had then nothing to do, as everybody supposed, but, with the needful complement of persons and suitable equipments of stores, to return to that spot with all convenient despatch; and, arrived there, to take possession at once, and set to work, without an hour's unnecessary delay, in laying the foundations of the first rude town.

"How have those anticipations been justified by the event? If we are to believe the concurrent testimonies before the public—and we see no reason to question their truthfulness—we can come to no other conclusion than that, in thinking the gallant Superintendent all right, we were all wrong. We must infer from those testimonies, either that on his return to Port Curtis by the *Lord Auckland*, His Honour was as undetermined as to the exact place of settlement as when he first beheld its shores from the deck of the *Cornubia;* or that his five weeks' loitering on the inhospitable sands was less excusable than it might be deemed on any other supposition."

Mr Gladstone's new colony had no more merciless and unscrupulous assailant than the Sydney barrister and journalist who, a couple of decades afterwards, was sitting by his side on the Treasury Bench of the House of Commons as Chancellor of the Exchequer. In the columns of the *Atlas*, Robert Lowe employed all his resources of biting epigram, caustic humour, stinging satire, and burlesque solemnity on North Australia in general, and Colonel Barney in particular.

With that faculty of humorous exaggeration which he subsequently developed at the expense of the English democracy, he held that the first Deputy-Governor of North Australia should be "equal to Cortez or Pizarro in enterprise and discovery, a Solon in legislative capacity, a Draco in executive vigour, grasping at once in his comprehensive mind the minutest details and the most remote results, quick-sighted, clear and resolute, patient of fatigue, hunger, and danger, with a head to conceive, and a hand to execute the most daring resolutions, under the most desperate circumstances." Then he proceeded to point out how far Mr Gladstone's choice had fallen short of this ideal, and he wound up a scorching editorial article with the amiable suggestion that Mr Gladstone, in making such an appointment, must have intended "that the North Australian exiles should toss the Governor and all his officers in a blanket, fraternise with or massacre the soldiers, pillage the stores, appropriate the marquees, ducks, pigs, cows, turkeys, geese, mules, and ladies, and when these supplies became exhausted, retire into the interior, and form themselves into bands of organised banditti."

The two satirical poems inspired by the incidents attending the colonisation of North Australia are certainly the wittiest productions of the pen of Robert Lowe during his colonial career. The first derives much of its point and effectiveness from the skilful style in which certain mistakes, attributed to Colonel Barney when he was engaged on public works in Sydney and its vicinity, are exaggerated to the extreme of absurdity :—

> How blessed the land where Barney's gentle sway
> Spontaneous felons joyfully obey ;
> Where twelve bright bayonets only can suffice
> To check the wild exuberance of vice !
> Where thieves shall work at trades with none to buy,
> And stores unguarded pass unrifled by ;
> Strong in their new-found rectitude of soul,
> Tame without law, and good without control !
>
> Bless'd land ! what mighty works thy future hides !
> What zigzag roads shall climb thy mountain sides !
> Where travellers shall view with proud disdain
> The shorter path across the neighbouring plain !

What harbours bristling with unsounded reefs
Shall shield the Navies of thy future chiefs !
What aqueducts shall bear thy river's bed,
Free from the modern heresy of lead,
To slake some parched city's thirst profound,
Built ere a single water-hole was found !

In that blest region sure 'twill natural seem
To bridge the dry and ford the turbid stream,
And each invention there will meet success,
Which makes the labour more and produce less.
Windmills in swamps and water-wheels on high,
This shall the stream eschew and that the sky ;
The sail shall steam, the oar the sail disgrace,
Oars change to paddles, paddles poles replace,
Till one by one each art and science fall,
And Barney's intellect is all in all.

The second piece was written on the receipt of the news of the misadventures that spoiled the official ceremonial landing of Colonel Barney at Port Curtis. It purports to be an inscription on the monument to be erected on the spot where the Colonel's foot first touched the soil of the new colony :—

Here Barney landed—memorable spot,
Which Mitchell* never from the map shall blot—
Leaving his steamer stranded on a bank,
Regardless if the sailors swam or sank.
Obeying Nature's most esteemed command—
Self-preservation—here did Barney stand.
What did he there ? The venerable man !
He came an embryo city's birth to plan ;
Wiser than Solomon, when first he traced
Tadmor and Balbec, cities of the waste.

For six long hours he did the search pursue—
For six long hours—and then he thirsty grew ;
Back to the rescued steamer did he steer,
Drew the loud cork and quaffed the foaming beer ;
Then ate his dinner with tremendous gust
And with champagne relieved his throat adust ;
Fished for his brother flatfish from the stern,
And thus, victorious, did to Sydney turn !

---

* Sir Thomas Livingstone Mitchell, the then Surveyor-General of New South Wales.

Weep not, my Barney! tremble not, my Brown!
Nor dread abatement of your high renown;
What though the Commissariat growl to pay
Your steamer's hire at thirty pounds a day;
What though your city on the northern shore
Remain as much a phantom as before;
Though people ask you for their *quo a quid*,
And say: "'Twas ever thus that Barney did.
Thus did he build a quay beneath the tide—
Thus scoop a basin where no ship can ride—
Thus carry roads on lowlands and o'er highlands—
Thus spoil our harbour—thus blow up our islands."

Weep not, my friends! Who knows, or who can tell
How well yourselves he served, and us, how well?
Oh! had some fever with its breath of flame
Blighted heroic Barney's stalwart frame;
Or had some savage, ignorant and dull,
Spiked the electric battery of his skull,
Then had our cup of woe indeed been full.
But now, let envy howl, let faction groan,
Yet, Barney! yet we have thee all our own.
Critics may cavil, governors may chafe,
We've lost a thousand pounds—but Barney's safe!

CHAPTER V

THE VETO OF EARL GREY

EARL GREY succeeded Mr Gladstone as Secretary of State for the Colonies on July 3, 1846, and one of his first official acts was the complete reversal of the policy of his predecessor with respect to the founding of the new colony of North Australia. While still in Opposition, he had more than once manifested an unsympathetic attitude towards the experiment that Mr Gladstone had initiated on the shores of Port Curtis.

On May 19, 1846, from his place in the Upper House, he inquired whether any measures had been taken for establishing a new colony to be called North Australia. It appeared from the papers before the House that such a colony was to be constituted almost exclusively of persons who had undergone the sentence of transportation, and were called emancipists. Lord Lyttelton, Mr Gladstone's Parliamentary Under-Secretary, replied that the scheme had already been carried out to a great degree, and that all the necessary proceedings, so far as they depended upon Her Majesty's Government, had been taken. This new colony was to be a settlement within the boundary of New South Wales in the north of Australia. It was not necessarily to be occupied entirely by emancipists. It was certainly intended to ameliorate the condition of those convicts who had gone through their punishment in Van Diemen's Land, where there was now no demand for their labour, and, in consequence, many of this unfortunate class were entirely destitute. Those persons would have facilities afforded them of proceeding to the new settlement of North Australia, and it was also intended that facilities should be given to the poorer classes in England to proceed there, as well as to prisoners at Pentonville and Parkhurst. By this means it was hoped to relieve Van Diemen's Land of its surplus convict population.

On November 15, 1846, Earl Grey wrote to Sir Charles Fitzroy, informing him that, on a full review of the subject, Her Majesty's Government had determined to abandon the design entertained by Lord Stanley, and carried into effect by Mr Gladstone, for establishing in North Australia a colony for the reception of pardoned convicts who might be unable to find the means of maintaining themselves in Van Diemen's Land. Earl Grey said he could not conceal from Sir Charles that Her Majesty's present confidential advisers dissented from the view taken of this subject by their immediate predecessors, both in reference to the state of facts under which they acted, and the considerations by which they were guided. But he would not enter on a discussion that might assume a controversial aspect, and which had become entirely superfluous. Since Mr Gladstone's decision in the matter was taken, there had been such a change in the condition and circumstances of society in the Australian Colonies as would, could it have been foreseen, have doubtless been regarded by the authors of the project as conclusive against its adoption. In making this observation, Earl Grey said he was referring especially to the cessation, during at least two years, of transportation to Van Diemen's Land. He also had in view the increased and increasing demand for manual labour throughout the Australian Colonies, as well as the methods which the new Governor of Van Diemen's Land, Sir William Denison, had devised for the employment of the convict and emancipated population in that colony—a duty in which he would be aided by his extensive experience acquired in the discharge of analogous duties in the Mother Country. Under these circumstances, Earl Grey had come to the conclusion that the establishment of the projected colony of North Australia was now an impolitic and needless measure, even if he could acknowledge that it was originally the reverse.

Her Majesty had therefore been advised to revoke the letters-patent, under which North Australia had been erected into a separate colony. The establishments formed there were immediately to be discontinued. Colonel Barney and the subordinate officers associated with him were to be recalled without delay, and employed, as opportunity offered, under the Government of New South Wales. Earl Grey concluded by expressing his personal pleasure in the knowledge that to Colonel Barney himself this change of purpose would not be a disappointment, as his engagement to serve in North Australia had been, by his own desire, limited to a period of two years. The officers who had been engaged in the foundation of North Australia would be paid salary for one year dating from their landing in Sydney.

In the first chapter of the second volume descriptive of his colonial policy, published by Bentley in 1853, Earl Grey enters more fully into the reasons that impelled him to reverse the decision of Mr Gladstone in the matter of creating the new colony of North Australia. The plan, he says, which had been determined upon by his predecessor at the Colonial Office, and in which he did not think it advisable to persevere, was to send a certain number of convicts, emancipated by pardon, by length of service, or as exiles, to form a settlement on a part of the mainland of North Australia, which was still unoccupied. It was, in the first instance, to be occupied by exiles from England, who were to be settled on small lots of land; and when, by the assistance of these men, sufficient preparations had been made, convicts from Van Diemen's Land, whose sentences had expired, or who had obtained conditional pardons, were to be sent there. To this scheme of Mr Gladstone's it appeared to him there were decisive objections. In the first place, if convicts were sent to a still unoccupied territory, where there were no settlers to employ them, no buildings prepared for their reception, and no roads of any kind, everything being in a state of nature, it was obvious that the expense to be incurred must be very large, as every fresh attempt to form new settlements had clearly demonstrated, and that the whole of the convicts who might remain in the settlement would for a long time be entirely dependent upon the Imperial Government for their support. The necessity of providing for them would not be averted by giving them allotments of land. From these allotments they could not possibly procure a subsistence until much time and labour had been expended in reclaiming and cultivating the land, and in the meantime they must be provided for by the Government. They could only cease to be dependent upon the Government for their subsistence when, by industry and good management, they were enabled to obtain a living from the soil. It had always been found a difficult and a costly undertaking to establish men who had no capital of their own as settlers on wild land, even when the experiment was tried with carefully selected labourers from rural districts. It was therefore little likely to succeed with emancipated convicts, whose habits were almost always improvident, and of whom much the greater number knew nothing of agriculture.

If it were necessary to provide for these men in the manner proposed by Mr Gladstone, clearly it might be accomplished with infinitely greater facility in Van Diemen's Land. There was plenty of good land still belonging to the Crown in that colony well adapted for the purpose in view, and far more accessible than North Australia. Besides, in Van Diemen's Land there were available for the undertaking all the resources offered by an existing colony and a large Government establishment. Roads to new settlements in Van Diemen's Land might have been formed by convict labour at a comparatively trifling expense; and no new establishment of police, judges, or commissariat, no additional troops, with the barracks and buildings necessary for all these departments of the public service, would have been required. The enormous amount of the charges which must have been provided for under these heads, if any considerable number of convicts had been settled in North Australia, might be inferred from the heavy expense that had unavoidably accompanied the formation of the penal establishment in Western Australia, although in that colony there were considerable resources of all kinds available, and many of the most costly preliminary preparations for taking possession of an unoccupied territory had already been accomplished.

But, further, the great object in the transportation of offenders was to avoid forming a society mainly composed of those who had been criminals. It was well known how great were the evils produced in the earlier days of New

South Wales by the preponderance of the "emancipist" element in colonial society, but Mr Gladstone's colony of North Australia would have been a society composed exclusively of men who had suffered punishment for their offences, unless a few free settlers were attracted by the Government expenditure.

Against these objections there was to be set but one real advantage that Earl Grey could perceive. Mr Gladstone intended North Australia to be peopled by emancipists, that is, by convicts over whom the Government no longer possessed the legal power of exercising any control, unless they should commit some new offences. Clearly these men would not have remained in the new settlement, but would have crossed the purely imaginary line separating North Australia from New South Wales to seek employment in the latter colony, where, no doubt, there would have been ample demand for their labour. But if this was the object of Mr Gladstone's new penal settlement, such, in Earl Grey's opinion, was not a legitimate mode of attaining it. He could not think it right to send the same class of persons, whose direct removal to New South Wales had been abandoned by the Imperial Government, to a new settlement immediately adjoining that colony, where there was nothing to detain them even for a single day, and from which there was no room to doubt they would immediately retreat to New South Wales.

The *Sydney Morning Herald*, the most influential and uncompromising opponent of the renewal of transportation in any shape or form, rejoiced exceedingly in its editorial columns at Earl Grey's decision to nip the Gladstone Colony in the bud.

"Seven years ago it was the lordly will of the powers that were to put down the hateful anomaly of mingling the transportation system with that of colonisation. Their successors, though they could not for very shame reverse the decree which had delivered New South Wales from the penal curse, had yet the conscience to wreak it with tenfold violence on the weaker colony of Van Diemen's Land. And when at length the cries of that sufferer had extorted a reluctant promise of at least partial deliverance, a new Secretary of State was made the instrument of attempting, under the most specious guise of modification, to revive the abomination in the elder colony. Concurrently with this attempt, a resolution was adopted to form a new penal settlement on our northern frontier. Without waiting to see how the overture to our own part of the territory would be received, Mr Gladstone, the Right Honourable successor of my Lord Stanley, at once causes letters-patent to be issued for erecting North Australia into a penal settlement, and sends out his officers with all needful instructions and appliances. No sooner, however, have these preliminaries been successfully carried into effect—no sooner has His Honour the Superintendent of North Australia set foot upon the soil placed under his charge—no sooner has a steamer been purchased and a ship chartered for the conveyance to its shores of civil officers, troops, convicts, and supplies—no sooner have the anti-transportationists amongst ourselves deplored these tokens of mischievous earnestness, whilst the opposite party have exulted in the brightening prospect of 'a stream of felons from the north'—no sooner has all this happened, than another change takes place in the Ministry, and the whole scheme is dashed to pieces! The letters-patent are revoked, the appointments are cancelled, and the nascent establishment ordered to be broken up!

"This, we joyfully admit, is one of the few instances in which the Ministerial wheel was turned for the better. It is a blessed turn. But who shall say how long its blessedness will last? Should the general election of the present year return a House of Commons unfavourable to the Russell Cabinet, another revolution among placemen may undo all that we are now exulting in. The orders of Earl Grey may be as summarily set aside as those of Mr Gladstone have been. There is something rotten in the state of Downing Street. We can place no dependence upon it.

"But whilst there is reason for our doubts, there is also good reason to hope. In the present distracted state of parties, the Ministry of Lord John Russell is more likely to stand than to fall; Earl Grey is more likely to keep the Colonial Seals than to have them plucked out of his hands, and without adverting to the general policy of those half-Liberal, half-Conservative statesmen, we have at least the consolation of knowing that on the penal discipline question they are the true friends of our adopted country. There is no chance, so long as they remain at the helm, of all the gaols and hulks of the United Kingdom disgorging their contents upon our sheep-walks.

"And even should the worst come to the worst, and the Russell Ministry be displaced by one predisposed to revert to Mr Gladstone's projects, we should still have hope, and stout hope too, that the numerous petitions that have gone home, testifying the abhorrence in which those projects are held by the great bulk of the colonists, would avert the calamity. At any rate, the colonists have done their duty, and though it is not for them to command success, they have deserved it."

When the bill of expenses in connection with the establishment and abandonment of the short-lived Gladstone Colony was sent to Downing Street, Earl Grey elevated his eyebrows, and promptly penned a despatch to Sir Charles Fitzroy, censuring him for not having exercised a more economical supervision of the affairs and arrangements of the new settlement. A memorandum from the Audit Office, Sydney, dated March 31, 1848, sets forth in detail the cost of the enterprise :—

NORTH AUSTRALIA.

Statement of expenses incurred for the Settlement at North Australia, as far as the same can be ascertained from the accounts at present in the Audit Office, viz. from December 1, 1846 to October 31, 1847, prepared pursuant to Treasury letter of February 1848.

	£	s.	d.
Pay of the Superintendent and of the Civil and Medical Establishments	2422	18	1
Allowances to Civil and Medical Officers	40	1	10
Expenses of Surveying the Settlement	900	0	0
Purchase of and fitting up the steamer *Kangaroo* and wages of the crew; hire of the *Lord Auckland*, the *Thomas Lowry*, and the *Sea Nymph*, to carry out the Expedition to North Australia and back to New South Wales, and other expenses of transport	8422	8	4
Pay of mechanics and boatmen; purchase of building materials; furniture for Government House; water-casks, seeds, stationery, and other contingent expenses	1184	8	6
Provisions, forage, fuel, and light for the use of the Settlement, and of the vessels conveying the Expedition	1546	15	4
Pay of Commissariat Officers	491	3	6
Pay of temporary clerks, issuers, and other subordinate persons of the Commissariat	259	2	6
Commissariat contingencies	5	0	6
Lodging allowance to Military and Commissariat Officers	130	7	7
	£15,402	6	2

Writing on September 30, 1847, Sir Charles Fitzroy deeply lamented that his proceedings in connection with the settlement of North Australia had met with the disapproval of the Secretary of State. He then proceeded to shift the responsibility on to the shoulders of Mr Gladstone :—

"I trust I may be permitted to point out to Your Lordship that the necessity for taking immediate steps for the formation of a settlement for the reception of the exiles was strongly urged upon me by Your Lordship's predecessor before I left England ; and that Colonel Barney, on his arrival in this colony, reported that ships having these people on board might be expected to arrive at Sydney early in January. If, therefore, I had acceded to Colonel Barney's suggestion of delay, I should have incurred the responsibility of detaining the exiles in Sydney ; a measure which, for many reasons, appeared to me to be extremely undesirable."

Sir Charles added that he was by no means satisfied with the first cursory examination that Colonel Barney had made of the coast and country in the vicinity of Port Curtis. Further exploration might have, and indeed had since, demonstrated the existence of an adequate supply of water not far from the coast. Colonel Barney had reported most favourably of the advantages possessed by Port Curtis as a harbour, and the safety of the vessels employed in the expedition was therefore assured while a closer search for permanent water was being made. Information had reached Sir Charles Fitzroy from persons acquainted with the locality, which had induced him to believe that the absence of water at the time of Colonel Barney's first visit was entirely accidental. Abundant rains had since shown the correctness of this information. Sir Charles concluded by assuring Earl Grey that the country around Port Curtis had been pronounced by every person who had returned from there to Sydney to be well adapted for settlement and adequately supplied with water, whilst the harbour was superior to any other along the coast, with the solitary exception of Port Jackson. Many persons had already left Sydney to settle at Port Curtis as private speculators, and numerous unauthorised squatting stations had sprung up to the northward of the 26th parallel. Parties of squatters were then travelling with their flocks and herds to occupy the rich pastures at the back of Port Curtis. He therefore asked Lord Grey to grant him the necessary authority to advantageously open up the Port Curtis district by free settlement in due and regular form, and under the circumstances to relieve him from the censure of having acted inadvisedly or without due consideration in the matter.

The *Sydney Morning Herald* came out with a strongly-written leading article in defence of Sir Charles Fitzroy, and in condemnation of Earl Grey for his "injustice," his "harshness," and his exhibition of "a spirit of discourtesy and snappishness altogether uncalled-for and inexcusable." The project for establishing the new colony of North Australia had cost the inhabitants of New South Wales considerable anxiety and no small agitation. It had seduced an influential section of the Legislature into the grievous error of consenting to the degradation of their country, and it had roused nearly the entire population to a vehement resistance of the measures by which that degradation was to have been inflicted. And now it was proclaimed on official authority that this same experiment had cost the good tax-payers of old England the sum of £15,000, a sum with which 1500 starving Britons might have been rescued from destitution and settled in the Australian land of plenty. This Ministerial whim, having been found so costly, was now disowned by its Ministerial parents. Ministerial shoulders, unwilling to bear the burden of their own responsibility, would fain transfer it to the shoulders of Sir Charles Fitzroy. His faithful execution of the orders he had received personally from Mr Gladstone on the eve of his departure from London had been rewarded by Mr Gladstone's successor with disapproval and censure. From the circumstance of his having been in London while the North Australian scheme was being moulded and fashioned by the authorities of Downing Street, Sir Charles had become thoroughly informed as to the views and wishes of Her Majesty's Government with regard to it. His personal interviews with Mr Gladstone and other Members of the Cabinet had given him a clearer insight into the policy of Ministers with respect to this grand penal experiment than could have been afforded by the most voluminous despatches. Sir Charles had come out to Sydney perfectly instructed as to the course of duty he had to pursue, and he pursued it with a zeal and intelligence which, had Mr Gladstone remained in office, would have encountered neither the dark frowns of censure nor the cold looks of disapproval. Mr Gladstone, as an enlightened and conscientious statesman, would not have shrunk from the weight of his own proper responsibility; still less would he have meanly sought to cast it upon the officer who had obeyed his instructions.

Mr Gladstone appears to have had but one Parliamentary opportunity of explaining and defending his action in connection with the establishment of North Australia.

On March 8, 1849, an important debate on the transportation system was initiated in the House of Commons by Viscount Mahon, Member for Hertford. Mr Gladstone was amongst the speakers, and several references were made to his projected penal colony in North Australia. Lord Mahon charged Earl Grey, Secretary of State for the Colonies, with having changed his views on transportation no less than five times in the short space of twenty months. As a result of the cessation of transportation to New South Wales in 1840, the convicts were concentrated in Van Diemen's Land to an extent that made that colony a loathsome sink of pestilence and infection. The complaints of the colonists reached England early in the spring of 1846. Mr Gladstone was then Colonial Secretary, and in conjunction with Sir James Graham, the Home Secretary, came to the conclusion that it was necessary to suspend the tide of transportation to Van Diemen's Land for two years. Transportation was thus checked, but Mr Gladstone accompanied this check by another measure. Lord Stanley had, some time before, sanctioned the establishment of an additional colony in North Australia for the reception of convicts, and Mr Gladstone made preparations for carrying out this plan. But on the 15th of November, Earl Grey wrote to Sir Charles Fitzroy, and by one stroke of his pen arrested the establishment of the new colony of North Australia. And that was not the only false step the noble Earl made at the time. Lord Mahon then proceeded to discuss in detail the various changes and contradictions that had characterised Earl Grey's proceedings in the matter of transportation.

Towards the close of his speech, Lord Mahon strongly urged that the colony of North Australia should be re-established on the lines laid down by Mr Gladstone. He was convinced that great advantage would accrue from constituting the convicts the pioneers of free emigration in that region. In the petition from Van Diemen's Land of the previous year, the abandonment of Mr Gladstone's North Australian project was one of the grounds of complaint.

Sir George Grey, as the spokesman of the Government, delivered a lengthy speech in reply. Lord Mahon, he said, had suggested that they should recur to the proposed penal settlement of North Australia. He doubted whether the noble lord had read the papers which had been published with regard to that settlement, and which showed the impolicy of adopting any such course. The result of such a step would be to create a colony exclusively of criminals, with scarcely any hopes of future amelioration or improvement. Exiles from Pentonville Prison were first to be sent there. The success of the system of sending exiles from Pentonville to the colonies had hitherto depended on their immediate dispersion, by which means they were blended with the population generally, and thus ultimately lost as a distinct class. Now the plan of North Australia was that it should be peopled by exiles and emancipists from Van Diemen's Land, who were to be induced to keep together by grants of land being given to them. All he could say was that he saw nothing but doubt and hesitation in the despatches of Mr Gladstone on the subject of North Australia, and subsequent consideration had only convinced him that the prosecution of such a scheme of colonisation would have involved enormous expense, and that the evils of an unmixed criminal population to be produced by it would be equal to any that existed under the previous system.

Mr Gladstone, who rose towards the close of the debate, entered at some length into the working of the probation system in Van Diemen's Land, and animadverted on what he called the "great precipitancy" in the conduct of Earl Grey with respect to transportation. He thought the noble Earl would do well to always keep in view the immense importance of extending as far as possible the area in which transportation took place. In fact, he was sorry to say that in this department, as in many others of colonial policy, it must be admitted that they had degenerated from the wisdom of their ancestors. In former times the principles on which transportation could be advantageously conducted were better understood than at the present day. The States of the American Union received convicts, but in numbers so small that they were easily absorbed in the rest of the population, and the evils which might arise to the community were reduced within the smallest possible limits. At the present day less caution was exercised, difficulties of a political character had been occasioned, and the very name of transportation had been brought into bad odour with the colonies. It was mainly from the difficulties which had thus been created that he felt strongly inclined to direct the attention of the House to the colony of North Australia. He felt the difficulties which now surrounded the subject—difficulties occasioned by the evil of compressing the convicts within a small space, and by the ill odour into which transportation had fallen with the Australian Colonies; but he hoped that, with the opening of a new door, transportation was not to be discontinued. It was his hope that North Australia would not be made a permanent penal colony, but that one or two cargoes of exiles from Pentonville should be sent there as pioneers, and not to Van Diemen's Land, for in the latter colony so plentiful was labour as compared with the demand, and so great the number of emancipated convicts it supported, that North Australia had been founded partially as a relief to Van Diemen's Land. He admitted that the whole question was surrounded by great difficulties, but he hoped that Her Majesty's Government would always take for their cardinal principle the importance of having as extensive an area as possible for the location of the convicts, for if they were to continue the practice of sending convicts by thousands to one penal colony, until it was drenched with iniquity, the very worst consequences would certainly ensue.

On April 7, the steamer *Kangaroo* left Sydney for Port Curtis with Earl Grey's despatches, transmitted by Sir Charles Fitzroy to Colonel Barney, ordering the abandonment of the Gladstone Colony. How the news was received by the pioneers of North Australia is described in a letter dated April 18 :—

"We have been anxiously awaiting the arrival of the *Kangaroo*, which made its welcome appearance here on the 15th inst., bringing the joyful intelligence that the colony was not to be proceeded with, and that we were all to return to Sydney. When first seen in the distance, the news spread like wild-fire through our camp, and every one was on the tiptoe of anxiety and hope to learn the nature of her despatches. Many and various were the conjectures afloat—one that the colony was to be abandoned; another that it was to go on; a third that the establishment was to be reduced and remain in abeyance until Parliament decided the question, but by far the greater number ardently hoped for the first. We were for a time in a state of tantalising suspense, but after about three hours, a boat was seen approaching, and our hearts were soon warmed with the news that we were again to be restored to our homes. I, for one, had made up my mind to leave by the first opportunity, but there were many whose circumstances would not admit of this, and to them in particular the news came like honey-drops from Heaven. Some few, indeed, who

'Dreamed bright dreams of future glory,'

might be seen mopish and melancholy at being thus so suddenly deprived of their short-lived honours, but they were lost — annihilated — amidst the general gladness that was diffused around. It will not be wondered at that we were thus rejoiced, when it is considered that for twelve weeks we have been living on soldiers' rations, some of which were so bad that they were altogether unfit for consumption, and that during that long period, in wet and dry weather, we have had no covering for our heads but canvas tents, which were totally inefficient to protect us from either heat, cold, or rain. And again we have had no water to depend upon but surface water, procured from the drainage of the ground; and this is now becoming very scarce, as we have had no rain for upwards of a month. I feel assured that, with the heavy dews which wet our bed-clothes through the canvas, together with our salt rations and bad water, illness would soon make its appearance amongst us; and I venture to prophesy that unless we have very fine weather indeed, those of us who may have to remain until a second ship is sent from Sydney, will feel the effects of wintering under our present circumstances. It is only fair to state that His Honour the Superintendent and his worthy and much respected family, have participated in all our miseries, Mrs Barney having remained amongst us up to the 4th inst., when in consequence of illness, induced, I believe, by the heavy morning dews, she, with her daughters, removed on board the *Thomas Lowry*."

The *Thomas Lowry* returned to Sydney on May 9, with sixty-seven of the North Australian settlers, including Mrs Barney and her daughters, Mr and Mrs Billyard, and Lieutenant de Winton in command of thirty-one of the rank and file of the 99th Regiment. One of the officials of the short-lived colony lost no time in proclaiming his belief in the suppressed settlement. "Notwithstanding that the present Ministry have come to the determination of abandoning North Australia, I cannot," he wrote, "see any obstacle to prevent private speculators from taking up that country." Then he added a prophecy, that has since been amply verified by the event:— "Many years will not elapse before we shall hear of a flourishing colony around the now-abandoned Port Curtis." He declared the climate to be exceedingly good, as was proved by the fact that the first settlers, although exposed to inevitable hardships and privations, continued in perfect health. The heat, though apparently great, was really not so oppressive as in Sydney, being tempered by the constant sea breezes blowing. Few or no storms or sudden changes were experienced. The harbour was the second best that Australia could boast, with deep water, sufficient for the largest ship afloat, for nine or ten miles, and backed by a magnificent range of mountains. Down to the water's edge there was an abundance of rich grasses, and there could be no possible doubt that the surrounding country was well adapted for grazing purposes.

CHAPTER VI

THE VINDICATION OF COLONEL BARNEY

As the proceedings of Colonel Barney at Port Curtis were subjected to the severest, most violent, and most abusive criticisms, specimens of which have been quoted in previous pages, it is only right and proper that he should be heard in his own defence and justification. His official report, covering the whole period of his career as Superintendent of the colony of North Australia, is dated Sydney, July 20, 1847. He states that the preliminary survey in search of a suitable site for a first settlement embraced Bustard Bay, Rodd's Bay, Port Curtis, and Wide Bay. In carrying it out he was assisted by Commissary-General Darling, Dr Silver, and Mr M. H. Browne. They came to the conclusion that Port Curtis alone offered desirable requisites for a settlement—a good and extensive harbour, requiring only a few buoys to render the access perfectly secure; a fair site for a settlement about eight miles within the port, offering ready means of drainage, good positions for wharves, and secure anchorage in five fathoms within half a mile of the shores; a creek admitting of vessels of large size being hove down in perfect security; an unlimited quantity of excellent timber, brick-earth, and shells for lime; and in the vicinity land fit for agricultural purposes. A most important essential, however, was not to be found—fresh water—and the Colonel feared at first that this drawback would lead to a decision unfavourable to the permanent occupation of Port Curtis. But on further investigation, the conviction was borne in upon him that a long and exceptional period of drought had occurred in the district. All the sources of water to which Captain Flinders and others had previously resorted were dried up, but the number of creeks and waterholes in the locality left little doubt in the Colonel's mind that a supply of water, equal to the early requirements of a new settlement, could be readily secured by constructing dams to catch and preserve the periodical rains.

Port Curtis having been selected as the best available site for the headquarters of North Australia, the ship *Lord Auckland* was chartered to convey the officers and stores from Sydney, but this vessel proving inadequate to accommodate the whole expedition, a second ship, the *Thomas Lowry*, was engaged, and it was expected that the latter would be ready for sea within a month. A small steamer, the *Kangaroo*, was also acquired for service in the further examination of the coast.

All arrangements having been completed, the *Lord Auckland* sailed from Sydney on January 6, and after a tedious passage, reached Port Curtis on the 25th, but, in the words of the Colonel, the ship "unfortunately grounded on the flats, about four miles east of Gatcombe Head, which led to the immediate disembarkation of the families, and a camp was formed on a projecting point of land, adjoining Gatcombe Head." The vessel continued to strike heavily during the night, and it being evident that she was in a critical position, the Colonel ordered all the necessary baggage and stores to be promptly landed. This having been done, it was discovered that the ship had sprung a leak. The Colonel became alarmed for the safety of the provisions and stores, and a party of soldiers were sent on board to assist in working the pumps. No measures were taken by the captain to lighten the ship, which continued on the flats for three days, when happily she moved into the channel, and finally anchored within the port about five miles from the encampment. Fortunately, the weather was fine while she was aground, but the equinox soon set in most violently, and throughout February and the early part of March continuous gales of wind, accompanied by heavy rain, were experienced. Had the *Lord Auckland* been caught aground in such weather, she would inevitably have broken up in twenty-four hours. During this period, the party encamped on shore were not only exposed in tents to the inclemency of the weather, but also to a want of fresh provisions and vegetables. Indeed, the privations and discomforts were of no ordinary character, but the Colonel was pleased to be in a position to record that no sickness occurred, and that all the pioneers bore their difficulties with patience and good humour.

The non-arrival of the *Thomas Lowry*, a month overdue, added considerably to the anxieties of the Colonel, but his peace of mind was restored to some extent by the appearance of the schooner *Secret* and the cutter *Harriet* on March 10. Both the schooner and the cutter were laden with cargoes of timber of a kind very serviceable for the construction of temporary dwellings, so the Colonel effected a purchase, and had the timber landed on the South Shore Head, the site he had prospectively fixed upon for the permanent town or metropolis of North Australia. He did not consider it advisable to remove the party from the original encampment, because the site had proved perfectly healthy, and it also possessed materials for the construction of temporary cover before the winter set in. He had determined not to come to any final decision as to the site of the settlement until he had satisfied himself that he was on the best spot the coast and the country afforded; and, as he had not heard anything of the sailing of the exiles from England, he did not feel himself called upon to come to any hasty decision on so important a point. He had, however, examined a considerable extent of country around Port Curtis, and had found that the late rains had filled all the creeks and water-holes, so that he was relieved of anxiety on that score for the immediate future. Indeed, he had formed an opinion that a permanent supply of water could be obtained by means of pipes from a creek not more than three miles distant.

The *Thomas Lowry* entered the harbour at last on March 14, with the remainder of the officers and stores. The whole of the stores of the *Lord Auckland* had been previously disembarked, owing to the unseaworthy condition of the vessel, which was leaking to such an extent as to require the pumps to be kept constantly at work. A rough building had to be constructed for the protection of these stores. On April 15, the steamer *Kangaroo* arrived, bearing instructions from Earl Grey, through Sir Charles Fitzroy, to break up the establishment, and return to Sydney with the least possible delay. These instructions were carried into effect with the utmost attainable expedition.

Colonel Barney concludes his narrative with a panegyric of Port Curtis. He had satisfied himself that it offered the most desirable position for a settlement in the northern part of Australia. With a better knowledge of the harbour, it had improved in character as to access and secure anchorage. Its waters abounded in fish. The extent of land suitable for agriculture within a few miles of the coast far exceeded the anticipations he had formed on his first visit. Timber for dwelling-houses and ship-building was abundant and of the best description. Within five miles of the South Shore Head, pipe-clay, brick-earth, ironstone, freestone, granite, trap, slate, and indications of coal were to be found. Apart from the large supply of shells for lime on the immediate site, there was at the head of one of the navigable creeks a fine fresh-water stream running over a bed of limestone. A second creek, navigable for ten or twelve miles, terminated in extensive water-holes. Indeed, within the port there were four inlets or creeks, navigable from ten to fifteen miles, each terminating in fresh water. The Colonel did not anticipate a frequent occurrence of the drought of the previous year. During his five months' occupation, the longest period without rain did not exceed four weeks. He considered the climate to have been fairly tested. The *Lord Auckland's* party of eighty-eight persons were landed under most unfavourable circumstances, at the worst period of the year, on the verge of the autumnal equinox, exposed under canvas for five months, and for nearly three months without fresh provisions or vegetables; yet during the whole period no serious case of sickness occurred.

As for the blacks, they were at first thought to be both numerous and hostile, but the Colonel was not disposed to consider either surmise correct. The largest party he had seen numbered eighteen males, who subsequently brought the females and children to the camp as a sign of amity and friendship. The Colonel emphasised his conviction that the position and extent of Port Curtis—the third harbour in

Australian seas, inferior only to Port Jackson and Hobart—must shortly lead to a permanent settlement on its shores, offering security to the numerous whaling vessels which were then compelled to go to Sydney for repairs and supplies, and becoming an important depôt for the supply of coal to steamers *en route* to India. He had reason to believe that coal would be found in abundance within a few miles of the coast. He had no doubt also that Port Curtis would become a celebrated ship-building centre, possessing as it did timber of the highest quality and facilities for the construction of docks. The adjacent country was capable of affording both tropical and European produce, and was specially adapted to the breeding of stock. "Indeed," wrote the Colonel to Sir Charles Fitzroy, "I believe I am correct in saying that numerous parties, with stock to a very large amount, are now within a short distance of Port Curtis, taking up stations, not only with a view to the supply of the projected settlement, but also to the shipment of wool, tallow, etc., direct to England. The occupation of the country by those parties must shortly lead to the formation of a settlement under private enterprise, and I submit for the consideration of your Excellency whether it may not be advisable to adopt some measures for the protection of the Government rights in this important and valuable position."

In accordance with this latter opportune suggestion, Sir Charles Fitzroy wrote to Earl Grey:—

"I beg to draw your Lordship's attention to that portion of Colonel Barney's report which refers to the advantages possessed by Port Curtis as a harbour and site for a settlement. Captain Owen Stanley, of Her Majesty's ship *Rattlesnake*, who is now here, informs me that the survey of Port Curtis will be one of his first duties after leaving Sydney; and I have requested him to furnish me with a report on the subject at his earliest convenience, in order that, should the result of his survey prove Colonel Barney's opinion to be correct, I may take such steps as will secure the possession of the adjacent country for the Crown, and prevent its occupation by private enterprise in opposition to the rights of the Government. When I am better prepared to offer an opinion as to the best means of effecting this object, it will be my duty to put your Lordship in possession of it without loss of time ; but, as far as I can form an opinion at present, it occurs to me that it would be desirable to proclaim an extent of country in the vicinity of Port Curtis as a county, and thus bring it under the regulations within the settled districts of the colony of New South Wales."

CHAPTER VII

THE GROWTH AND DEVELOPMENT OF GLADSTONE

THE official career of the new colony and the philanthropic experiment, on which Mr Gladstone had bestowed so much time, thought, and labour, was now at an end. North Australia was a thing of the past—wiped out of existence by the unceremonious edict of Earl Grey. But the little town of Gladstone, the intended metropolis of the new colony, remained as an established entity on the shores of Port Curtis, and although Earl Grey could abolish North Australia with a stroke of his pen, it was beyond his power to prevent or to check in any way the growth and development of the town of Gladstone. That town was destined to be the one direct and permanent outcome of the colonising project of the great statesman whose name it bears and perpetuates. An indirect but not unimportant result of Mr Gladstone's experiment was to expedite, and bring within the range of practical politics, the creation of the present colony of Queensland, which covers all the territory that Mr Gladstone had assigned and set apart for North Australia. For, brief as was the official existence of the colony of North Australia, it lasted long enough to draw the attention of adventurous and ambitious young men in the southern districts to the fact that splendid areas of unoccupied pastoral country were to be found in the vicinity of Port Curtis. The result was that while Colonel Barney and his pioneers were retreating to the south, under orders from Earl Grey, other bands of pioneers were travelling up from the south, overland, driving their flocks and herds before them. These newcomers spread themselves over the Port Curtis district, squatted on the rich grassy flats, grew by degrees into an important and influential community, and thus paved the way for the advent of the great colony of Queensland, which may be metaphorically described as the imposing superstructure erected on the temporarily-abandoned foundations of Mr Gladstone's North Australia.

Some time before Colonel Barney received his marching orders to return to Sydney, the course of events was clearly foreseen by at least one Sydney journalist, who wrote:—

"What is there to restrain our squatters and our settlers, who, like Lot in ancient times, will naturally have an eye to the best watered runs, from advancing into the regions so highly praised by the explorers, and, forsaking the barren realms of New South Wales, adding to the population and pastoral wealth of North Australia? There they will find fresh grass, abundance of water, a free country, and there, unterrified by the £1 per acre clause, and not having the fear of the Commissioner before their eyes, they may make hay while the sun shines; that is, until Colonel Barney can summon up courage enough to start a few Commissioners of his own; which, by the way, would be one of the wisest things he could do. It will be but a short time before cattle and drays will be finding their way to the at present unknown embouchures, or heads of navigation of the great rivers that must enter the ocean somewhere in the neighbourhood of the new settlement."

Gladstone thus grew apace, and developed into the nearest and most accessible port of a considerable area of pastoral country dotted with sheep and cattle stations, the port to which the squatters sent their wool, tallow, hides, etc., for exportation, and from which their drivers brought back dray-loads of all the requisite supplies for their stations. By one of those right-about-face evolutions which are by no means rare either in British or Colonial politics, Gladstone, from being originally the *bête noir* of the Sydney Government, became in a few years its particular *protégé*, its "pet township," as Mr Pugh says in his historical sketch of Queensland, the favoured spot for the expenditure of Treasury subsidies. Mr (afterwards Sir Henry) Parkes, the Prime Minister of the future, then a young Member for the city of Sydney, and a zealous economist of the public funds, was repeatedly indignant at what he considered this wasteful expenditure upon Gladstone, and made many vehement speeches on the subject. No doubt the animating motive of this complete change of policy on the part of the Sydney authorities was their conviction that separation was imminent and inevitable, and they naturally preferred that the capital of the new colony, which would soon be created in the north, should be a town at a considerable distance, such as Gladstone was, rather than the only other possible capital, Brisbane, which was close enough to their own doors to be regarded as an unpleasant and undesirable rival metropolis. Hence, all the efforts of the Sydney Government during the years preceding separation were directed towards thrusting Gladstone into the forefront, and pushing Brisbane into the background. These efforts, as we know, were not ultimately crowned with success. When separation did come, and the colony of Queensland was constituted by the Imperial Parliament, Brisbane, as the site of the first settlement and the possessor of the larger population, was deemed to have superior claims to Gladstone in the choice of the capital. In other respects, Gladstone unquestionably would have been the better choice. It had what Brisbane could make no possible pretence to—a magnificent harbour, and it possessed the great merit of a central and commanding position on the coast. Indeed, one glance at the map is sufficient to show that the situation of Brisbane is positively ludicrous and entirely indefensible as a metropolis, being at the remote south-eastern corner of a territory stretching away for some 1300 miles to the north and 1000 miles to the west.

One of the most important steps taken by the Sydney authorities with a view to pushing Gladstone into all possible prominence, and qualifying the place for metropolitan honours, was to constitute it the seat of a Government Resident. Having regard to the remoteness of the town at that early stage of its existence, the absence of regular communication with Sydney, and the consequent necessity of acting largely on his own responsibility and depending on his own resources, the position of a Government Resident under such circumstances approximated closely to that of a Governor of an isolated Crown colony. The Sydney authorities made an

admirable selection when they nominated Sir Maurice Charles
O'Connell as the first Government Resident at Gladstone at
the beginning of 1854.

A few days afterwards he was also gazetted as Police
Magistrate and Commissioner of Crown Lands at Gladstone.
This gentleman, who was a kinsman of Daniel O'Connell,
the emancipator of Catholic Ireland, had entered the Army
as an ensign in 1828, when he was in his seventeenth
year. He accompanied his regiment, the 73rd Foot, to
Gibraltar and Malta, and in 1835 he obtained permission to
raise an Irish regiment for service in Spain to uphold the
cause of Queen Isabella against the Carlists. Of this
regiment, the 10th Munster Light Infantry, he was gazetted
Lieutenant-Colonel. He was in command of this regiment
for nearly two years, during which he took part in a number
of engagements and achieved considerable distinction. At
the close of the campaign he was a General of Brigade, and
a Knight of three Spanish orders. In 1838 he accompanied
the 28th Regiment to Sydney, and on its recall he sold out
and settled in the colony, devoting himself with considerable
success to pastoral pursuits. After serving for three years
in the New South Wales Legislative Council as Member for
Port Phillip, he was appointed a Commissioner of Crown
Lands in the Burnett district, an office from which he retired
at the end of 1853 in compliance with a request from the
Government to superintend and establish the permanent
settlement on the shores of Port Curtis. It is the career of
Sir Maurice O'Connell, as Government Resident at Gladstone,
that specially comes within the scope and purpose of the
present work, but it will be convenient at this stage briefly
to summarise his subsequent history. He remained in
official charge of the Gladstone district until 1859, when
the colony that Mr Gladstone had projected, and partially
established under the style and title of North Australia,
became an actual and permanent political entity under the
name of Queensland. Sir Maurice O'Connell was nominated
a Member of the first Queensland Legislative Council, and
rendered valuable assistance to the Ministry of Sir Robert
Herbert, to which he was unofficially attached. In 1861 he
was elected to the Presidency of the Legislative Council, and

he continued to hold that high office up to the day of his death, discharging its important duties with a dignity, impartiality, and courtesy that commanded general respect and esteem. On four occasions he was called upon to officiate as Acting-Governor of the colony. His death, on March 23, 1879, was deeply and sincerely deplored throughout the length and breadth of the colony; his remains were honoured with a public funeral, and a life pension was conferred upon his widow by the Parliament of Queensland.

On the same day that it announced the appointment of Sir Maurice O'Connell as Government Resident at Gladstone, the *Herald* published a lengthy article of three columns, discussing in detail the agitation that had arisen for the erection of a new colony in the northern district of New South Wales. The establishment of such a colony was deprecated as premature and unnecessary, but in the event of the Imperial Government deciding otherwise, it was strongly urged that Gladstone, and not Brisbane, should be the northern capital.

"In appointing the centre of a colony, a secure and easily accessible harbour is a desideratum that first presents itself, and, by all accounts, few on the coast can compete with Port Curtis in either respect. This place is admirably fitted to become the site of a capital. Its situation, close to the commencement of that Great Barrier Reef which forms so singular and formidable a feature of the north-eastern coast, is calculated to confer upon it additional importance, and, when combined with its easy access and secure anchorage, will always ensure its being frequented by steamers and other vessels navigating along the coast. If, therefore, a northern colony must be formed, it would appear that its limits can only be properly defined, and its capital fixed upon, after the settlement of Port Curtis has been thoroughly explored."

As a result of the appointment of Sir Maurice O'Connell to the Government Residency at Gladstone, and the pervading belief that Gladstone would be the chosen capital of the new colony that must sooner or later be proclaimed in the north, a considerable amount of public interest was concentrated on the first sale of Government land around the shores of Port Curtis. It was held at the Colonial Treasury, Sydney, on February 8 and 9, 1854. There was keen competition for Gladstone town and suburban lots, and the aggregate sales realised nearly £14,000. Archbishop Polding, the then Catholic Primate of Australia; Sir James Martin, afterwards Chief-Justice of New South Wales; and the Hon. William Forster, afterwards Prime Minister and Agent-General for New South Wales in London, figure prominently in the list of purchasers. But from the frequency with which such names as Moses, Mendelson, and Cohen occur, it is evident that Jewish speculators were chiefly responsible for the Pactolian stream that flowed into the Colonial Treasury as a result of the first sale of Gladstone lands. A newspaper correspondent, writing shortly afterwards from Brisbane, the rival candidate for northern metropolitan honours, remarked :—

"We were rather surprised on learning the high prices paid for ground at Port Curtis. The result of the first sale of allotments at Gladstone proves that I was correct in all along maintaining that the public would attach a high degree of importance to that place."

The same correspondent, writing on March 9, and discussing the petitions to the Queen for the separation of the northern district from New South Wales, observed :—

"The approach to unanimity is not so close as was supposed. In the north they are inveterately opposed to the measure, if Brisbane is to be the capital of the new colony. Under the circumstances, it seems impolitic in the Brisbane people to press their petition. Its consideration is likely to bring forward what many consider to be the superior claims of Port Curtis to form the capital, and it is worth their while to reflect whether it would not, on the whole, be better for them to maintain the present connection with Sydney than to see their respectable borough eclipsed by a metropolis so close to them as Gladstone."

A letter from Sydney to England, dated March 20, 1854, refers to the opening-up of the Port Curtis district under the administration of Sir Maurice O'Connell as "the most important feature in our recent affairs." The departure of Sir Maurice from Sydney, "with a well-appointed staff of working pioneers," is recorded, and it is added that the first operation to which Sir Maurice would direct his efforts would be the development of every available means of internal communication. He would commence by constructing a road from Gladstone to Gayndah, the then most northerly post-town in Australia, a distance of a hundred miles.

"Whether as regards the pastoral, mercantile, or maritime interests of the colony, the opening of this new settlement offers a most promising subject of consideration. The results of the first sales of lands, already surveyed in the town of Gladstone, give evidence as to the great interest with which the new settlement is viewed. For twenty-one town allotments, the upset price of which was £20 per acre, £318 per acre was given. For 215 acres of suburban lots, whose upset price was from £2 to £2, 10s. per acre, £9 per acre was obtained."

In the speech from the Throne at the opening of Parliament in Sydney, on May 10, 1853, Sir Charles Fitzroy referred to the great increase of pastoral settlers in the Port Curtis district, the growing importance of Gladstone, and the necessity of making that town the headquarters of an adequate force of police. Provision, he added, would be made upon the estimates to meet this essential expenditure.

Simultaneously with this Vice-Regal statement was published a report of a very interesting character, on the progress of settlement in the districts around Port Curtis. It gives some graphic particulars of the perils to which the pioneer squatters and settlers were subjected. We are told that before the organisation of a force of mounted native police, under Commandant Walker, murders by the wild blacks were of almost daily occurrence: white men could not travel at all unless well mounted and well armed; hut-keepers would not venture down to the creek to get a bucket of water without a double-barrelled gun; workers would not journey along the road on foot unless in bands for mutual protection, and tree-fellers at each blow looked behind them, expecting to see a spear levelled at them by some lurking savage. Chinamen who had been imported by the squatters to act as shepherds were so scared by the ferocity and hostility of the blacks, that they deserted *en masse*, or "bolted," to use the more expressive phrase of the report. But when a certain number of the blacks were civilised, organised into companies of mounted native police, officered by white men of military experience, and trained to run down, shoot, or capture their wild marauding brethren of the bush, the condition of the country around Port Curtis rapidly improved. The marvellous qualities of these native troopers are thus depicted :—

"In a country intersected with thick scrubs, and well supplied with fruits, game of all kinds, and water, hordes of savage blacks swarm, issuing forth in bands, attacking the shepherds, and driving away the stock to slaughter at their leisure. In almost all attacks made upon them by the whites, the latter were worsted, being unable to penetrate the scrubs, but the native policeman, when once he has passed the sagacious searching examination of the Commandant, and is reported fit for duty, can go anywhere and do anything. He is an expert swordsman, a perfect light dragoon, and one of the best skirmishers of any troops in the world. When dismounted and fighting on his own hook, nothing stops him, nothing daunts him, he scales the highest mountains like a goat, traverses the plains in pursuit with the swiftness of a deer, rushes through the scrub like a wallaby, and loads and fires with the precision of an old soldier."

At the time this report was prepared, all the best lands for hundreds of miles in the vicinity of Port Curtis had been marked out by adventurous pioneer squatters for occupation as sheep and cattle stations as soon as Governmental sanction could be secured. Some appear to have anticipated the formal official permission, for it is recorded that "James and Norman Leith Hay, with 40,000 sheep, have crossed the dividing range and occupied a splendid country close upon the borders of Port Curtis. Other gentlemen are about to follow with more sheep, and before twelve months have passed, the whole country, up to the Peak Range, will be clothed with cattle and sheep upon a thousand hills. Nothing can stop the onward march of the Australian squatter, protected as he now is by Commandant Walker's native police. All this is due to their civilising influence."

The *Brisbane Courier*, on April 1, 1854, wrote :—

"Within the last few months, since northern separation has appeared inevitable in Sydney, there has been a great outcry about

Port Curtis, which has been played against Moreton Bay, and the land at which place has realised large sums, owing to the flourish of trumpets so interestedly sounded in its behalf. But if a colony is to be established with a centre at Port Curtis, we may reasonably expect the limits of such colony to extend some three or four degrees further to the northward; and in such a temperature the sheep-farmer, who alone could be a profitable colonist in a new country like that, might soon bid adieu to his calling, for the wool of his sheep would soon become too coarse to pay. If sheep-farming can be profitably carried on as far north as the Tropic of Capricorn, it is as much as can be expected. What other branch of industry, then, would be the means of introducing and supporting a population there? Certainly, agriculture without a market will never do; and all that remains is the mere chance of a gold-field being discovered. Any attempt, then, to fix the centre of a colony at Port Curtis, deprived of the succour and support of the wealth and population of the Moreton Bay District, must end in disappointment and disaster."

The Brisbane organ was willing to recognise Port Curtis as an important outpost of the new colony, which might, in process of time, develop into a large and populous centre. In that case, and if in the future Gladstone should become the most eligible site for the seat of Government, the *Courier* acknowledged that "the future Governor of Northern Australia would have a right to remove thither."

Commenting on this Brisbane view of the rival northern centre, Gladstone, the *Sydney Morning Herald* pointed out that the statement that sheep-farming could not be successfully carried on beyond the Tropic of Capricorn, owing to the alleged deterioration of the wool in low latitudes, was a mere surmise.

"There are sheep now running and producing wool of first-rate quality in situations which would have been pronounced a few years ago, simply on account of the lowness of the latitude, altogether unsuitable for the growth of the great colonial staple. In fact, every movement of sheep northwards towards the Tropic during the last four or five years has been undertaken more or less in the way of experiment, and as these movements have always succeeded, it is difficult to say where the true northern limit to the successful growth of wool is to be drawn in Australia."

The *Herald* proceeded to soundly rate the Brisbane folks for fancying that their interests required them to depreciate Gladstone as the future centre of a large exporting district, and lightly estimate its probable pastoral resources. The folly of disparaging what was evidently designed as the natural outlet of a vast extent of valuable territory, the lapse of a very short time would clearly establish. Cotton, sugar, coffee, rice, and maize could in all probability be most successfully cultivated in the Port Curtis district, while the auriferous prospects of that extensive region were of the most inviting character. As for the objection that Gladstone was unsuitable as the capital or centre of a new northern colony, because it was too near the existing northern limits of white settlement, the *Herald* contended it was an objection that could at any time be removed by the simple process of extending those limits.

"To what extent this ought to be done, in the supposition that it is intended to make Gladstone the capital of a new colony, will depend partly on the line that may be adopted as the southern boundary of that colony, and partly on the extent of inhabited country to the north-eastward, of which Port Curtis shall be found to form the natural harbour."

Sir Charles Fitzroy commenced his career as Governor of New South Wales by faithfully carrying out the instructions he had received from Mr Gladstone, both in conversation and correspondence, in regard to the establishment of the new colony of North Australia, and there was a certain appropriateness in the fact that one of his last Vice-Regal acts, prior to surrendering the reins after an exceptionally long tenure of office, was to voyage to the town of Gladstone, the sturdy and prosperous child of vanished North Australia, and formally instal Sir Maurice O'Connell as Government Resident. Sir Maurice sailed out of Sydney Harbour on board the *Tom Tough* on March 1, 1854, accompanied by Lady O'Connell, Captain Prout, Mr Riddell, Mr Moore, Mr Sheppard, and fifty-two in the steerage. Three days later, Sir Charles Fitzroy embarked at Sydney on board Her Majesty's ship *Calliope*, for the purpose of making a tour through the northern district of the colony, and officially establishing a Government settlement on the shores of Port Curtis. All the leading officials of the colony assembled at Government House and accompanied His Excellency to Fort Macquarie Stairs, where he was received by a Guard of Honour from the 11th Regiment with the band and the Queen's colours. On His Excellency's leaving the shore a salute was fired from Fort Phillip, and on his reaching the ship, his flag as Vice-Admiral of Australasia was hoisted and saluted with seventeen guns.

"The main and chief object of the trip," wrote the *Sydney Morning Herald*, "is to establish a settlement at Port Curtis, to form, in fact, what may hereafter be considered by geographers, under whatever name it may be designated, the Northern Province of the Australian Continent. Such an object is of the greatest importance to the whole community. A Government Resident for the district has been appointed, and competent people have been sent down to report on the natural capabilities of the country. To predict anything of good, to augur anything of evil, would be most improper, but we shall look most anxiously for the results of this expedition."

After a brief stay at Brisbane, Sir Charles proceeded to Port Curtis and arrived off the infant town of Gladstone on the afternoon of April 16. Sir Maurice and Lady O'Connell went out to meet him, and remained on board the *Calliope* until nightfall. On the following morning Sir Charles Fitzroy and suite officially landed, amidst the cheers of the assembled Gladstonians, white constables and black being drawn up in military array. The latter, called the Native Mounted Police, were under the command of Lieutenant Murray. Repairing to the extemporised Government House of the settlement, Sir Charles received an address of welcome, and formally installed Sir Maurice O'Connell in the office of Government Resident at Gladstone, expressing his hope and belief that the settlement, at whose inauguration they were assisting that day, would grow and prosper and play an important part in the future development of Northern Australia. His Excellency, after visiting the principal points of interest, was entertained at a banquet, and in responding to the toast of his health, spoke in eulogistic terms of the delightful scenery by which

F

Gladstone was surrounded, and of the many advantages offered by Port Curtis as a harbour and distributing centre for the northern districts when they became thoroughly opened up, as they assuredly would be in the early future.

During his stay at Gladstone, Sir Charles Fitzroy called upon the oldest inhabitant of the place, Mr Willmott, and took lunch with him. After the abortive colonising experiment of Colonel Barney, Mr Willmott, with a firm faith in the future of the place, established himself on the shores of Port Curtis, and his courage, enterprise, and foresight did not go without their reward. His Excellency also made several excursions into the country around Port Curtis. He was much interested in the discovery of specks of gold on the banks of a certain river, and strongly urged Sir Maurice O'Connell carefully to prospect the locality with an eye to the discovery of a permanent and payable goldfield. He christened the river the "Calliope," and in a few years the "Calliope goldfield" became an established and recognised fact.

The voyage back to Sydney was exceedingly tempestuous, and the *Calliope* was forced to run for shelter under the lee of Lord Howe's Island. A small party braved the elements and ventured ashore. They found four families, numbering twenty souls, living on this lonely spot in the Pacific. Five children were baptised by the chaplain of the *Calliope*, the Rev. Mr Carwithen, who was the first clergyman seen on the island. Being struck by a squall of exceptional violence, the cable of the *Calliope* snapped, and she was compelled to put to sea in very rough weather, which did not moderate for several days. Sydney was reached on the morning of May 10.

In opening a new session of Parliament on June 6, Sir Charles Fitzroy thus referred to his visit to Gladstone in the Speech from the Throne :—

"My recent visit to the northern districts of the colony has been of material assistance to me in forming an opinion of their value and importance, and I shall be prepared to submit for your consideration in the course of the session certain measures calculated to increase their trade and develop their resources. The new settlement at Port Curtis promises to be, at no distant day, of great value to this colony, on account of the excellence of its harbour, its genial climate, and the fertility of its soil."

The official recognition of Gladstone by the visit of the Governor, and his confident predictions of its coming prosperity and importance, appear to have had an immediate effect in attracting people to the place, for in a letter from Gladstone, dated May 20, 1854, the constant arrival of new settlers and citizens is recorded. Most of them came overland from the south, "cutting and marking as they came what will probably be ere long a fine road into the interior," to quote the words of the letter.

"We constantly hear," the letter proceeds, "of new water-holes and excellent water being found by ramblers and bushmen, and Gladstone is now no worse off than Sydney in this respect. Plenty of cattle, too, are daily expected with the overland parties. Everything in its way is assisting to make Gladstone greater than many towns that are twenty times its age, and its harbour, above everything, must make it the envy of every sea-port on this coast, scarcely excepting Port Jackson itself."

In the Legislative Council at Sydney on August 29, Sir Henry Parkes inquired whether in founding the new settlement at Gladstone any reserves of land had been set apart for the use of the blacks? The Colonial Secretary replied that reserves for the use of the aboriginal population were always set apart when new districts were colonised. In the case of Port Curtis no reserve had yet been proclaimed, but it was intended by the Government to provide one, if not two, as soon as it was known what the habits and requirements of the natives were.

A letter, dated September 8, 1854, says :—

"There seems to be no doubt that the country in the immediate neighbourhood of Gladstone is possessed of considerable agricultural capabilities, and this of itself will, in time, when labour is more abundant, confer upon the place a considerable degree of importance. As yet there does not appear to be much investment of capital going on, either in buildings or territorial improvements.

By selling the Gladstone allotments in Sydney, a higher price was unquestionably obtained, but in taking this course, the Government have unquestionably retarded the progress of their infant settlement. Purchasers closer to Gladstone would have improved their properties by buildings or cultivation forthwith, whereas the allotments, having been mostly acquired by Sydney speculators, will, in all probability, be left untouched for years in the hope of an augmentation taking place in their value."

On July 25, 1855, Sir Henry Parkes attacked the Government for what he conceived to be the extravagant amount of money they had expended on the establishment of the new settlement at Gladstone. He objected to voting £3300 as salaries for the officials engaged in creating what he characterised as a "New Utopia," and a further sum of £7000 for the starting of public works at Gladstone. He also attacked the appointment of Sir Maurice O'Connell to the Government Residency. The Colonial Secretary, in reply, said he regarded the new settlement at Gladstone in the light of an important dependency, and as a most advantageous expansion of the colony in a northerly direction. The Hon. Member for Sydney had charged the Government with going to great expense for a private purpose, and in order to bestow an appointment on a certain gentleman. He could assure the House that the gentleman appointed as Government Resident at Gladstone, had been selected on account of his special knowledge of the country and its capabilities, as well as for his conspicuous intelligence and ability. When it was determined to establish a settlement at Gladstone, it was obviously necessary to despatch a vessel with a surveying party in the first instance, and when the district came to be partially settled, it was no less necessary to send a native police force to remove from the minds of the settlers all apprehension of attacks from the aborigines. The Governor-General had from the first taken the proper and statesmanlike view of the circumstances and necessities of this new dependency, and had acted most judiciously throughout.

CHAPTER VIII

THE EXPERIENCES OF A PIONEER SQUATTER

In the course of an interesting speech, delivered in Sydney on the first of May, 1854, Mr T. S. Mort, one of the greatest names in the history of the Australian wool trade, made a noteworthy reference to the prominent part played by the pioneer squatters in the opening-up and development of Australia in general, and the Port Curtis district in particular. He pointed out that the squatting interest was the primeval interest of the colony, the interest which had brought the colony into its present prosperous position, and if the colony were to continue to flourish, this interest must be encouraged until improved means of internal communication had rendered the interior fully available for settled enterprise. The squatters had universally been the pioneers of civilisation throughout Australia. He could say from his own personal knowledge, that the first white men who had trodden the solitudes of the Port Curtis district were the brothers Hay, pioneer squatters. They depastured their flocks there at an expense to themselves of £1400; they lost five companions who had joined them in the enterprise; they lost many bales of their wool, but they succeeded in opening up the country around Port Curtis. Recently lands in that district had been sold to the amount of £30,000. The Colonial Treasury had been enriched to that extent by the energy and enterprise of the much-maligned squatters.

I have been privileged to peruse the unpublished autobiography of one of the first squatters to venture into the unexplored regions around Port Curtis, and from the manuscript of this gentleman—who was destined to become in later years the holder of one of the highest offices under the Government of Queensland — I extract the following graphic and interesting narrative of his impressions and experiences as a pioneer explorer:—

"Having some years before read an account of Sir Thomas Mitchell's discovery of Fitzroy Downs and Mount Abundance, it occurred to me that, according to his description, that beautiful country could not be very far to the westward of the most outlying station on Darling Downs, and, after some consultation, my brother and I agreed that it would be worth while making an attempt to find it. We therefore set to work to make the needful preparations for an exploring trip into the wild west. With a young white man and a black boy, named Darby, I set off, armed with a couple of guns and a brace of pistols, and equipped with three saddle and two pack-horses carrying provisions, blankets, etc. Leaving the River Condamine, we struck off to the north-west, and on the third day, calculating that we had attained a position due east of Mount Abundance, we changed our course westward, and after forcing our way for ten miles or so through a thick briggalow scrub, we emerged on a patch of open downs country, with a creek running through it to the north-eastward. Camping here in a downpour of rain, we started again next morning, and continued our westward course for five days through a succession of scrubby ridges, occasionally varied by a few square miles of open country. On our left was a range of low hills, to the top of which I climbed to view the surrounding country, but nothing could I see save scrub, scrub, all around for miles, with occasional glimpses of open country between. The first of these hills I named Mount Disappointment, and the second Mount Deceitful, because there was a fair-sized piece of open country at its foot, which at first promised well, but on closer inspection turned out to be a mere patch of a few square miles surrounded by the inevitable scrub. Here we camped for the night on the bank of a larger creek than we had yet seen. This was our nineteenth day out, and there was as yet no prospect of our dropping upon the Fitzroy Downs. No natives could we see to enlighten us. We had caught a glimpse of one the day before. He was up a gum-tree hunting an opossum, and the first we knew of his presence was seeing him drop from the tree about twenty yards from us, pick himself up, and, uttering a succession of short howls, run crouching towards a creek close by, into which he pitched himself headlong and disappeared. Our provisions were diminishing alarmingly, as we had only been able to shoot half-a-dozen ducks and a few pigeons. We lay awake discussing whether we ought to abandon the quest of the Fitzroy Downs and return to our point of departure. During the first part of the night, when we were tired, hungry, and depressed, we rather favoured a retreat, but after a few hours' sleep, a pint of tea, and a morsel of damper and beef, our spirits revived, and we determined to continue our westward course for another day or two, in the hope of accomplishing our aim, and being the first to find the way from Darling Downs to the splendid country described by Mitchell. We agreed to be satisfied with two meals a day, consisting of a small bit of biscuit and a still smaller bit of salt beef. After getting the horses saddled and ready for a start, I suggested that, as there had been a good deal of rain, it would be well to fire off our arms and reload, to make sure that there would be no miss-fire if any occasion should arise for using them. After firing our salvo of six barrels, there was a moment's stillness, and then arose a yell of men's voices and a screaming of gins and piccaninies that made the welkin ring, and showed us that we were in the immediate vicinity of a big camp of blacks. The knowledge of this made us reload our arms rapidly and mount our horses without delay, for although we would have been glad of an interview with one or two for the sake of obtaining information about the country, I had been taught by experience that with blacks, as with other members of the human family, numbers give confidence. They had large numbers, and we had not, so we lost no time in resuming our westward journey with as much speed as was compatible with dignity, viz., a smart walk. That night we fortified our camp by placing all the saddles on edge round our heads to fend off any missiles that might be thrown at us from the scrub, for it was possible that the blacks were following on our track. But the night passed in profound sleep, and next morning we continued our course. About noon a scrubby ridge on our left rose into a low isolated hill, and while our horses were having a bite of grass, a drink, and a roll in the dust to refresh them, I climbed to the top in eager anticipation of seeing open country to the westward, but no such luck was mine. Dense scrub greeted my view in every direction, not even varied by the open patches we had seen during the earlier part of our journey. Descending in a not very amiable temper, I avenged myself by naming the hill Mount Horrible; and, much mollified by this, we mounted and proceeded on our way.

"Towards evening I noticed a slight improvement in the country and the grasses, and when we had camped, I saw the sun sink clear to the horizon without the intervention of scrub, the first time that such a phenomenon had greeted our eyes during the whole journey. Next morning, while Darby was bringing in the horses, I shouldered my gun, and walked up the sloping and open ridge at the foot of which we were camped. The country kept on improving as I advanced; whinstone soil, thinly timbered with white box, and a good sprinkling of herbage began to prevail. The top of the ridge was level for about half a mile, and I continued walking on to its western edge, when at the foot of a long slope before me appeared a large valley, its sides formed by open undulating downs country, with a good-sized creek meandering through it. Above the top of the opposite slope appeared in the remote distance the summit of an isolated mountain, which I at once concluded must be Mount Abundance. The sudden transition from great despondency to joy at this grand discovery was almost too much for me in my rather reduced condition, and I flung myself down at the foot of a box-tree, and for many minutes sat gloating over the squatters' paradise that lay spread out before me. Returning to camp with a light step and in a serene temper, in marked contrast to that in which I had quitted it, I communicated the glorious news to my fellow-travellers, who fully shared in my jubilation at this happy result. After saddling up and finishing our breakfast (which did not detain us very long), we started off to have a nearer view of the glorious scene that had so unexpectedly greeted my eyes. Descending into the valley I had seen, we crossed the creek and then ascended the long succession of sloping downs that formed the western side of the valley, and which were covered with abundance of the very finest grasses and herbage. On arriving at the summit of these slopes, a vast extent of open country lay spread out before us, stretching for miles to the south, to the west, and to the north, where appeared the mountain I had seen looming large against the sky, while behind us to the east lay the black and desolate-looking mass of scrubby country through which we had made our way. What would I not have given to spend a week in exploring this grand stretch of country? But alas and alack! our provisions were now reduced to so low an ebb that starvation stared us in the face, and we had to content ourselves with one day's exploration, edging off all the time to the southward, and leaving the mountain behind us gradually sinking beneath the horizon. As we were riding along the top of a high plateau of open downs, a black speck appeared before us in the distance, which Darby pronounced to be a blackfellow, but which, on our getting nearer, turned out to be a "gin" or black woman busily engaged in digging up the ground with her long yam-stick, and searching either for edible roots or for ant-grubs. So absorbed was she in these operations that she never noticed us until the jingling of the hobbles and the tin pots on the pack-horses reached her ears, when she looked up and saw us. Never was poor mortal more terrified. With a shriek she fled, giving utterance to a series of moans, and never looking behind her lest the dreadful vision should appear again and strike her dead. I told Darby to ride after her and "head her back," which he did at a canter. She never stopped, but kept running on and on, until at last, finding that she could not escape, she flung herself on the ground, hid her face in her hands, and lay stock still, uttering the most heart-rending moans. I was much concerned for the poor creature, and would gladly have left her in peace to recover from her fright, but we were anxious to get information about water, always the most important element in exploring new country. Dismounting, therefore, I took her gently by her raven locks with one hand, and with the other removed her hand from her face, so that her eyes became visible, and then, assuming my very blandest expression of countenance, nodded and smiled upon her, at the same time making signs to her to rise. This she did, and cast a timid glance at me, when I noticed that the expression of horror on her sable countenance was not quite so marked. I next told Darby to speak to her in his native tongue, for although I knew she was not likely to understand the dialect he spoke, I thought it might soothe her to find that one as black as herself could associate with white men and horses, and yet live. The experiment succeeded; she stared wistfully at Darby, the expression of her face gradually became calmer, and horror was succeeded by astonishment. Taking out our biscuit bag and putting a piece in my mouth, I handed her some, making signs to her to eat it, which she did, but apparently with more surprise than relish. I then took a pint pot, and putting it to my lips, went through the form of drinking, pointing at the same time in various directions with a note of interrogation on my face. Suddenly a look of intelligence appeared on her countenance, and pointing to the westward, she signified with animated gestures that there was a plentiful supply of water in that direction. Where she pointed we could see an extensive plain with lines and clusters of trees, which we assumed to be in native phrase "yarra," or flooded gum-trees, a sure indication of a creek or a river, but in that direction we dared not go. Our steps had now to be directed as rapidly as possible to the east, to the east, to the land of the whites, and I felt like the Irish fisherman that 'if any one came between me and my last resource, I'd run him down av he was my father.' Parting therefore from our sable friend, now much calmer and almost restored to her seven senses, we continued our way across those lovely downs, and in the evening camped on a delightful spot, where our horses had a grand time, up to their eyes in magnificent grasses and herbage. Next morning the country began to change from downs into low iron-bark ridges with patches of scrub, and about noon, as we turned the angle of a creek, we saw before us, about a hundred yards off, a camp of about fifteen blacks, with gins and piccaninies, who, greatly to our surprise, held their ground. They neither ran away nor attacked us, but awaited our approach with tolerable equanimity. Some of the men showed evident symptoms of fear, not unmixed with a desire to try conclusions with us. This was evidenced by the determined manner in which they grasped their spears and scowled at us. Others scrambled up the trees and stared at us in mute astonishment. We pulled up about thirty yards from their camp, when out stepped an elderly gin, who began to talk to us in a mixture of the language of the blacks and the slang that served as a medium of communication between the two races on the border-land of civilisation and savagery. She was the one member of the party who had seen white men before, having visited, as she gave us to understand, one of the outlying stations on the Darling Downs. Doubtless it was owing to her persuasion that her friends had neither run away nor attacked us. We asked her, 'where big fellow water sit down' (meaning the River Condamine), and in reply, turning to the south-eastward, she flung out her skinny arms and exclaimed, 'Good way.' I was sorry that we could not afford to give the old lady some token of good-will, for of food we had hardly any left, and the taste for tobacco had not yet penetrated into these remote wilds. Leaving the blacks with every outward appearance of friendliness on both sides, we pushed on as vigorously as possible for the rest of the day. Early on the following morning I despatched Darby to search for big water-holes or lagoons, where ducks might be found to replenish our scanty larder. He only succeeded in losing himself, and we lost valuable time in searching before we found him. Towards evening, however, we came across some billabongs (anabranches) and lagoons, which made us aware that we were near a large river, and furnished us with a couple of ducks for supper. Next morning we divided the last crumbs left in the bottom of our biscuit bag, about a handful to each, and this was the last of our farinaceous food. Our flour had been finished a couple of days before, our sugar-bag was empty, and all we had left was a good supply of tea, together with a few pipes of tobacco. Our ammunition was also very scant, and our distance from the nearest station could not be under one hundred miles in a straight line. Turning once more to the east, we reached the Condamine at last, and followed it up, pushing our way through a succession of scrubs, billabongs, and large flats. We had to keep carefully to the valley of the river and its bordering lagoons, for on them depended our supply of water-fowl to keep us from starving. Darby was fortunate as a sportsman, and by taking advantage of every cover, crawling close up to his victims, and blazing into the middle of the swimming flocks, in defiance of the laws of sport, he managed nearly always to hit one or two, and occasionally three, at a shot, and thus kept us supplied with ducks while the powder and shot lasted. But these soon became very scarce, and on the third day our prospects became very gloomy. Only a couple of charges were left, and the necessity of sacrificing one of our horses to keep us alive until we reached the nearest station was discussed. We had even fixed upon the victim, my pack-horse, a lazy, useless brute, but in fair condition, when next morning, just as we had crossed a creek, we came upon some fresh horse-tracks going up it. Needless to say, we followed them up with all possible alacrity, and in a few minutes we were delighted to meet an outward-bound exploring party, headed by Mr Connor. They generously replenished our supplies of powder and shot, while we in return gave them some useful information about the country we had been traversing. After a very pleasant and, to us, providential meeting, we parted, they for the west and we for the east. A scrub soon appeared ahead of us, long and unbroken, and rather than follow it round, we kept our course and plunged into it. Hour after hour we forced our way along, but we had to camp in the middle of it. We dared not hobble out our horses, as they would have strayed off in search of water, and the poor beasts had therefore to be tied up, the only time that such a misfortune had befallen them on the journey. We started again at dawn, and eventually emerged upon open country, where a chain of lagoons greeted our longing eyes and furnished us with a breakfast of duck, washed down with a pint of tea, refreshing though sugarless, and followed by a pipe of the soothing, narcotic weed.

After giving the horses a few hours to make up for their night's starvation, we again pushed on for a couple of days. Again our ammunition was getting short, and again we began to cast wistful and longing eyes on the pack-horse. Our last charge, when expended, brought us a brace of ducks, and on these we both supped and breakfasted. Towards nightfall we struck a large creek flowing towards the Condamine, which we knew must be Dogwood Creek, and that being so, we could not be more than twenty or thirty miles from a station. Thus cheered and encouraged, we pushed on with the utmost speed that we could extract from our fagged and jaded horses, and at last, to our intense joy and relief, we came upon some sheep tracks, which led us to an outlying station belonging to Mr Ewer, who was then the furthest pioneer squatter in that direction. In a few minutes the hospitable hut-keeper had placed before us a large piece of damper (bread baked in bush fashion beneath the piled-up embers), some first-class mutton chops, and a pot of exquisite tea. What I enjoyed most was once more having sugar in my tea, a luxury of which we had long been deprived. Of our attenuated condition and dilapidated wardrobes, I need only remark that a more haggard and ragged trio could seldom be seen even in the slums of London.

"After resting and recruiting for a time, we decided to make another journey to Mount Abundance in order to effect a more thorough exploration of the country than was possible under the circumstances of our first visit. This time I was determined that we were not to suffer from hunger if I could help it, so, besides a far larger stock of tea, sugar, flour, and beef on two pack-horses, we took with us an extra pack-horse, loaded with flour as a stand-by in case of accidents, together with an ample supply of ammunition and fishing tackle, which latter we stupidly omitted when starting on our former journey. This time we revelled in luxurious plenty. It was a complete contrast to the last trip, when hurry, hurry, or starve was the order of every day. We arrived at Mount Abundance in due course, and spent six days in a thorough examination of the glorious Fitzroy Downs, with the result that we determined to occupy this new and promising country as soon as possible."

CHAPTER IX

THE GREAT GOLD RUSH

FROM 1854 to 1858 the little town of Gladstone made quiet, solid, and substantial progress under the beneficent rule of Sir Maurice O'Connell and the benevolent patronage of the Sydney Treasury. Squatters gradually increased in the surrounding territory, and their exportation of wool and importation of supplies from the town of Gladstone naturally increased in proportion to their numbers. Gladstone was thus developing into a thriving centre of commercial and shipping activity, a town characterised by steady progress and placid prosperity, too remote and isolated to be appreciably affected by the feverish, high-pressure existence that was then led by most of the southern Australian communities. But in July, 1858, an event occurred that rudely interrupted the quiet progress of the place, induced a heterogeneous invasion from all quarters, and threw the whole of Australia into a condition of uncontrollable excitement bordering upon temporary insanity. As recorded in a previous chapter, Governor Sir Charles Fitzroy, on the occasion of his official visit to Gladstone, had impressed on Sir Maurice O'Connell the importance of exercising energy and vigilance with a view to the discovery of a permanent goldfield in the district. Sir Maurice had kept the injunction constantly in mind, but it was not until the middle of 1858 that he felt himself justified in officially reporting to his superiors in Sydney the existence of payable gold in the vicinity of Gladstone. The result was wholly unforeseen and unprecedented, and no one was more surprised than Sir Maurice himself at the startling and unexpected consequences that flowed from his words. They wrought an immediate and general commotion in the mining centres of the southern colonies, and not only the large army of unsuccessful diggers, but many of the moderately successful as well, lost no time in packing up and preparing to start as soon as possible for the new El Dorado of the North, the spot where, they had persuaded themselves, immense and easily acquired fortunes were awaiting them a few feet beneath the surface of the soil. The *Melbourne Argus* was not exaggerating in the slightest degree when it described the rush to Port Curtis as "the most remarkable episode in our goldfields' history."

Under the heading of "Discovery of a Rich Goldfield in the Northern District," the *Sydney Morning Herald* of July 27, 1858, published a lengthy communication from its correspondent at Gladstone, dated July 13. From this letter it appears that seven months previously a gentleman who had been travelling in the district, declared that he had found gold in the neighbourhood of the Fitzroy River. This report aroused considerable interest amongst the citizens of Gladstone, who promptly started a subscription and fitted out a party to prosecute the search for the precious metal in the locality indicated. This party started in December, 1857, but returned without having achieved any substantial results. Nevertheless, the belief in the existence of a payable goldfield in the vicinity of their town continued to occupy the minds of the people of Gladstone, and in February, 1858, Sir Maurice O'Connell despatched Mr W. C. Chapel, a gentleman with considerable practical experience of the Australian goldfields, to the Fitzroy River, with instructions to make a minute and thorough investigation of the country, in order to ascertain whether a goldfield really existed in the neighbourhood. Information reached Gladstone in the middle of the following June that Mr Chapel's party had found gold in paying quantities, and Dr A. C. Robertson, who had been for some years Government Resident-Surgeon at Gladstone, proceeded at once to the Fitzroy to determine the accuracy of the report. He and Mr Chapel soon returned with specimens of the gold they had discovered, and a crowded meeting was held in the Gladstone Hotel, on July 9, to receive their report. Mr John Murray, J.P., was voted to the chair, and

Dr Robertson was greeted with loud cheers on rising. He submitted seven samples of the gold he had discovered, and called particular attention to the primitive manner in which the search had been conducted. The cradle in the possession of the party had been found useless, and most of the specimens had been obtained by washing in tin dishes. One specimen he had taken from a creek, in which he had seen the precious metal shining as he passed. From his previous experience on the Californian goldfields, he had no doubt that a man could average fifteen shillings a day on the new field. Mr Chapel next addressed the meeting, and described the geological strata of the country. He had discovered indications of gold in various parts of the district. He had first found the precious metal on the Fitzroy River near Canoona, and he had subsequently discovered it near Mr Clarke's station on the Calliope River. He thought it probable that gold would also be discovered throughout the mountainous country between the Boyne and the Dawson Rivers, but not yet having developed that district, he was not prepared to state it as a fact to the meeting. But he was prepared to open the south-west end of that range of country with a paying goldfield, where he had proved that any man not afraid of work could earn twenty shillings a day by surface washing, and without any of the better sort of appliances which were generally used on the other Australian goldfields. He had no doubt that the field, when fully worked, would prove as rich as any hitherto discovered. In proof of this assertion Mr Chapel produced a number of fine specimens of coarse gold as the result of two consecutive days' washing. On the motion of Mr C. J. Clarke, seconded by Mr William Miller, it was unanimously resolved:—

"That the best thanks of this meeting are due to Dr Robertson for his services in proceeding to the Fitzroy, and for the very handsome manner in which he has come forward and placed the whole of the information there obtained at the disposal of the people of Gladstone."

It was further resolved:—

"That a subscription be at once opened for the purpose of presenting Mr Chapel with a suitable testimonial in acknowledgment of his valuable services in the opening of the goldfields of the Northern District."

In support of this latter resolution it was urged that Mr Chapel had undergone many hardships in his search for the precious metal, had lived for months in the bush, and had frequently been without rations, but still he persevered until his labours were crowned with success. His discovery of this goldfield would vastly improve the value of property in the town of Gladstone and its vicinity, and the citizens should therefore evince their gratitude to Mr Chapel in the most practical manner.

A letter published in Sydney on August 11, alleged that there was no longer any doubt that a remunerative working goldfield had been discovered, and that the town of Gladstone had been deserted by its residents, who had hastened to the scene of the discovery. Working-men were washing out gold and earning from fifteen to twenty-five shillings a day. Six men in five days had secured one and a half pounds' weight of gold. Excitement ran high, and the impression prevailed that the most remunerative goldfield in Australia had been revealed. The credit of the original discovery was ascribed to Sir Maurice O'Connell, who brought down the first specimens to Gladstone, and took immediate steps to have the search he had commenced satisfactorily completed.

On August 16, it was announced that steamers were beginning to arrive with crowds of passengers intending to try their luck at the new goldfield, that numerous nuggets had been found quite close to the surface, and that the town of Gladstone was practically uninhabited, so general was the exodus to the neighbouring El Dorado.

On the 26th, the *Sydney Morning Herald* devoted its first leading article to the subject. It pointed out that the news from Gladstone respecting the recently opened-up goldfields in that district was bound to attract considerable attention. Assuming the accuracy of the accounts received, there was a prospect of gold production equalling, if not surpassing, anything hitherto known. At the same time, all such representations were to be received with caution. Men, excited by particular instances of success, were too apt to generalise and to imagine that the impression produced on their own minds would be communicated to the world. But if a valuable and permanent goldfield should be developed in proximity to Port Curtis, and a large body of people attracted to the locality, a new direction would be given to commercial enterprise, and fresh political and financial arrangements must ensue. The northern district, when it was erected into a separate colony, would, in that case, have neither Brisbane nor Ipswich as its metropolis. Gladstone must necessarily be the Imperial City of the North.

Private letters published on the same day proclaimed the richness of the new field, and gave a number of individual instances of success. It was added that large orders for stores had been sent to Sydney. On the 30th it was announced that from forty to fifty ounces of the precious metal had been brought into Gladstone, and that gold was being found at only eighteen inches from the surface. Next day a despatch from Gladstone informed the public that £600 worth of gold had already been procured, and that old, experienced diggers had given it as their opinion that the field would prove the richest in the colonies. The gold was generally found in patches, either on the surface of the ground, or a few inches below. The great recommendation of this new field was that the gold was impartially distributed over a large expanse of country.

On September 2, the first symptoms of the great historical rush became manifest. The Sydney papers of that day report "considerable excitement in consequence of the news from the North." A number of steamers were advertised to sail for Port Curtis immediately, and parties of intending diggers were in process of formation in all directions. The *Herald*, in its first leading article, declared that the colonisation of the region around Gladstone was so desirable on every ground that "we should rejoice greatly if all these projects end in the most perfect satisfaction." In the general intoxication of the moment, the *Herald* even went the length of predicting that "no doubt the growth of a new community in that portion of Australia will soon occasion the establishment of direct relations with Europe, and vessels will sail from the port of London to Port Curtis." The fact

G

that in 1852 the Rev. W. B. Clarke, the most eminent of colonial geologists, had expressed a conviction that an important and valuable goldfield would one day be found in the vicinity of Port Curtis, was now recalled, emphasised, and quoted as conferring scientific corroboration of the discoveries reported in the letters from Gladstone.

"Considering," wrote the *Sydney Morning Herald*, "how fortunate Mr Clarke has hitherto been, not only in the original statement of geological facts, but in the confirmation of his opinions, when they have been disputed, by subsequent discoveries, we are certainly justified in placing considerable reliance upon the opinions he has expressed in regard to the auriferous prospects of the Port Curtis district."

Four days later, more nuggets and letters from Gladstone arrived in Sydney, and intensified the excitement. As a specimen of the latter, the following, written by a daughter in Gladstone to her mother in Sydney, is worth quoting for the sake of its amusing *finale :—*

"I suppose you have heard of the goldfields. I have seen the gold, and I think it is the richest I ever saw. There is one very fine nugget, and all the others are small, like shot. All the men that went up are making from £1, 15s. to £2 a day with a tin dish. The man who first found the gold is named Chapel, and he tells me that a man can make £1 a day by merely washing surface stuff, and I am sure it is very fine gold. The boats' crews have gone, and the constables are all gone except two. And now, I think, I have let you know all the particulars about the gold; so, if father likes to come up here, he can, for now, I think, is the time to make money."

The arrival of the *Jenny Lind* in Sydney from Port Curtis, on September 6, determined many cautious waverers to hesitate no longer, for this vessel brought gold, not in single nuggets as heretofore, but in parcels, consigned to various firms, and thus all doubts as to the reality of the reports already published were dispelled. The *Herald* of the following day printed a number of letters from Gladstone brought by the *Jenny Lind*, all couched in the most confident and alluring terms. Here is one by way of specimen :—

"GLADSTONE, *August* 28.

"I am happy to inform you our goldfields are turning out even better than my most sanguine anticipations. Every one is doing well, and people are passing through the town by hundreds. This place is likely to become of immense importance in a very short time. I forward you by the *Jenny Lind* twenty-seven ozs. eleven dwts. twelve grs. gold. I shall send you a larger parcel by the *Uncle Tom*.

"R. HETHERINGTON."

Another letter mentioned that all the private houses in Gladstone were entirely without servants, and that all the employees of the squatters in the surrounding country had also deserted to the diggings.

By September 11 the "rush" may be said to have fairly commenced, as is sufficiently evidenced by the opening sentences of the *Herald's* leading article on that day :—

"Our advertising columns show how strong the current has set in towards the Port Curtis gold-diggings. It is a topic which has almost superseded every other, especially amongst the sanguine and the necessitous."

The *Herald* proceeded to ask the very pertinent questions :—

"What is the Government doing to facilitate and protect the movements of the gold-diggers ? What preparations are made for the preservation of order, for the protection of the revenue, and for the security of property ? Where so many people rush to one spot, and everything has to be provided, there must of necessity be much confusion, and there may be much needless obstruction."

But although the praises of the new goldfield were being sounded at this time in all directions, there were not wanting men of shrewdness and foresight to utter words of warning and common-sense. One of these, published on September

13, was a letter that proved a very accurate forecast of what eventually transpired. He wrote:—

"I have observed, amongst those who are going to try their luck, a number who, I have no hesitation in saying, will find themselves unable to meet several difficulties which they will have to overcome. They have been employed hitherto in capacities far from requiring the exercise of their physical energies, and although they may be desirous of bettering their fortunes, they are ignorant of that with which they will have to contend, and have but a very slight acquaintance with the meaning of the words 'roughing it.' This new goldfield lies so far distant from their homes, and from any settlement where the unfortunate digger could recruit his finances in the event of his failure, that I cannot but recommend a careful consideration of the position to those about to proceed to Port Curtis, and who come under the designation of the inexperienced."

But nobody was in a mood to pay heed to cool commonsense of this description. The excitement generated by the reports from Gladstone of fresh golden discoveries had become so great and so general, that, on September 15, Sydney was described by its leading journal as—

"Suffering from a veritable fever. Its effects are seen everywhere. In every family circle, in every shop, at the corner of every street, it meets the eye in some form. Among some classes of society it has spread with tremendous force, absorbing the faculties, incapacitating people for their employment, filling them with unnatural exaltation, with anticipations of a high and flourishing future, and in the meantime causing them to venture their money with remarkable indifference. The fever is specially prominent in ironmongers' stores, in carpenters' workshops, in shipping offices, on the wharves, and in general wherever men resort for the purpose of migration. One of its symptoms was a violent inroad upon the savings bank. It required an effort to keep order among the throng who were suddenly seized with a desire to draw out their savings, not because they distrusted the security, but because they were impatient to be gone. The disease, like intoxication, shows itself in forms which vary with the peculiar temperament and character of the patient. Thus, affectionate persons, in view of separation from the domestic hearth, are moved to tears, but the selfish show a more than usually stolid indifference to the consequences, so far as their wives and children are concerned. Some show the progress of the fever by incapacity to comprehend a question, or to return an answer having any reference to the query. Upon all projects of steady employment or progress they look with contemptuous scorn. The objects of their former envy they regard as persons under a thrall. They rather pity all who cannot possibly escape from their counters, their offices, or their professions. Any person who has walked the streets and seen the groups in agitated and earnest conversation, and who has marked the signs everywhere of the existence of this fever, must be conscious that the city is passing through a crisis."

Melbourne, Brisbane, and other leading Australian centres were naturally infected by the general and feverish excitement that prevailed in Sydney. A letter from Brisbane, published on September 18, described business in that city as completely suspended, the new goldfield in the North being the sole topic of conversation. Numbers had already left for the scene, and parties were being rapidly organised, not only in Brisbane itself, but in all the surrounding districts. Alike in Sydney, Melbourne, and Brisbane, the universal question was: "When are you off to the diggings?" Vessels for Port Curtis filled up with passengers as fast as they could be "laid on." The publication of the first official despatch from Sir Maurice O'Connell to Sir John Robertson, the political head of the goldfields department at Sydney, increased and intensified the popular excitement in the Australian cities. It was dated "Gladstone, September 7, 1858." It formally reported the discovery of the new goldfield in the Gladstone district, and intimated that the population on the field, and the yield of gold, necessitated the immediate adoption of the measures of protection and police, contemplated by the Goldfields Management Act. Sir Maurice added that "instances of great individual success in obtaining gold are reported," and cited the good fortune of a couple of men who in two days had washed out seventeen ounces of the precious metal. Eighty ounces had been transmitted to Sydney, but the diggers, said Sir Maurice, were not disposed to sell their gold until its actual value at the Mint was ascertained, and therefore the great bulk of the gold obtained was still held by the finders. It amounted in the aggregate to as large a yield as had been procured in any goldfield in the colony. In addition to this official despatch, the *Sydney Morning Herald* published a further instalment of private letters from lucky diggers, all breathing the same sentiment—" Plenty of gold to be got with very little trouble." In its editorial columns, the *Herald* pronounced the latest news from Gladstone "most gratifying," and, in pointing out that a vast population would now move from all quarters into a country comparatively uninhabited, urged that they should "move under the shadow of British law, administered with intelligence, with firmness, and with irresistible energy."

Amongst the letters published on September 23 was one from an old Californian gold-digger to his "mate," in Sydney. He wrote:—

"We arrived in Gladstone to-day. The people here are all going mad. I have seen one man who has been at the diggings for a fortnight, and the first week he got twenty-two ounces himself. He has just come to Gladstone to try if he can get a horse and cart. Everybody says there is no mistake about the diggings being as good as any that have been found for some time past."

Further despatches from Sir Maurice O'Connell were published on September 29. They reported the "progressive increase of the yield of gold" as "meeting the most sanguine anticipations," and this authoritative confirmation of the earlier announcements had the effect of impelling many cautious and hesitating persons to join in the now general exodus. Sir Maurice mentioned that 350 ounces had been sent to Sydney, "but," he added, "the principal portion of the gold obtained is still in possession of the diggers." This element of mystery, the general belief that marvellous discoveries of the precious metal had been achieved in the Port Curtis district, but were kept secret for selfish and prudential reasons, was perhaps the most potent factor in generating and fostering this unexampled rush. Sir Maurice concluded with an urgent appeal to his Sydney superiors for police reinforcements, pointing out the large and sudden advent of a miscellaneous population from all quarters, the risk of riot and disorder, and the fact that the town of Gladstone was practically deserted by its male population, so that the women and children were exposed to outrage and attack from the wild and lawless blacks of the neighbourhood. This application from Sir Maurice was not sent a moment too soon, for in several of the numerous private letters published simultaneously with his despatches, there are accounts of a collision between certain Chinese and European diggers over the disputed ownership of a claim. The Chinamen used their guns, and had to be disarmed by the Europeans. A public meeting was then held, a code of regulations drawn up, and an order for the general disarmament of the Chinese on the goldfield adopted. The Sydney Government promptly despatched a force of mounted and foot police, in addition to appointing a Commissioner to govern the new goldfield, a Sub-Commissioner, a Gold Receiver, and various officials for the administration of justice and the protection of the revenue. By October 2, the exodus had assumed such enormous proportions that the *Sydney Morning Herald* described it on that day as "astounding." The advertising columns of the Sydney, Melbourne, and Brisbane papers were crowded with announcements of the early departure of steam and sailing ships for Port Curtis, and the scenes that accompanied the leaving of the vessels were of the most exciting and enthusiastic description. The piers were thronged by vociferous crowds, and the sanguine cheers from the regiments of red-shirted and white-hatted gold-seekers on the decks and in the rigging were returned with interest by the thousands who were reluctantly left behind, but who hoped to be able to start very soon. The all-pervading anxiety to get away to Port Curtis as speedily as possible was thus hit off by a facetious observer:—

SCENE: SHIPBROKER'S OFFICE.

[*Enter, in great haste, intending passenger.*]

Passenger: "I want a cabin passage in the vessel you advertise to sail on Thursday for the new diggings."

Broker: "I am happy to tell you the cabin is full."

Passenger: "My mates are on board, and I want to go with them. Can I have a berth in the intermediate?"

Broker: "Full too."

Passenger: "Or in the steerage?"

Broker: "Full too."

Passenger: "I am determined to go in your vessel; I'll take a passage in the main-top."

Broker: "Had you been ten minutes earlier you could have gone there, but the tops were secured by the parties you met on entering the office."

Passenger (nonplussed): "What shall I give you to *tow* me there?—for go I will."

One of those scenes of departure is thus graphically depicted by the special correspondent of a Sydney journal:—

"There could not have been less than 3000 persons assembled to witness the departure of our good ship. Of these the larger proportion were women, many of them with children, come to take a farewell of husbands, brothers, or sweethearts. Through a complicated mass of confusion, tears, laughter, farewells, oaths, and wishes of good luck, the cargo was put on board in an incredibly short space of time. Then came the inspection of the tickets, from which the unfortunate clerk, who performed this disagreeable duty, came out such a rumpled, tumbled, heated, and flattened spectacle that he was barely recognisable. He would, doubtless, have disappeared altogether, but for the stalwart arms of two policemen, who protected him and occasionally fished him out from a denser rush than ordinary. Then came a warning from the bell, then a rush or two to the fore-hatchway, as some rival claimants to a berth settled their respective rights by an appeal to fisticuffs, then a sudden silence from the steam, then a heavy splash or two as the paddles revolved, and then broke out from the dense crowd that lined the wharves and shipping a cheer so loud, so hearty, as to send a thrill through one's frame, and to sound as the very augury of success. Every vessel, as we passed, gave us a hearty cheer, which was, on each occasion, responded to with alacrity by the human freight that crowded our decks, and as we passed the Artillery Barracks the band, which was at the time playing in the balcony, struck up 'Cheer, boys, cheer,' and wound up with 'The girl I left behind me.'"

CHAPTER X

A MARVELLOUS WILD-GOOSE CHASE

THE most graphic, entertaining, and trustworthy history of this phenomenal rush is the one written by Mr Frederick Sinnett, an accomplished and versatile journalist, who was despatched to the scene by the proprietors of the *Melbourne Argus* as their special correspondent. He was a son of Mrs Percy Sinnett, a once well-known and popular English authoress and translator.

Mr Sinnett describes the rush to Port Curtis as a marvellous wild-goose chase, the most remarkable and distant rush recorded in the annals of the Australian goldfields. At that time, and indeed all through the fifties and the early sixties, the nomadic habits and the unsettled condition of the great gold-digging class were frequently illustrated in "new rushes." A rumour reached some centre of digging population that a rich deposit had been discovered, and immediately the more restless and dissatisfied diggers started off for the scene of the reported rich "find." If the rumour proved groundless, the abortive rush was seldom heard of beyond its own immediate neighbourhood, but if the good news proved true, armies of diggers at once took the road from all directions for the new field. Along with the regular rank and file, as in the case of other armies, marched a body of camp followers, often even more numerous than the main force on which they depended.

The active and energetic competition then pervading every kind of business in Australia was an assurance to the digger that wherever he went there would be very few consumers on the ground before purveyors for their various wants appeared in force. Under such circumstances it only needed a few weeks to convert a solitary gully—in which the settlers' cattle had hitherto undisturbedly browsed, and which, except for the occasional visits of the stockman, had not been seen by mortal eye from one end of the month to the other—into a regularly organised town, with its mile or two of crowded streets, its stores, and shops, and public-houses, its theatre, and other places of amusement, its newspaper, and even its own little Circumlocution Office and Governmental centre. One thing, indeed, commonly regarded as essential to towns, was not to be met with in those "new rushes," viz., a house. Houses might come in the course of time, but they were regarded as of secondary importance, as refinements for which there was no immediate hurry, as much too fixed an investment to be ventured upon at once. Ten thousand persons might flock to a place in the course of a few weeks, and a few weeks afterwards not as many hundreds might remain. Canvas is the best building material for a nomadic people, and the digging population of Victoria was not only nomadic, but nomadic in a sense of which the world had previously had but few examples. Bedouins pitch their black tents in small groups. Tartars wandering to find pasturage for their flocks and herds do not crowd greatly together, but the Victorian digger was a citizen as well as a nomad. He had many of the habits of a townsman, although as itinerant as a Tartar; and while he was as ready to strike his tent and march off to some distant spot as if he were a Pawnee on a hunting excursion, whither he moved, the population, the divided labour, the organisation of a town, and often a large one, quickly followed.

The first rumour of discoveries of gold at Port Curtis reached Sydney in July, 1858. On the 25th of that month the *Jenny Lind* arrived with the intelligence that rich gold-fields had been discovered near Gladstone, but beyond that general announcement not much detailed information was procurable. On August 24, the *Coquette* arrived at Sydney with specific news calculated to produce an impression on the public mind. Letters announcing the discovery of a first-rate goldfield near Port Curtis were delivered, and specimens of the auriferous wealth of the place were forwarded by way of positive proof. So much interest did this news excite, that the steamship *Eagle* was at once laid on for Port Curtis, and left Sydney full of adventurers bound for the new rush. The *Jenny Lind* returned to Sydney a second time on September 7. She brought further accounts from the diggings, together with sixty ounces of gold. Letters were published, stating that the gold was found near the surface, and that twenty-seven pounds of the precious metal had already been raised. On September 18 the *Uncle Tom* arrived at Sydney from Port Curtis with the news that there were 400 men upon the diggings, who were making from £6 to £7 per week. An official despatch from the Government Resident, Sir Maurice O'Connell, dated September 7, communicated the stamp of authority to the private reports. Sir Maurice stated that there were 300 persons on the spot, that there were individual instances of great success, that about eighty ounces of gold had been sent to Gladstone, and that it was desirable to officially proclaim the goldfield. Simultaneously with the publication of Sir Maurice's despatch, private letters from Port Curtis were printed to the effect that the news from the goldfield was astonishing, that one man had secured twenty-two ounces of gold in a week, that another had obtained £100 worth of gold in a fortnight, and many other reports to the same effect. The *Sydney Morning Herald* wrote:—

"We meet daily with persons who affirm that letters have been received privately, containing facts of an astounding nature, but that self-interest induces their suppression for the moment. We can scarcely imagine that all these statements are false; still, we have been very unsuccessful in tracing them to reliable authority. In some instances, they have evidently been mere rumour, and probably the rumour has been due to sinister motives. At the same time, if the whole be founded on delusion or deception, its authors are entitled, at least, to the very doubtful credit of success. The effect produced has certainly been very marked, and even marvellous. Eighteen vessels have left during the past three weeks, and 1580 passengers, from the 1st to the 20th September, for the Port Curtis goldfields. Twenty vessels, including steamers, are now advertising—some for the conveyance of passengers only, and others for the exclusive conveyance of goods."

About the middle of September the excitement produced by the reports from Port Curtis not only raged fiercely in New South Wales, but spread to the adjoining colony of Victoria. There the flame burned more and more fiercely every day. Not only did diggers troop down to Melbourne from all the Victorian goldfields, north, south, east, and west, but appointments were thrown up and paying businesses abandoned by hundreds of men who were carried off their feet by the all-pervading excitement. Every dead-wall in Melbourne and Geelong was covered with flaming placards announcing the immediate departure of ships and steamers for Port Curtis. The new El Dorado was obtruded upon public notice in multitudinous ways. Every shopkeeper found some article to display in his window with a label recommending it as specially adapted to supply some pressing want of Port Curtis diggers. Every puffing advertiser used Port Curtis as his catch-word. The Press certainly did not stimulate the prevailing excitement, but all the attempts to check it which public writers made were quite unavailing. It was in vain that the risks to be run were urgently pointed out day after day. The excitement grew by what it fed on. No one could be brought to believe that every one else was wildly acting upon the vaguest information. "A" could not believe that "B" and all the other letters of the alphabet were as mutable as himself. Almost every one of the multitude that joined in the rush was persuaded that so great an effect must have a proportionately great cause. When ships began to sail for Port Curtis with hundreds on board, sagacious reasoners far and near began to conclude that "there must be something in it," and booked their passages at once—themselves to become arguments in favour of the departure of others. At the end of September, thirty vessels of all classes were laid on in Melbourne and Geelong for Port Curtis. Some enthusiasts even rigged out boats of five or six tons' burden, and boldly set out on a voyage of 1500 miles in such small and perilous craft, while steamers and large passenger-ships carried their hundreds at a time. But in the midst of this large exodus of people it was to be noticed that comparatively few merchants made ventures in goods. There were plenty of men ready to hazard their lives in a wild experiment, but men of business were not to be persuaded to risk their goods upon such slight information. So little was generally known about Port Curtis, indeed, that the most contradictory accounts of its climate were published in the newspapers, some alleging it to be a low, swampy region, from which the hot tropical sun drew forth pestilential vapours, amid which no European could labour and live.

Mr Sinnett felt a great curiosity to know what the truth about the Port Curtis goldfields really was, and he therefore resolved to go and see for himself. He proposed to the proprietors of the *Melbourne Argus* to visit the "new rush" in the capacity of their special correspondent, and his offer was accepted. On October 2, he was ready to leave in the steamer *Admella*, lying at the Port Melbourne pier. As he drove down to Port Melbourne, or Sandridge, as it was then called, with a tent and other suggestive equipments protruding from the conveyance, he and his friends became objects of envy and attention. On that very day one man had thrown up a good position, telling his employer that if he were to die for it fifty times, he must and would go, for he had heard that a friend of his was getting five ounces of gold an hour. There was a belief in some quarters that Port Curtis was a New Guinea coast, but at once richer and more deadly than that fever-stricken storehouse of barbaric wealth.

The Port Melbourne pier was so thronged with spectators and friends of the passengers about to leave by the *Admella*, that it was no easy matter to squeeze one's way on board. And even when there, the crowding was scarcely lessened. Quantities of goods were in process of loading, and passengers' luggage was being thrown in promiscuous heaps about the decks. The noise, dirt, and confusion were indescribable. The passengers were of all nations and tongues, but high over all predominated the vocal jerks and drawls peculiar to the utterance of Brother Jonathan, for, needless to say, the percentage of Yankees was considerable in the case of such a speculative proceeding as the Port Curtis rush, and equally, of course, the proportion of friends that came down to take one last long lingering liquor with each adventurous "old hoss" was prodigious.

When late in the afternoon the warps were cast off the

jetty, it was densely crowded by shouting and cheering friends and spectators, and amid hurrahs and hat-waving, and the strains of a brass band concealed somewhere in the mass of people, the *Admella* stood out into the Bay. About a mile off she came to a standstill, while the emigration officer came on board, and while some attempts were made to evolve order out of chaos, after the encumbering swarm of visitors had been got rid of. The task was no easy one, for the vessel had far more passengers than she was entitled to carry. The unfortunate agent, who had made himself conspicuous by mounting a magnificent crimson fez, was incessantly assailed by relays of murmuring, menacing, or reproachful steerage passengers who could not find berths. Nevertheless, all the offers of the agent to return the passage-money and set the complaining ones ashore were received with derision. So determined were the people to go, so convinced were they of the fortune that only needed to be picked up a week from that time, that they would have stowed themselves away in the cross-trees rather than lose a day. Boats full of men that could not go came alongside to look with envious eyes on those that could. One old waterman who had brought a passenger on board, and who stood balancing himself in the bows of his boat, holding on by the rope's end that had been cast to him, observed with an evident sincerity that would probably not have gratified the absent lady: "Ah, if they'd only hoist my boat aboard, and take me and she together, I wouldn't so much as ask to go and say 'good-bye' to my old woman."

Next morning Mr Sinnett was confirmed in an impression that he had formed the previous afternoon—that the *Admella* was not a very carefully or well-governed ship. When he went on deck he found it still lumbered up with goods, while the ordinary nautical observance of washing decks appeared to be altogether disregarded. There was no room for walking, the quarter-boats being swung in over the poop, although the weather was beautifully fine and the sea smooth. A good deal of room was also taken up by a small steamer, which was being conveyed to Port Curtis as a speculation. Its stern overhung one side of the *Admella* and its stem the other, so that it had to be passed under with crouching contortions of the body if one wanted to go forward. A quantity of bags of coal also encumbered the decks, and had been trodden by hundreds of feet until the bags had burst. There was scarcely an inch of clear deck to stand upon. Below in the steerage, owing to the berthing provision being inadequate to the number of passengers, the clamour of complaint was loud and general.

After surmounting a variety of difficulties and having once been in imminent danger of going on the rocks, the *Admella* entered the port of Newcastle, about half-way between Melbourne and Port Curtis. There reports the reverse of rose-coloured about the "new rush" were in circulation. Some of the passengers were so discouraged that they sold their £10 passenger tickets for 10s. One man was so disgusted that he lighted his pipe with his ticket and booked his passage back to Melbourne. Nevertheless, for one that wanted to return, there were many anxious to proceed. Each vacated berth was readily filled up at Newcastle, while many applicants for passages had to be left behind.

"Port Curtis within five days," was the alluring advertisement placarded in Melbourne in connection with the departure of the *Admella*, but, as a matter of fact, the voyage covered a period of ten days. Every night the floor of the saloon was occupied by sleepers who could find no berths or room in the steerage. As the *Admella* steamed into harbour, "hundreds of hands," says Mr Sinnett, "along the bulwarks of a large ship at anchor waved us away; while, amid a hurricane of voices, clearly rose the ominous words, 'Go back!' 'Go back!' 'Shicer!' 'Shicer!'" This latter expression is diggers' slang for an unsuccessful quest of the precious metal. But the pilot and visitors from the shore gave much more sanguine accounts of the "new rush," and pointed out the absurdity of attaching any importance to the impressions of people who were frightened back from the threshold of the place they had come so far, and with such high hopes, to reach.

Proceeding up the Fitzroy River—"a noble river running through a noble country"—Mr Sinnett arrived on a Sunday evening at the scene of the "rush." "It was already dark," he writes, "but by the light of the moon we saw the tents of the diggers standing in considerable numbers, and presenting all the outward appearance of a Victorian goldfield. The tent in which I was to pass the night was at the far end of the diggings, so that we had a fair view of the transitory canvas town as we went along. Everything looked cheerful enough; the fires were burning brightly, and the men were moving about, talking and laughing, and enjoying their after-Sunday-supper pipes. There were a good many women to be seen, too, but I cannot say that they added much to the pleasant appearance of the scene. A diggings rush is certainly not woman's sphere." Mr Sinnett's slumbers during his first night on the Port Curtis goldfield were repeatedly broken by a party of Shakespearian inebriated revellers in an adjoining tent. "Macbeth" was their favourite tragedy, and the still night air rang with peculiarly impassioned passages, interrupted by occasional notes and parentheses not to be found in the authorised edition, such as:—

"Before my body I throw my warlike shield. Lay hon, *Macduff*, and damned be he that fust cries, 'Old, enough! 'And us the pannikin, old man."

Next morning Mr Sinnett was out early amongst the tents and washing-places. He found the Canoona flat, on which the diggers were mostly congregated, covering an area of forty or fifty acres, surrounded on three sides by lightly-timbered slopes, with a mountainous background. Down the middle of the flat ran a small creek, whose banks constituted the chief scene of activity. Here many wells, whips, windlasses, cradles, and washing-dishes were busily engaged. In answer to questions, the diggers replied that any man could make his rations on the field, and some were making a good deal more. After breakfast Mr Sinnett paid a visit to the Government Camp, where he made the acquaintance of Sir Maurice O'Connell, who had just come in from a tour of inspection, and was about returning to his headquarters at Gladstone. Sir Maurice expressed a very hopeful view of the auriferous prospects of the district, although he was somewhat alarmed at the possible consequences of the extensive rush that had set in—a rush for which the old residents of the district were altogether unprepared and utterly unable to account. Sir Maurice estimated the quantity of gold so far procured at about 2000 ounces, and he showed Mr Sinnett a parcel of twenty ounces which had been placed in his charge that morning. As a proof of the general dissemination of gold in the district, Sir Maurice also exhibited a paper containing specimens collected by a black boy attached to the Government Camp, who was persuaded to go off and imitate the white men's proceedings with a tin dish. Sir Maurice, speaking particularly of Gladstone, where he had long resided, gave a very favourable account of the climate. The heat was rarely excessive, and the nights were almost invariably cool and pleasant. A great advantage enjoyed by this portion of Australia was almost complete freedom from hot winds.

At spots called Chinaman's Gully and Golden Point, which had proved the richest parts of the field, Mr Sinnett found a good many diggers at work, but they were only gleaners after the harvest. The great yield of gold was in a thin stratum of soil, rarely above a foot deep, overlying the bed-rock. A number of gleaners were at work scraping away the remaining earth from the surface of the rock, and thereby obtaining a modest livelihood. Many others were trying their luck in places where the soil, if less rich, was more readily secured. The man who gave the best account of what he was earning on new ground reported that he was getting half an ounce of gold to the load.

All over the goldfield unlicensed grog-selling was undisguisedly carried on. "Talking of hotels and unlicensed victuallers," Mr Sinnett observes, "I should mention that there are no licensed ones. Bottles and glasses stand openly on almost every store counter in the place. The law does not wink at this sly grog-selling. It looks at it with calm unaverted eyes, and it is generally understood that until due notice has been given, and the machinery for issuing licenses is complete, there is to be no restriction upon the sale of alcoholic drinks." Mr Sinnett does not think that there was any appreciable increase of drunkenness from this indiscriminate and unchecked sale of intoxicants. In such a heterogeneous and suddenly collected community a large amount of drunkenness was inevitable, but the evil would have been augmented if the drinkers had been concentrated in a few crowded licensed establishments. Incessant quarrelling and fighting would have been the rule, and the pernicious bibulous rivalry that the practice of "shouting," or calling upon all present to drink at the caller's expense, engenders, would have come into the fullest operation. But the unlicensed grog-selling store-keepers only satisfied a more moderate and unstimulated demand for liquor amongst their general customers, and would not permit their places to become scenes of drunken and riotous clamour.

Every goldfield has its distinctive humours and its peculiar catch-word. The latter at the Port Curtis rush was composed of the affectionate phrase: "Oh, dearest Emma." Just after dark somebody would shout this amatory ejaculation at the top of his voice, and immediately the cry would be taken up and repeated all over the field in every varying tone of mock admiration. At first Mr Sinnett was under the impression that Emma was an actual flesh-and-blood personage running the gauntlet of playful pleasantries from the gay young diggers, but he soon discovered that Emma existed only in the realms of local imagination. It was simply an inexplicable but an established rite of the Port Curtis diggers to shout "Oh, dearest Emma," from time to time at the highest pitch of the voice. Occasionally the cry was raised during the day, but the practice was an essentially nocturnal one, lasting from seven o'clock until midnight, and attaining its maximum between nine and ten. Now and then a digger would vary the entertainment by adding to "Oh, dearest Emma," "'ow my 'art aches," but the majority contented themselves with merely apostrophising Emma. Sometimes, if tolerable quiet had reigned for half an hour, she would suddenly be addressed with startling vehemence, and the cry would then be passed on from voice to voice, until the farthest passionate appeal could be barely heard. Just as one dog beginning to bark, or one cock commencing to crow, rouses all the dogs or cocks within hearing, and sends the signal along a line of sentries for many miles, until the last answer seems but a faint and distant echo, so was it with the shouts of "Oh, dearest Emma," and "'Ow my 'art aches," at the Port Curtis rush.

Mr Sinnett returned to Melbourne under the impression

that when the Port Curtis district was thoroughly prospected, important discoveries would be made.

"It certainly seems to me improbable," he wrote, "that in a country where gold is found in minute quantities almost wherever sought over a large area, it should turn out that the little patch near Canoona was the only rich spot extant. If I may venture to give any general opinion about this place, it is that it will not turn out a 'Shicer' so far as gold-digging is concerned, while that it is a fine field for colonisation in other respects I have little doubt."

CHAPTER XI

THE HOST OF DISAPPOINTED DIGGERS

Towards the middle of October the first whispers of failure, disappointment, and an impending disaster, that would necessarily entail the most calamitous consequences, began to circulate in Sydney; but so widespread and overmastering was the madness of the hour, that no appreciable diminution in the crowds sailing from every Australian capital to Port Curtis was produced by these ominous and well-founded reports. Sir Maurice O'Connell wrote to the Government:—

"I look with some alarm at the vast numbers who are said to be now on their way hither, as I fear there will be much disappointment and individual distress, more particularly to those who come unprepared to submit to several weeks of delay before the search for gold becomes profitable. Hitherto the price of provisions has been very moderate, but the pressure of so large an increase of population in a new district has already raised the price of meat to sixpence and eightpence per lb., and I fear that the high price of carriage (twenty-five shillings per cwt.) will have the effect of equally raising the cost of all other articles of subsistence at the diggings. Until the last two days, all the reports I have received, both of individual and aggregate success on the diggings, have been most favourable; and all the original diggers who left their employments in Gladstone to seek for gold have remained steadily at work, many of them taking their families up to reside with them."

Mr William Archer, the uncle of the now well-known London dramatic critic of the same name, wrote to his Sydney merchants:—

"This excitement is very alarming, and I fear a great deal of evil will result from it. The country is so dry that people cannot prospect, and gold in paying quantities has yet only been found in a few acres of ground. I have no doubt gold will ultimately be found here over a large surface when the wet season sets in, but what are people to do in the meantime? It is, of course, to our interest that the country should be settled, as the people must raise the price of stock; but I foresee a great deal of misery, and wish you would give some extract from this letter to the papers, and thus deter those who are madly rushing towards this part of the colony."

In explanation of some allusions in this letter, it may be added that the Archer Brothers were amongst the earliest and most adventurous squatters and settlers in the Gladstone country. Mr Thomas Archer arrived there as early as 1848. The exploring and opening-up of the Port Curtis district were largely due to the energy and enterprise of the Messrs Archer. Here is an instructive passage from another private letter:—

"Many of the diggers come up here improperly equipped, and having no means of support, even for the distance of thirty-five miles to the goldfields, have wandered from the road, and been discovered by the Native Mounted Police in the bush in a state of extreme exhaustion. Some, laden with a roll of blankets behind and a cradle or something else to balance in front, have sunk under the excessive heat of a tropical sun. Picks, shovels, blankets, etc., have been cast away, and are frequently met with by the roadside."

A third private correspondent concluded his letter thus :—

"I hope it is not true that a great many people are coming from Sydney. What the poor wretches will do I cannot tell. There is no employment for men here."

An old digger was driven to moralise and describe the discomforts of his position in these feeling terms:—

"Please God, if I live and have good health, I will never go to any more gold-digging rushes. This will teach me better sense for the future. I am here in perfect misery—what with the flies, and the heat, and no prospect of getting any gold, bad living, and bad water. I would not bring you down here for anything" (he was writing to his wife), "not if the country was running over with gold. I am sure it would kill you; it is as much as I can do to stand it. The flies at this moment are almost eating the eyes out of my head."

Here is a further letter of the same date, but in curious contradiction to the foregoing :—

"We have had conversations with Sir Maurice O'Connell, the Commissioner, and Mr Archer, the squatter. Both confirm the general opinion that there is a large extent of auriferous country, but they are unwilling to add to the excitement by saying too much. They are both perfectly astonished at the virulence of the gold fever. The climate is very beautiful just now, not so hot as I expected. This is really a splendid country. I have not yet seen a mosquito or any other annoyance in the shape of flies, but they may be bad enough in hot weather."

The woes of the disappointed digger were thus depicted by one of themselves, under date October 11 :—

"I have seen many bad fields, but this beats all. You could not get anything for tents or tools. Our party made up their minds to leave, and we endeavoured to get something for our tents and tools, which cost some £10 in Sydney, but we could not sell them, so we gave them away, as did plenty of others. Men were to be seen in all directions begging a few shillings for tools that had cost pounds. Any person might have loaded a dray with new picks, shovels, tin dishes, and tools of all kinds. The road down to the coast was strewn with them. Men, unable to get anything for them, attempted to carry them down, but being overcome by the heat, weary and footsore, gradually threw them away to lighten their loads."

The Sydney journals of October 12 called upon the Government to take prompt action, and save the self-deluded thousands, who had hurried off to Port Curtis in the infectious madness of the moment, from the consequences of their own rashness and folly. It was pointed out that from ten to twenty thousand men had flocked from all quarters into a primeval country that could not possibly absorb them or supply their necessities at such extremely short notice.

"Let the Government calculate what is the consumption of such a multitude, and what the agency required to bring supplies together. Even were they an army, a commissariat would be tasked to supply their wants at a moment's notice. What resources would be necessary against the inevitable casualties of such a campaign? Is it not morally certain that, if gold is not procurable in sufficient quantities to supply the wants of these multitudes of poor wretches, there will be found among them men who will prompt them to violence? It would be a nice piece of casuistry to know in what the position of the men at Port Curtis, if without food or money, will differ from the position of passengers on board a ship. In the last resort they certainly would not hesitate to appropriate any private store to prevent a general starvation. Whether such casuistry will be applicable to that distant region or not, we cannot doubt, from the murmurs we have already heard and the dark forebodings of correspondents, that a rush on the stores will take place, should dire necessity seem to justify peculation. It is clear that if ever there was a time when a Government would be justified in stepping out of the ordinary course, it is now, when nothing but Governmental interference can prevent the spectacle of disgraceful disorder, the violation of law, probably private vengeance, the interruption of commerce, even the utter failure of the goldfields, and finally a wasting away of human beings, who will die upon that desert shore. This is a case in which private charity cannot and ought not to be expected to interpose. What is necessary must be done by the whole people, and if it should turn out that we have afforded to the world a spectacle of heedless folly on the one side, let us not grudge the cost of vindicating the colony from the reproach of heartless indifference."

It was doubtless in compliance with these journalistic exhortations that the Governor, Sir William Denison, promptly despatched H.M.S. *Iris* from Sydney to Port Curtis to watch the development of the situation. Yet, strange to say, simultaneously with the stories of disappointment and disaster, there were not wanting reports of a hopeful and encouraging character to maintain the "rush" to Port Curtis, though naturally in a much diminished volume. Thus, for instance, as late as October 18, the *Sydney Morning Herald* published a letter to a leading Sydney firm, in which these passages occur :—

"People are leaving the diggings in hundreds, dissatisfied with their success, and plenty of them without even putting a pick into the ground. Very many of the old hands on the field continue to do well, but not so well as at first. Many of the most experienced diggers are of the belief that gold in great abundance is to be found here. My partner took down a considerable quantity of gold to Gladstone to be forwarded to you, and we shall send you some more in a few days."

On October 19 questions were asked in the Legislative Assembly at Sydney, with respect to the intentions of the Government in the matter of affording "relief to those persons who have inconsiderately and improvidently left their ordinary employments for the purpose of joining in the rush to the Port Curtis diggings; and who, in consequence of the failure of those diggings to realise their expectations, have found themselves in circumstances of temporary inconvenience." Sir Charles Cowper (Premier), in reply, stated that Sir Maurice O'Connell had been authorised to use his discretion with respect to giving employment to those who had improvidently placed themselves in a position of difficulty, and affording temporary relief to the destitute. At the same time, Sir Maurice had been informed that it would be necessary to be careful in the exercise of his discretion in the matter, as the expenditure would have to be justified by the Government. On October 23 the *Sydney Morning Herald* described the rush as over for the present, and it was now possible to calmly speculate on the course and characteristics of the extraordinary movement of the population which had taken place. The wharves were no longer crowded with departing adventurers; men were no longer throwing up their situations and selling their properties, and vessels were no longer laid on for the golden river. Those who were so tardy as not to have committed themselves before the reaction set in could congratulate themselves on their lucky escape, while those who were caught in the first whirl of the excitement had leisure now to ruminate sorrowfully on their imprudence. The terrible disasters which would have occurred, had not the mad migration been stopped in time, had been fortunately averted. There must have been many cases of individual distress and impoverishment, but there had been no wholesale starvation, no outbreak of disease, and no violation of social order. Thousands of the too easily allured adventurers had been restored to their homes with no worse results than the loss of their passage money. There was evidently some special charm about the Port Curtis goldfield which had acted on the population with magical effect. The willingness of the people to believe in wonderful discoveries that would stimulate the prosperity of the colony had, no doubt, something to do with it. The wish was father to the thought. But three causes apparently principally operated. First, the spot was so easy of access that, in case of failure, retreat was easy; secondly, many were so unsatisfactorily employed, that they were movable on very slight provocation, and the excitement caused by their starting off being naturally infectious, the most impressionable and incautious part of the population were drawn into the whirl; and thirdly, the rumour that the gold lay near the surface, and was obtainable with very little labour, had an irresistible effect on the minds of many. It was this last fact that operated with special force on the diggers at Ballarat, then the richest goldfield in the world, but the precious metal had to be extracted there at the cost of much labour and expense. Deep sinking had yielded large returns, but the process had also been very exhausting. So when the Ballarat miners, who had been accustomed to sink shafts from 100 to 500 feet in depth, heard that nuggets of a respectable size were to be picked up at Port Curtis within a few feet of the surface, the news was altogether too much for their philosophy. They deserted the windlass and rushed to the ship.

On October 26 there was a crowded meeting of the citizens of Sydney to devise means for the retention and the profitable employment of the host of unemployed diggers, who had returned from the Port Curtis rush, and many of whom were then walking the streets of Sydney in a destitute condition. Resolutions were adopted, calling upon the Government to employ the destitute diggers on public works, and inaugurating a public subscription to enable such of them as wished to establish themselves on the permanent goldfields of the colony to do so. It was urged that a million and a half had been spent on the importation of labour from the Mother Country, and that therefore it would be the height of folly to take no steps to secure the large amount of labour of a very superior class, that had been thrown by circumstances on the streets of Sydney, and whose advent had not cost the Colonial Exchequer a single penny. As a result of this meeting a considerable sum of money was raised, which enabled the Committee to draft many of the diggers from Sydney into the interior, where they settled down and contributed a valuable element to the population of the parent colony. The neighbouring colony of Victoria also took prompt action, and despatched a Government steamer, with a large supply of provisions, to Port Curtis to bring back the Victorian diggers who had joined in the rush. The Sydney Relief Committee speedily raised a sum of £2000, and this was supplemented by a Government grant of £2500. In a few days the Committee were able to "announce to their subscribers and the public, that they have forwarded into the interior, and placed in a position to develop the resources and capabilities of the colony, the labour and skill of 1100 men—diggers and others—many of whom arrived in Sydney from Port Curtis with means completely exhausted, and in a state of utter destitution." The promptitude and energy of the leading citizens of Sydney at this crisis were not without their effect at Port Curtis, for a special correspondent at the diggings, writing under date November 11, remarked :—

"There seems to be a regular competition between the representatives of the Governments of New South Wales and Victoria, the one vieing with the other in doing as much as possible for the destitute diggers. Rations are served out, passages are provided, and comforts are supplied by each. The diggers may be heard discussing the relative merits of the colonies, prior to making their decision as to which they will patronise with their presence. The movement that has been made in Sydney in favour of the diggers has, I know, had a very great effect in influencing a decision in many cases, and many will now proceed to Sydney who would otherwise have taken passage to Melbourne."

One party of destitute diggers, assisted up country from

Sydney, soon dug up 100 ounces of the precious metal in the neighbourhood of Sofala.

A special correspondent's letter, dated October 29, described the disappointed diggers as listlessly roaming backwards and forwards, congregating on vacant ground, gathering around the liquor stores, or sitting in apathetic indolence upon anything that offered a sufficient basis for the purpose. Soured by disappointment, and doubtful as to their immediate future they were excitable and irritable in the extreme. This excitability was shown in the eagerness with which, on the least symptom of a "difficulty," the whole population collected on the scene of action; and, as the slightest spark would set the inflammable mass into a blaze, thoughtful men trembled lest any moment might bring about an explosion. There was a large number of "rowdies" on the spot, who had everything to gain by disorder. It was agreed to hold a public meeting to consider the situation, and one of these "rowdies" volunteered to act as bellman. His manner of notifying the holding of the meeting was by making a series of short inflammatory speeches, charging the Government in general, and Sir Maurice O'Connell in particular, with having cajoled them all to Port Curtis for some unknown purpose of their own. His speeches generally concluded in this style, omitting sundry sulphurous expletives :—"If you're half men, you'll pull that wretch (indicating Sir Maurice O'Connell) out of his tent and pitch him into the river. Only stand by me, and I'll do it quick." But Sir Maurice O'Connell was too popular and too generally respected to be in any danger from such a brutal and barbarous threat. Always accessible, always ready to give advice or assistance, explaining, reasoning, urging, or entreating, according to the varying circumstances of the hour, his personal influence was undoubtedly the most potent factor in preserving peace and order in the midst of a miscellaneous, disappointed, and exasperated concourse from all quarters of Australia. Sir Maurice attended the meeting, and so far from being lynched in the manner suggested by the amiable bell-ringer, was heartily cheered by the assembled thousands of diggers when he detailed the steps he had taken to provide them with employment, and promised, as the representative of the New South Wales Government, that no man on the field would lack the necessaries of life.

Captain Moodie, the local representative of an important Australian steamship company that had conveyed a large proportion of the gold-seekers to Port Curtis, had an unpleasant experience with the host of disappointed diggers who wanted to get back to Sydney and Melbourne. He had received instructions to charge £3, 10s. for the passage to Sydney, but his tent was besieged by an indignant and clamorous crowd who refused to pay that figure. For two hours the question was debated between the angry multitude and the captain. One digger, getting weary of the protracted discussion, and longing to return to civilisation as soon as possible, offered to pay the amount claimed. But he was summarily seized by the excited crowd and narrowly escaped being pitched into the river. Eventually a compromise, providing for a substantial reduction in the amount demanded by the captain, was arrived at.

Mr Edwin Carton Booth, the author of "Australia Illustrated," gives a graphic description of the rush, based on personal observation and experience. The year 1858, he says, was one of very considerable depression on the goldfields of the older colonies. The large fortunes realised in the earlier days had, many of them, been spent, recklessly speculated with, or dissipated. The diggers had not yet learned to look upon moderate earnings or savings with content. The modes of working were still primitive, and although gold, alluvial and in quartz, existed in plenty, the appliances for obtaining it were rude and inefficient. As early as the June or July of 1858, water for gold-washing purposes began to fail, and a long and dry summer was predicted. If repeated and painful experiences of failure could have taught gold-diggers wisdom, those of the southern parts of Australia would have been very wise long before 1858. With the exception of the rush to the Woolshed Creek, in the Ovens district, nearly every expedition to far-off fields in search of gold had proved a failure. They were as a rule unfortunate, and in some instances disastrous in their results. Wisdom was not to be known however, or the time for its practice had not arrived. Omeo and Kiandra, the Snowy River, and the Lachlan, had imparted their lessons in vain. A voyage across the seas to Panama, ending in worse than disaster and a deliberate fraud, attended with much loss and suffering, were all powerless to divert the mind of the gold-digger from the desire to grow rich in a hurry. Just when the miners were most likely to be easily affected, before their savings were exhausted, and when the desire to make up for bygone losses was keen upon them, news came to the effect that somewhere up in the North, far beyond where diggers had ever been before, in a corner of the country hitherto given up to sheep and cattle alone, gold in plenty, and lying close to the surface, had been discovered. The news spread as only such news among such a people can. At first the information was of the most indefinite character imaginable. Nevertheless, it told of an ever-flowing river, of rich alluvial flats, and "made hills," having gold-bearing drifts and rocks for their bases. This was sufficient. Fast as ships were laid on the berth, they were filled with gold-diggers. From every goldfield and up-country township diggers flocked into Melbourne and Sydney in thousands. Quiet, easy-going South Australians and Tasmanians joined in the mad stampede, and within a month fully 40,000 men had been landed on the hitherto unthought-of shores of the River Fitzroy. In New South Wales and Victoria stage-coaches reaped a rich harvest. Colossal vehicles, each of them carrying from fifty to sixty passengers, started from all the more important towns to the coast, three or four a day. All the highways and many of the cross roads of the colonies, leading from the goldfields towards the sea, were filled with lines of stalwart men, many of them carrying heavy weights upon their shoulders, bound in the same direction. Ships' agents had to improvise passenger offices, in which clerks were employed taking passage-money from morning till night. Day by day the crowds poured into the towns, and ships sailed from the ports, without any definite information having been received from the so-much-thought-of new diggings. When the diggers were asked their reasons for the migration, the most vague answers possible were given: somebody had heard of the discovery of gold, and had given the information to some one else. This was sufficient: all the early glories of Ballarat, of Bendigo, and of Forest Creek were to be repeated within the line of the tropics.

Mr Booth was a passenger in the last ship that sailed from Melbourne to the new El Dorado of the North, and he thus describes the scene that met his gaze at the end of the voyage:—

"The first dawn of the next morning saw the ship that had carried the last of those who joined in the mad stampede moved up to the ordinary anchorage, and within an hour she formed one of as fine a fleet of ships as the mercantile navy of the world could boast of. They hailed from every naval nation in the world, and it was a singular sight to see the flags of the various nationalities streaming out to the wind in one of the most out-of-the-way corners of England's dominions. One little vessel was easily distinguishable from the rest, and gave a peculiar characteristic to the whole scene. A gun-brig of the English Royal Navy was there, and her mere presence was all that was needed to keep in order one of the most heterogeneous crowds ever gathered together. The crowd was soon dispersed, and within a month the Fitzroy and the country round about—save for the remains of the camping-places on its banks, and the numberless holes that had been sunk in search of gold—had resumed their ordinary appearance. The story of the leaving of the country is almost as strange as that of the entrance thereto, but it need not be told here. Suffice it to say, that with the immigration of an undisciplined, disorganised, and unreasoning mass of men commenced the development of a colony so prosperous that its ultimate destiny overpowers the desire to prophesy its future greatness."

Sir William Denison, in forwarding his annual report on the condition of the colony to the Duke of Newcastle, enclosed a comment on the Port Curtis rush by Mr C. Rolleston, the then Registrar-General of New South Wales. Mr Rolleston referred to the disappointment occasioned to the thousands who, by reason of exaggerated rumours of the discovery of rich auriferous deposits in the Gladstone district, were tempted to leave their occupations and desert their families in search of fortunes. The sudden repute and as sudden failure of these gold-diggings formed too remarkable a feature of the history of the year under review to be soon forgotten; but, although the distress and disappointment that resulted from the rush were great, there were some compensating grounds of satisfaction in the opening up of a very rich district on the extreme northern frontier, which, under ordinary circumstances, would have attracted but little attention for some years to come, except as an outlet for pastoral enterprise. The existence of rich deposits of gold on the western slopes of the ranges between Port Curtis and Broad Sound was still credited by many people who had had the opportunity of examining the auriferous indications with which the country abounded.

Sir William Denison himself, in the first volume of his "Varieties of Vice-Regal Life," page 453, embodied some unofficial and outspoken observations of his own on what he characterised as "a most curious rush of diggers to a place to the north of Port Curtis." Rumours of the discovery of gold in that region had been started, and the gold-digging public chose to fancy that great wealth was to be found there, "so a stream set in that direction, which kept increasing, till from Melbourne and Adelaide thousands joined it, who were fools enough to sacrifice good present wages to a most absurd hope for future wealth. Upwards of 8000 left Melbourne for these diggings, which have turned out to be an isolated patch of about two acres in extent." Sir William estimated the number that left the Australian capitals for Port Curtis during the rush at more than 16,000. Writing on November 6, 1858, he added: — "The bubble has now burst; thousands are streaming back. I think these rushes speak most unfavourably for the state of the people who are engaged in them. They appear to be bound by no ties; they leave home, wife, children, carried off by a most intensely selfish spirit; they do not think of any duty which they owe to their country, or to their family, to say nothing of that which they owe to God; but every impulse of their selfish nature is obeyed on the instant; and the Government, if it can be so called, is in such dread of these people that, instead of opposing the evil which is sapping the foundations of society, it pats these fellows on the back, feeds them at the expense of their better-behaved industrious neighbours, and brings them back to play the same trick again as soon as an opportunity offers." This latter prediction has not been verified. During the four decades that have since elapsed, there have been minor sporadic "rushes," in various parts of Australia; but there has never been any repetition of the all-pervading excitement, the general madness in the air, the communication of a contagious impulse to all sections of the population, and the simultaneous stampede of thousands from every quarter of the southern continent towards a particular locality, which were characteristic of the great rush to Port Curtis. That was an event which, by reason of its magnitude, its rapidity of development, and its psychological interest, is without a parallel in the chequered history of our Colonial Empire.

Amongst those who were in Australia at this time, and who were interested eye-witnesses of the phenomenal movement of the colonial population towards the golden shores of Port Curtis, was Mr E. P. Hingston, the business manager of Artemus Ward as a lecturer, and the author of an entertaining volume of reminiscences of that popular American humorist. Mr Hingston writes:—

"Port Curtis has made a sensation in Sydney. It is the topic of all talk, the theme of all discussion. Few, if any, regard it as a Utopia; on the contrary, every one seems to think that it will throw all the auriferous glories of Victoria into the shade. The man who has not gone to Port Curtis is going if he can; the man who cannot go laments his inability, and believes that he is an injured individual. Maps of Port Curtis attract you in every shop window, and at hotels they give a map to every one who purchases a drink. There are crowds on the wharves, waiting all day to take their passage, and there are similar crowds around the offices of the shipping agents. Every carpenter in Sydney is now cradle-making, for there are piles of new ones at every corner. The rockers of these will be from every class. Waiters are leaving the hotels, comedians are deserting the theatres, while stationers, fruiterers, tailors, and shoemakers are closing their shops and joining in the common cry: "I believe in it, and I'm off."

At the same time, Mr Samuel Mossman, an early colonist himself, and the author of several valuable books on Australia, wrote :—

"Doubtless, the rush to Port Curtis will precipitate the separation of the northern district from New South Wales. It will be a remarkably parallel case to that of Port Phillip, which became the independent colony of Victoria simultaneously with its gold discoveries. In all likelihood, the seat of Government in the new northern colony will be fixed at Gladstone instead of Brisbane. The former is decidedly the better site of the two for a shipping port, as Port Curtis is easily accessible, and has a depth of water sufficient for ships of any tonnage."

Here are some reminiscences of the rush by a Victorian digger who took part in it :—

"Exaggerated reports were circulated of a second Ballarat. The coaches from the large Victorian mining centres, notably Pleasant Creek, the scene of the last great rush, came down crowded with diggers and their swags. Others arrived in town in large parties, with their traps in drays, walking, as a matter of economy. Tradesmen, storekeepers, and mechanics were throwing up their places by hundreds. Tent-makers, blacksmiths, and tin-workers were working all hours to supply the demands made upon them, while the city of Melbourne was covered with posters announcing the different sailing-vessels and steamers which had been laid on for the new El Dorado. We decided for the ship *Salem*, 1800 tons register, of the Thames and Mersey line. After clearing Port Phillip Heads we took stock of our shipmates—old diggers from Pleasant Creek, old hands from all parts, and men of all descriptions, who had resolved to try the rush. Whenever we overhauled any other craft, there was a banging of tin dishes, waving of shovels, firing of guns, and cheering. One night we had a determined fight over cards between a digger and an old Derwenter.* It lasted about two hours, during which the uproar was deafening. For threatening the life of the captain, the old Derwenter had to be put in irons and bundled into one of the quarter-boats, with a tarpaulin to cover him. As we neared our destination a steamer approached us. Some experienced diggers, who had been at rushes before, were talking, and then

---

* An ex-convict from Van Diemen's Land.

one hairy-chested being, with his big arms covered with tattoo-marks, shouted to her while she was still a mile off: 'A shicer, by thunder!' he said; 'too many hands on that craft for the rush to be any good.' His diagnosis proved true.

"On arriving at our destination we found a population of from 5000 to 6000. The bush was thick with tents. Firearms continued to be discharged from all directions until after midnight—a precaution to ward off intruders. The scene from the front of our tent was something to be remembered—huge fires burning, tents lit up, showing the inmates in curious positions by the shadows cast on the canvas, some card-playing, some singing and drinking, some loading firearms, and others attending to watch-dogs, of which there was a great number chained up in front of the tents. Groups gathered around the fires, gesticulating and shouting, while about a hundred yards in front of us a fire lighted at the butt of a hollow tree had mounted up the pipe, and was roaring out at the top like a furnace.

"In the meantime, a main street was forming. Billiard saloons, concert rooms, rifle galleries, and shanties were going up continually. Surveyors marked off streets, and bush ovens were built to make bread, which was badly wanted. So matters went on for a week. Things then began to look serious, as some were getting hard up. Great dissatisfaction was felt with the steamship companies, it being openly stated that they were aware of the failure of the rush while they encouraged it, but a climax was arrived at when they raised the fares by 10s. to go back to Sydney. Fights and scrimmages were of daily occurrence; the growling and discontent became alarming, and the Government officials had to find employment for as many as they could. As I was strolling about I heard a 'coo-ee' from my mate, who told me there was a row over at the Steamship Company's tent, the diggers threatening to pull the place down if the fares were not lowered. I started off with him, and sure enough an angry and excited mob were round the tent with knives drawn, while one of the officers—Captain Moodie, I think—was trying to pacify them. I eventually got back to Melbourne on a vessel chartered to convey 112 passengers, but which had over 400 on board."

One special correspondent on the scene of the rush descried a tent bearing the inscription: "Letters written for a shilling." Entering, he found several miners of neglected education awaiting their turn. The digger in possession proceeded with his dictation in these terms: "Tell him he ain't no call to mind them blessed yarns in the papers." "Do not be led away by newspaper statements," echoed the scribe, reproducing the sentiment in polite and grammatical English.

Mr Sinnett, in his closing reflections on the rush, remarks that the failure of hope, disappointment in all sorts of shapes, is common enough, and there is nothing new about embarking on an enterprise in high spirits, and cheered on by numerous friends, and some time after struggling out of the fray somewhat torn and battered and cast down. But the contrast between hope and disappointment was certainly unusually conspicuous in the present case. The expectations of those who started in the ill-fated rush were wildly high. The failure of those hopes was absolute and complete. Mr Sinnett strongly suspects that most of the 300 who returned with him were mingling, with calculations of what they had lost, self-reproaches for their folly in having come, and the scarcely less annoying anticipations of the ridiculous figure they would cut as prodigals returning amid the merriment of their good-natured friends. This latter feeling seemed indeed to predominate in a good many of those with whom he got into conversation upon the subject of the rush. A young gentleman, whose friends resided in Melbourne, contemplated passing through that city with his hat drawn over his eyes, without stopping, and first notifying his return from Port Curtis in a letter dated from the Ovens, or Indigo Creek. "I hope we shan't get into Melbourne by daylight," another man said to me; "I know I shall feel the same as if I'd stole something. I'd like to slink away home in the dark." And so it was with many more.

The crestfallen diggers who had expressed an ardent desire to "slink" home in the sheltering darkness had their wish, for it was ten o'clock at night when Mr Sinnett and his 300 disgusted fellow-voyagers were absorbed into the population of Melbourne. Next day Mr Sinnett found that the people of Victoria had become as unreasonably apprehensive about Port Curtis as they had been unreasonably hopeful at first. Wild and extravagant stories about the sufferings and destitution of the adventurers who had gone there had succeeded the previous wild and extravagant stories about their enormous gains. The war steamer *Victoria* had been despatched from Melbourne, and H.M.S. *Iris* from Sydney, with stores to relieve the numerous starving diggers that were alleged to be unable to get away from Port Curtis.

That there was some foundation for these reports, and a not entirely remote risk of catastrophe, is sufficiently evidenced by an official letter from Sir Maurice O'Connell to the Colonial Secretary, dated October 29, 1858, in which he relates that on returning to the diggers' encampment after a brief absence—" I was immediately surrounded by an excited crowd, all clamorous for food, employment, or the means of getting back again to the places from whence they came. After addressing this crowd, and not without some little difficulty pacifying the tumult, chiefly I think by an assurance that no person would be allowed to starve, I was enabled, comparatively free from interruption, to inquire into the causes of discontent, and consider the remedies within my power. I found that within the last three days from 1500 to 2000 people had arrived, chiefly from Melbourne, and that considerable numbers of these were, according to their own accounts, without means of subsistence, even for a week after landing. In fact, they had thrown themselves as paupers upon these shores in the anticipation of getting gold immediately on their arrival." Sir Maurice adds that a mass of discontent was thus collected, which, "under the dread of starvation, was fast ripening into sedition and outrage." Recognising the necessity for immediate and vigorous action, Sir Maurice employed as many men as he could on relief works in the Gladstone district. He also held a conference with the captains of nine vessels that had brought 1660 passengers from Melbourne, and under the influence of a Government guarantee against eventual loss, persuaded them to take their living freight back again to Melbourne. The Colonial Treasurer at Melbourne, the Hon. George Harker, subsequently presented to the Victorian Parliament a "little bill," to the tune of £15,000, in connection with the Port Curtis Relief Expedition, for miscellaneous expenses and the passage-money of 5000 destitute diggers. A letter, dated November 20, thus records the final dropping of the curtain on this strange, chequered, and swiftly-moving drama of the Port Curtis rush :—

"The *Victoria* has just embarked the remnant of the distressed diggers, ninety in number, and all wearing a subdued and penitent demeanour, befitting those who have wandered from their homes like wayward little children, involving the employment of a beadle to bring them back."

The special correspondent of the *Sydney Morning Herald*, writing on November 20, declared the feeling of hope in the ultimate success of the Port Curtis country as a goldfield to be much more widely extended than would be believed after the numerous and recent scenes of disappointment and panic. Many of those who had left, some of them veteran and widely-experienced gold-diggers, had assured him they were certain a rich goldfield would be discovered there some day. On being asked why, holding that belief, they abandoned the place, they replied that the "some day" might be a distant day, and they had no means of bridging over the interval, even if they were inclined to lose the time.

The predictions of these veteran and experienced diggers were afterwards abundantly verified, for the strangest part of this strange story has yet to be told. Most people have read that wonderfully analytical and artistic study by Edgar Allan Poe, "The Purloined Letter," a document that eluded all the efforts of the most acute, experienced, and energetic of the Parisian police and detectives to discover its whereabouts "by dint of being excessively obvious, too obtrusively and too palpably self-evident." While they were searching all over the premises, looking through every page of every book in the library, examining secret drawers, unscrewing the legs of chairs and tables, and applying the microscope to every possible receptacle, the purloined letter of enormous value was all the time literally staring them in the face, being, with calculated carelessness, thrust into a card-rack dangling beneath the middle of the mantelpiece. The Minister of State, who had committed the robbery, had, in the words of the author, "deposited the letter immediately beneath the nose of the whole world by way of best preventing any portion of that world from perceiving it." So it was in real and sober truth with the thousands of intending gold-diggers who flocked to Port Curtis in 1858, and who, after a few weeks, rushed back indignant, disappointed, and semi-starved. A few miles from the spot on which they had congregated to dig for the precious metal, and which was speedily exhausted by the immense number of men at work on such a limited area, was a genuine mountain of gold, the now world-renowned Mount Morgan. As in the case of the purloined letter, it was too directly under their noses to be visible. Many of them, in prospecting parties, must have walked over and around it without suspecting that beneath their feet lay undiscovered wealth beyond the dreams of avarice.

CHAPTER XII

THE CORRESPONDENCE OF SIR MAURICE O'CONNELL

For the purposes of the present volume Lady O'Connell has very kindly placed at my command the correspondence of her distinguished husband, while holding the office of Government Resident at Gladstone, and my best acknowledgments are also due to Mr Denis O'Donovan, the accomplished Parliamentary librarian of Queensland, for valuable assistance in arranging and summarising a correspondence of a somewhat varied and voluminous character.

Before leaving Sydney to enter on his duties as Government Resident at Gladstone, Sir Maurice O'Connell addressed several communications to the Colonial Secretary with respect to the policy he meant to pursue. For instance, on February 7, 1854, in applying for permission to detain the Government steamer at Port Curtis until such time as communications were so far opened up with other parts of the colony as to relieve Gladstone from the risk of suffering from the want of supplies, or other evils incidental to its isolated position, he remarked:—

"I deem it the more incumbent on me to take this precaution, as in this instance the Government has gone in advance of private enterprise, and sold the lands of the Crown, previous to their occupation by squatters, and will therefore be held more than ordinarily responsible that all possible protection is given to those who locate themselves under its auspices in a portion of the country in which the first settlers will, doubtless, be subject to some risks and privations. It appears to me that the first object to which my attention should be turned is that of opening up the communications with the interior, and this will be more apparent when it is considered that the township of Gladstone is entirely isolated from all other portions of the colony as yet under occupation, and that, in fact, there is no occupation of sufficient magnitude to afford supplies for the present population even within a hundred miles of it. I would therefore propose at once to take measures to open a road to Gayndah, as the shortest and most direct route to the southward, and as bringing Port Curtis at once into connection with the nearest point of postal communication with Sydney."

On May 9, 1854, Sir Maurice O'Connell officially reported to the Colonial Secretary his arrival in Gladstone, and shortly afterwards he acquainted that Minister with the fact that he had received letters from the Messrs Archer, W. H. Walsh, and W. A. Brown, applying for lands in the Port Curtis district. After pointing out that the lands in question had not yet been surveyed, Sir Maurice proceeds :—

"It would appear, therefore, that either the lands referred to must be allowed to remain idle and unoccupied for some time to come, that is to say, until the survey of the counties in which they are included is sufficiently advanced to allow the provisions of the above-mentioned section to come into force, or special regulations must be made to meet the case. Should His Excellency the Governor-General deem it proper under these circumstances to provide for the immediate pastoral occupation of the greater portion of these lands, and I think it would be desirable so to do rather than wait what, in the present state of the labour market, must, I fear, be the slow progress of their survey, I would venture to recommend that all lands within the counties of Clinton, Deas Thomson, and Livingstone, situated at a greater distance than twenty miles from the outer limits of the township of Gladstone, should be open to pastoral occupation at £1 per section on annual lease, renewable without competition until surveyed or required for sale, and with a right of pre-emption over 160 acres or any less quantity on which valuable improvements have been made, the applications for such lands to be addressed to the Government Resident or Commissioner of Crown Lands at Gladstone, priority of claim to be allowed according to date of application, and all conflicting tenders to be submitted to public competition, as in the unsettled and intermediate districts. I do not think it is necessary to allude to the particular views or the personal claims to consideration put forward by each of the gentlemen whose letters I enclose (Messrs Archer, Walsh, and Brown), as of course the question at issue can only be decided upon grounds affecting the general public good, but I believe them to be fully entitled to the merit of having shown much energy and enterprise in pushing out to, and exploring the country in this neighbourhood."

A letter, dated the following November 1, gives some interesting details concerning the little force of black police on whom Sir Maurice had to rely for the preservation of law and order in the districts contiguous to Gladstone:—

"Referring to my letter of the 7th October, with its enclosures on the subject of the suspension of Lieutenant Murray of the Native Police, by order of Mr Walker, the Commandant of that corps, I have now the honour to report that Mr Murray has resumed his duties in pursuance to instructions from Lieutenant Marshall, who has, I understand, been temporarily invested with the authority Mr Walker had previously held. These changes have not, however, been effected without creating serious difficulty in regard to the native troopers, who were reported to me by Mr Murray to have determined upon going into the headquarters of the corps at Traylan with the mail escort, which left this on Saturday week last, and on questioning Sergeant Humphreys, who is the non-commissioned officer attached to the section at this place, I found he was also of opinion that the greater number, if not all the men would leave. This was rather a serious dilemma, as in the event of our being abandoned by the native police, it might have become a matter of much difficulty to keep open the communication between this settlement and the inhabited interior of the country, from which an unoccupied tract of some eighty miles still separates it. Moreover, the dangers attendant upon detached working-parties in the bush would have been so much enhanced, that I should have found it a serious increase to the difficulties, already sufficiently great, of carrying on the public works and buildings which have to be erected; and in addition to all this, postal communication would have been entirely stopped. Under these circumstances, I desired Mr Murray to have his men paraded for my inspection on the day previous to the departure of the mail escort, and, putting on my uniform, I rode over to the Native Police Quarters to try what effect an appeal to the men on the part of Government would have upon them, and I am happy to be able to add that the result of this attempt has been as successful as I could have wished it to be. I found the men, in the first instance, apparently determined upon going in to Traylan to see Mr Walker. They said they were getting too far away from their own country, and that they were anxious again to see their relatives and friends, and that they understood, if they lost Mr Walker, they would have to travel on foot to the distant places from which he had brought them. I then pointed out to them that it was the Government, and not Mr Walker, who had clothed and fed them, and that whatever undertaking Mr Walker had given them as to the means of their return to their own country, I pledged myself, on the part of Government, should be faithfully performed, and I appealed to their pride of manhood, explaining to them that the country they had served so well for the last five years was now at war with other white people, and that their services might yet be required as soldiers to defend the coast upon which they were stationed, and showing them by my uniform that I too had been a soldier, I told them that, in the event of an enemy's landing, I depended upon the native police as the only force at my disposal for the means of repelling him. They answered to this appeal gallantly, and seemed to feel as strongly as more civilised troops would do the disgrace of deserting their post in what might be the moment of danger, and on my again assuring them that opportunities should be given to them to revisit their relations, they unanimously declared their intention of remaining, and, as if to show their intention more significantly, they themselves, as Mr Murray assures me, asked permission from him to accompany me in a body to my own camp, which they did. So far, this difficulty has been overcome, but whether a similar one may not recur in consequence of further communication with Traylan, where, I understand, Mr Walker still is, it is impossible for me to say. He has, I am sure, great influence with the men, whom he himself enlisted and brought from their distant tribes, and at his suggestion, further difficulties might arise. However, I shall feel strengthened in endeavouring to combat these, if I learn that His Excellency the Governor-General approves of the steps I have taken, and sanctions the guarantee which I have given on the part of the Government that the troopers of the native police here, shall, as opportunity offers, be taken by their own officers to the districts from which they originally came; in fact, that they should have furloughs, and be aided by Government to visit their friends."

After several letters in connection with the plans of the town of Gladstone, the establishment of a post-office, court-house, etc., Sir Maurice, on July 4, 1854, made his first report on the subject of the aborigines. He said that when he arrived at Gladstone he found Lieutenant Murray in charge of the native police, and Mr Surveyor M'Cabe employed in laying out land for sale. Mr Murray had his headquarters then at a point on the Calliope River some twelve miles distant, but he had now, on the suggestion of Sir Maurice, established himself at Auckland Creek, close to the town of Gladstone.

"I have experienced no inconvenience," Sir Maurice adds, "from the display of any hostile feeling on the part of the aborigines. On the contrary, when two of my orderlies, in driving my horses and cattle over from Gayndah, came suddenly in contact with a large party of them, they showed every desire to establish a friendly intercourse by pointing out the most direct line of road, and assisting in driving the stock. A portion of this party, who had evidently never been in contact with white men before, came into my camp, and remained for two or three days, leaving again on the occurrence of wet weather."

On the same date Sir Maurice reported the completion of the road from Gladstone to Gayndah, and expressed his satisfaction that the former was now connected with Sydney by a continuous, well-marked overland route.

One result of the remoteness and isolation of Gladstone at this early period of its history was reported by Sir Maurice on September 11, when he informed the Colonial Secretary that "letters lately had not been stamped," for the good and sufficient reason that "there were no stamps in the post-office at Gladstone."

The provision of a permanent water supply was a matter that demanded the immediate and most serious consideration of the Government Resident. On November 6, 1854, he wrote to the Colonial Secretary, suggesting that dams should be thrown across some of the water-courses in the immediate vicinity of the town.

"The country in the neighbourhood of Gladstone," said Sir Maurice, "is an extraordinary jumble of steep ridges and hills of slight elevation, culminating at a point called Round Hill. These ridges and hills, with very narrow valleys intersecting the variation of their alignments, abut upon the shore, leaving very short courses, varying, I fancy, from one mile to three, for the streams which drain them ere they reach the sea. This construction of the ground accounts for the non-formation of actual reservoirs. The amount of water escaping from these ranges into the sea must be very considerable."

On November 16, 1854, Sir Maurice despatched a consignment of wool from Gladstone to Sydney by steamer, as an indication of the progress the settlement was making, and a fortnight afterwards he expressed his gratification at the prospect of a steamer, the *William Miskin*, running regularly once a month between Gladstone and Sydney. Early in the new year, 1855, he forwarded to the Colonial Secretary a memorial from the commercial citizens of Gladstone, praying that Port Curtis might be proclaimed a free port where vessels could receive and discharge cargo on payment of the regulated customs. Sir Maurice, in supporting the prayer of the memorial, mentioned that he had himself intended making this recommendation at the beginning of the wool season. He believed that its adoption would lead to the opening-up of a direct trade between Gladstone and Singapore and the East Indies, as the result of the removal of existing fiscal obstructions.

At the beginning of 1855, Sir Maurice reported that the rates of wages he was then paying on Government works were — stonemasons, £5 per week; carpenters, £4; and labourers, £75 per annum; in all cases with Government rations, and when married, a double ration. Towards the middle of this year, Gladstone was threatened with famine, in consequence of the protracted absence of the steamer employed in conveying stores from Sydney. Sir Maurice generously placed his private stores at the command of the community. On August 6, he wrote:—

"The steamer has not yet arrived. The number of those who have been put on rice diet has increased. There is great inconvenience and discomfort. I have only one week's supply of flour in my private store. The rice also is fast drawing to an end. With the exception of about thirty lbs. of flour of my own, the only flour in Gladstone is a supply of 780 lbs. in the hands of the contractor, who, in dread of the penalties attached to a breach of contract, will not issue it except as rations to persons entitled to such a concession as persons in the employment of the Government. There are about 500 lbs. of rice in a damaged condition in the hands of one of the storekeepers. These are our only resources independent of animal food. I trust that means will be found to ensure greater punctuality, as, even with the best arrangements, an unforeseen accident may leave this place without other resource than overland communication by dray, a trip of at least six weeks."

The steamer fortunately arrived before all available resources were exhausted, and the Gladstonians were relieved from an anxious and very unpleasant situation.

At this time the Surveyor-General of New South Wales was the distinguished Australian explorer, Sir Thomas Livingstone Mitchell, and with him Sir Maurice O'Connell had a little controversy over the manner in which the future town of Gladstone should be planned. Sir Thomas favoured the chessboard style of construction, and Sir Maurice objected to it. Writing on September 7, 1854, the latter remarked:—

"Here we have a very irregular natural surface, in consequence of which, under the proposed plan, it would become a matter of chance and not of arrangement whether the streets run through those parts which offer the greatest facilities to traffic, or whether they meet the ground where a considerable expenditure is required to make them passable. In laying out a seaport town, the great object is to conduct the traffic of the interior by the shortest lines to its point of exit on the seashore. This point in Gladstone is at present, and must be for some years to come, the shore of Auckland Inlet, and the course of the River Calliope on the northern side would indicate that, to reach this from any part of the interior, lines drawn to the cardinal points of the compass would be preferable ones for the alignment of streets. That is to say, the Calliope running north and south, and presenting no ford nearer than some fourteen miles from Gladstone, throws all the northern and western traffic from that distance on a north and south line, and the traffic from the southward will take the same direction naturally. Wherefore, any deviation from north and south lines with east and west cross streets seems rather a demerit than otherwise."

These objections of Sir Maurice were not approved by Sir Thomas Mitchell, whereupon the former rejoined that "although they may not be felt for some time, they will undoubtedly become very serious when Gladstone attains the commercial importance to which it is destined."

At the suggestion of Sir Maurice, no more sales of land in the Port Curtis district were held in Sydney, because, as he pointed out in a letter to the Colonial Secretary, the practice was detrimental to the interests of Gladstone, inasmuch as it led to a non-resident proprietary. The first sale of land at Gladstone was held on July 31, 1855, and Sir Maurice reported that all lots offered were sold at a considerable advance on the upset price, an average of £15 per lot having been obtained.

On August 24, 1855, Sir Maurice wrote to the Colonial Secretary, in terms of astonishment and indignation, with respect to certain charges of extravagance and alleged irregularities in the administration of public affairs at Gladstone, that were brought forward by Sir Henry Parkes, one of the members for Sydney, in the course of a speech on the estimates. These charges Sir Maurice had no difficulty in thoroughly repelling and exploding. In his own words, they were shown to be, for the most part, "emanations of Mr Parkes's imagination." In a lengthy letter of reply to this gratuitous and wholly unjustified attack, Sir Maurice wrote:—

"On the general policy of opening this port, it is sufficient to remark that it was opened at the repeated request of that portion of the public most interested in the matter, and that it has been confirmed by the purchase, at extraordinarily high prices, of the land offered for sale. The port having been opened and land sold to the extent of £11,000 or £12,000, it became incumbent on the Government to take every precaution for the care of the people placed in a position so isolated, and it was with this view I recommended, and the Government agreed to, the retention of the services of the steamer *Tom Tough*. I did not keep her longer than her services were absolutely necessary, and I seized the first opportunity, offered by the appearance of the *William Miskin* as a regular trader, to dispense with a stationary vessel altogether. I adopted this measure with misgivings, which were justified by the straits to which we were subsequently reduced. If the expenditure on the *Tom Tough* was greater than it ought to have been in proportion to her value, this must be attributed to the exorbitant rates demanded in Sydney at the time for everything. As to the comparative smallness of the community for whom this expenditure was incurred, they were, however few in numbers, entitled to protection from the Government; moreover, the paucity of numbers proved the economy with which the arrangements had been made. It ought not to be forgotten that this is the first settlement on the coast established without military protection."

Referring to the allegation of Sir Henry Parkes that the office of Government Resident at Gladstone had been created for his special benefit, Sir Maurice pointed out that this was sufficiently contradicted by the fact that his official salary from the beginning had been inadequate to the expenditure the position necessarily entailed.

"My expenditure for the year 1854 more than quadrupled my official income, and my expenditure for the current year, as far as I can form an opinion from the first six months, will more than double it. I do not think the present state of the colony requires any individual to sacrifice his own private interests on the altar of the public good; but, concurring in the policy which dictated the location of this settlement, I have been quite willing, in the commencement of the experiment, to suffer some temporary inconvenience and risk of loss, trusting that if the event shall justify my anticipations, my country will not deny me a fair reward for my services."

Early in 1856 Sir Maurice reported that on his return to Gladstone, after a brief absence, he found the place (at which hitherto the most friendly relations had subsisted with the aborigines) in much disquiet, owing to several daring and murderous attacks by the blacks on the settlers and the stations of the squatters. At Mr Young's, every white on the station was brutally killed; at Messrs Elliot's one man was killed, and Mr W. Elliot severely wounded; and Mr Charles Archer had demanded protection in consequence of the threats of large numbers of blacks in the vicinity of his station. These painful incidents impelled Sir Maurice to make strong representations to the Colonial

Secretary on the necessity of increasing the native police force. In other matters also the interests of Gladstone continued to be overlooked or neglected by the ruling authorities in Sydney. Sir Maurice forwarded to the Postmaster-General a petition from the people of Gladstone, praying for better postal communication, and bringing under his notice the very substantial grievance that "letters take as long going from Sydney to Gladstone as from London to Gladstone, viz. four months." A further desirable reform was indicated by Sir Maurice when he pointed out to the New South Wales Government that, notwithstanding the progress of settlement in the Port Curtis district, the town of Gladstone, as well as the adjacent counties of Clinton, Deas Thomson, and Livingstone, remained unrepresented in the Parliament of the colony.

In a letter of May 23, 1857, Sir Maurice indignantly remonstrated with his superiors in Sydney against a proposed reduction of the defensive forces at his command, and revealed some of the perils to which he was subjected at his outpost of civilisation in Australia.

"I may have a larger establishment than the returns of the district would seem to justify for the time, but the growth of this part of the country may be predicted without any chance of failure. It will not be asserted that the Port Curtis district is as yet in so quiet a state as to render it unnecessary to travel about without precaution to resist violence. The district is 200 miles in extent along the coast; it is thickly inhabited with blacks, and in all parts, except the town of Gladstone, there have been serious outrages by the aborigines, and much loss of life. Two nights before the receipt of the letter I am now replying to, I was, with three of my men, for several hours under arms, with spears and boomerangs flying against the walls of my house, and had I not had sufficient force to feel confidence in my power to resist attack, I should on this occasion have been compelled to have become the assailant and to drive away blacks, who eventually did no injury. Such scenes are not uncommon in the neighbourhood of my quarters, as to prevent their doing mischief elsewhere, I have, ever since my landing, encouraged the blacks to camp near me, and I have thus prevented any outrage in the town of Gladstone. Since my arrival at Port Curtis, I have been at an expenditure of more than £1500 per annum, hoping to gain credit for myself and expansion for my country at the risk both of my life and my private fortune. As an Australian, my object is, and for the last eighteen years has been, to serve my country."

On the following July 14, Sir Maurice, in a letter to the Colonial Secretary, makes reference to the infant township of Rockhampton on the Fitzroy River, in the vicinity of Gladstone, a settlement that was destined to expand into an important and populous centre, and to overshadow for a time the intended capital of Mr Gladstone's projected North Australian colony. Sir Maurice had been called upon to erect a court of petty sessions at Rockhampton and constitute it a new police district. He replied, urging the impolicy of this proceeding on the ground that, having regard to the manner in which the Government had undertaken the settlement of Port Curtis, and the large sums raised from the public by the sale of land in the town and neighbourhood of Gladstone, it would be a breach of faith to establish in its immediate vicinity another seat or centre of Government business. Besides, means of communication between Gladstone and the Fitzroy River were of the most ample and facile description, and the few persons so far located in Rockhampton and its neighbourhood had no adequate cause to ask for a separate court of petty sessions.

In these early years of its history, Gladstone was a very remote, lonely, and isolated little town, with but few facilities for communicating with the populous and important Australian centres. A letter of Sir Maurice O'Connell's, dated August 1, 1857, mentions that it took nearly three months to communicate by post with Sydney, and that improved postal communication was a crying necessity. He had called for tenders for the conveyance of the mails from Gladstone to Gayndah, the nearest town with an organised postal service to Sydney, but only one application had been sent in, and that was from a person who required to be supplied with twelve horses entirely on credit. In these circumstances, Sir Maurice offered to add to the multifarious duties he already discharged that of mail-carrier or general postman for the district. That is to say, he was willing to detach a

K

certain number of his servants to carry the mails, on condition that he was not to be considered a public contractor, and that he would not be held liable for any sudden break or cessation of the service. The proposal appears to have been accepted by the Sydney authorities, as Sir Maurice reported on the following September 14, that he had completed arrangements for a weekly mail between Gladstone and Gayndah, the men to be withdrawn as soon as a public contract had been entered into.

A letter dated November 25, 1857, is of special interest as giving an authoritative and first-hand account of the circumstances under which the great gold rush described in a previous chapter originated. Sir Maurice writes:—

"Having occasion to leave Gladstone on the 11th of last month on an extended tour to the northern portions of my district, and having long felt convinced that some part of the country I was about to travel over was auriferous, I took with me a very competent practical miner, and on arriving at the outside limit of present occupation on the northern frontier of the colony— that is, on the very last station—I, on Saturday, the 17th November, caused some pans of earth to be washed, and thus discovered, both in the beds of creeks and on the surface soil of the surrounding country, very promising prospects of gold; and then extending my researches over some four or five miles of ground adjoining, in almost every instance found spangles, or, as it is technically termed, the colour of the precious metal. I afterwards had some holes dug to a depth of seven or eight feet to what appeared to be the bedrock, but without reaching any more promising washing stuff than was found on the surface, and eventually after passing one day's journey beyond all occupation, and devoting about six to the development of this very important question, I succeeded in obtaining as a specimen only about half a dwt. of fine gold. But a report of this discovery has already brought up from Gladstone another party of four to continue the prosecution of the search, and they, although not well provided, and eventually disturbed by the aborigines, returned with some gold of a much heavier description than I had found, and, moreover, obtained in another and more southern locality than the one I had tried. In consequence of these discoveries, the inhabitants of Gladstone have provided rations and equipment for a party of ten or twelve persons, who leave this on Monday under engagement to prosecute the search for gold for a period of six weeks. I am fully persuaded, and all those practical miners who have had opportunities of examining the ground are of the same opinion, that there is a rich and extensive goldfield in this neighbourhood, and the existence of gold in the soil has been verified over a distance in a straight line of some sixty or seventy miles —that is to say, it has been found at different points within these limits. The geological features of the country, taken in conjunction with the fact of gold being actually found, are quite sufficient, I think, in the eyes of all who have some knowledge of the affinities of rocks and minerals in other localities, to warrant the belief that this is a metalliferous country. The principal rocks on the north bank of the Fitzroy—and the same formation appears again on the Calliope—are serpentine of very many beautiful varieties and in large masses, with considerable veins of metal-bearing quartz in close connection with calcareous spar and white limestone, and in addition to these, I observed clay slate, porphyry, and many pebbles of jasper, chalcedony, and ironstone."

On December 4, 1857, Sir Maurice reported that a Mr Sloman was cultivating cotton on a small scale, and had already forwarded some beautiful specimens to the Manchester Chamber of Commerce. Having regard to the dimensions which this industry subsequently attained, the comment of Sir Maurice upon the first modest experiment is noteworthy :—" Though not possessing any capital, or at any rate but little beyond his labour, yet if he cultivates but one acre, the result will be one of considerable interest."

Five days later Sir Maurice wrote to the officer commanding the native police, communicating a report that a white woman with two children, supposed to have been shipwrecked, had been captured and detained by a tribe of wild blacks on the Fitzroy River. Several friendly blacks had told substantially the same story—a white woman whose hands were tied by day, and two children along with her. Sir Maurice considered that it would be injudicious to attempt her rescue by any display of force, but undertook on behalf of the Government to offer a liberal reward of flour, clothing, blankets, etc., to any blacks who would bring her and the children to the town of Gladstone. He suggested that the native troopers should be employed to circulate the news of this reward amongst the blacks. On the following January 23, he transmitted his annual report on the aborigines of the Port Curtis district. Those who had frequented the neighbourhood of Gladstone, he said, had been remarkably well conducted, and had shown themselves willing to assist the townspeople, but some tribes at a distance of forty miles to the southward had been troublesome. They had killed three white men, and seriously wounded three others. He had no doubt these outrages might have been prevented by a thoroughly efficient native police force, which at present did not exist.

In one of the last official letters he wrote from Gladstone to the Colonial Secretary in Sydney, on the eve of his nomination to a seat in the Legislative Council of the newly-created colony of Queensland, Sir Maurice cast a retrospective glance at his career as Government Resident, and once more energetically protested against a further threatened reduction in the defensive force of the settlement on the shores of Port Curtis. He observed:—

"On the first establishment of this settlement, in March 1854, I took up the occupation of an isolated spot on the coast. I felt that I was undertaking a post of no little responsibility, as this was the first instance in the history of Australian colonisation in which an isolated settlement had been taken up with so scanty a force for its protection as that placed at my disposal. Moreton Bay had been occupied as a penal settlement, and for many years had a considerable number of troops stationed in Brisbane, and even then had not escaped many outrages from aboriginal violence. Port Curtis also, when previously taken up by the expedition under Colonel Barney, had a company of the 99th Regiment assigned for its defence. I felt, moreover, that I was not taking up the country in the ordinary mode of squatters' occupation, with a number of handy men alone, but that I was entering upon an attempt at colonisation, under which, as the representative of the Government, I was responsible to public opinion for the safety of women and children, and for that preservation of order which would allow persons engaged in trade and commerce to pursue their avocations without hindrance from lawless violence. The Government of the day gave me, however, all the assistance I asked for, and I entered upon my task with seven constables and four orderlies, or eleven available men in all, to protect the foundation of the settlement and open up its communications with the interior. I had likewise placed under my orders a detachment of native police, and I had authority to retain the means of communicating by water with other portions of the colony by having the *Tom Tough* placed at my disposal, so long as I might consider it necessary to detain her; and further, when I thought the time had arrived to dispense with the *Tom Tough*, I had a boat's crew of one coxswain and five men allowed me. Under these circumstances I felt I had a sufficient force about me to enter upon a policy of conciliation with the aborigines, and from the first year of our arrival I have allowed and encouraged their resort in any numbers they may choose to congregate into the town of Gladstone, and I have as much as possible induced them to camp in the immediate vicinity of my own residence as a place of resort for safety in all cases where they themselves have not committed crime or outrage. By these means, under the protection of Providence, the town of Gladstone has from the beginning been free from any outrage by aboriginal violence, nor have they been allowed to pilfer or steal as they do in many other places. On the contrary, the aborigines have been exceedingly useful to the townspeople, and have been in their constant employment as hewers of wood and drawers of water. But by degrees the small amount of protective force at my disposal has been decreased, until now I have only one chief and five other constables to depend on in the event of an emergency, and of these there are frequently two or three away at a time on escort or other duties. Under these circumstances, I no longer feel the same confidence in allowing an unquestioned resort to the town by the aborigines —sometimes so many as three or four hundred, who have been accustomed to resort to it—and yet it will be difficult now to prevent this without coming to an open rupture, and endangering the peaceful occupation of the settlement. . . . It is true there is a native police station within three miles, but for the last two or three years it has been very badly supplied with men, and when the party is complete, it is frequently absent on duty at a distance. Moreover, a resort to their use is of itself a declaration of hostilities which entails all the inconveniences I have detailed above, and, besides, amounts to a sentence of indiscriminate slaughter, which, for the sake of our common humanity, ought only to be resorted to after more serious outrage has been committed."

CHAPTER XIII

A GRIEVOUS ERROR OF MR GLADSTONE'S

CLOSELY connected with Mr Gladstone's colonising experiment in Northern Australia was a personal incident of an exceedingly painful character, which caused a considerable sensation at the time, and which, after the lapse of half a century, must needs be pronounced by the impartial historian to be the one ugly blot on Mr Gladstone's colonial administration. It will be remembered that the primary purpose of Mr Gladstone's new colony on the shores of Port Curtis was to act as a safety valve for Van Diemen's Land or Tasmania, which had become deluged with convicts from the Mother Country to an alarming extent. Mr Gladstone's predecessor at the Colonial Office, Lord Stanley, had sought to grapple with this menacing situation by instituting the probation system, the essence of which was the dispersal and distribution of the convicts over the island in what came to be very unfavourably known as "probation gangs." It was hoped that, by the adoption of this plan, not only would the evils incidental to the aggregation of large numbers of prisoners in a few centres be minimised to the utmost, if not entirely removed, but that the individual reformation of the convicts would also be appreciably promoted. Unfortunately, neither of those sanguine anticipations was realised in the result, and the last state of Van Diemen's Land became worse than the first. The immediate effect of the probation system was to multiply the few former centres of vice and pollution, and to create a reign of terror in the country at large. In the words of a contemporary chronicler: "Respectable people were afraid to walk along the roads, and robberies by men in the dress of probationers were of frequent occurrence." The circumstances of the colony at the time called for the highest powers of administration, organisation, vigilance, firmness, and foresight; and, although the reigning Governor, Sir Eardley Wilmot, Bart., undoubtedly did his best to cope with the evils and perils of the situation, it must be confessed that he was hardly strong, young, and energetic enough to combat or control, with any pronounced success or satisfaction, the combination of formidable difficulties by which he was surrounded. But that was his misfortune, not his fault; and, instead of being treated with the Spartan severity (culminating in a baseless charge and a pitiful death from a broken heart) meted out to him by Mr Gladstone, he was entitled to the utmost sympathy and consideration at the hands of his superiors in Downing Street.

Sir Eardley Wilmot had been sent out from England with the special object of inaugurating the new probation system, and carefully watching its working. One of the Members for Warwick in the House of Commons, for many years Chairman of the Local Quarter-Sessions, and exceptionally well-informed on all matters relating to convicts and prison-discipline, he was regarded as peculiarly qualified to assume the government of a penal colony, and initiate a reform of the character contemplated by Lord Stanley. But Van Diemen's Land at the time was a focus of intrigue and a hot-bed of discontent, and, like his immediate predecessor, Sir John Franklin, Sir Eardley Wilmot found himself hampered at every step and his ideas marred in their execution by official hostility and outside interference. A stronger and younger man might have borne down all such opposition, but, with the best of intentions, Sir Eardley Wilmot was unable to make much headway against the difficulties of the situation. Meanwhile, Mr Gladstone had succeeded Lord Stanley at the Colonial Office, and had developed a deep interest in the working of the probation system. He wrote several despatches to Sir Eardley Wilmot, seeking for detailed information on the subject—asking, indeed, for psychological particulars that it would be exceedingly difficult, if not absolutely impossible, for any Governor to supply.

In the course of one of those communications Mr Gladstone wrote:—

"The primary object of transportation, as of all other punishments, is of course the prevention of crime. But this is to be attained, not merely by exciting terror in the minds of those who may be meditating offences against the law, but by improving as far as possible the prudential, moral, and religious character of the convicts, who, unless so improved, must return at the end of their term of punishment to the perpetration of the same, or similar, or worse offences. Their good conduct, while congregated together in Van Diemen's Land, must also be an object of the highest interest to the whole vicinage. And considerations yet more sacred enhance the importance of it, for it is impossible to forget in how large a proportion of cases these unhappy people have every claim on our sympathy which the force of temptation, adverse circumstances of life, ignorance, and neglected education can afford to those who have incurred the penalty of the law."

The replies to these despatches were not satisfactory to Mr Gladstone, and he resolved to recall Governor Sir Eardley Wilmot from Van Diemen's Land and send out Sir William Denison, of the Royal Engineers, in his stead.

In a despatch addressed to Sir Eardley Wilmot from Downing Street on April 30, 1846, Mr Gladstone said it had become his painful duty to inform Sir Eardley that Her Majesty had been pleased to dispense with his further services in the administration of the affairs of Van Diemen's Land, and that he might expect the early arrival of a successor. His recall was due, not to any incompetency, either real or alleged, for the discharge of the ordinary duties of a Governor, but to the very defective manner in which Sir Eardley had met the special exigencies of the Government of Van Diemen's Land. Her Majesty's Government considered that he had altogether failed in a principal portion of his public duty, namely, the active care of the moral interests involved in the system of convict discipline then practised in Van Diemen's Land.

"You have been placed," wrote Mr Gladstone, "I freely avow, in circumstances of difficulty. So far as that difficulty has been economical and financial, you have given it your attention, and have endeavoured to meet it, if not always in such a manner as to command the concurrence of Her Majesty's Government, yet by no means so as, upon these grounds alone, to have necessitated the cessation of your tenure of office. But so far as the difficulty which you had to meet was a moral one, and this, I must add, was its chief characteristic, it has not only not been overcome, but it does not appear, from the information with which you have supplied me, that any adequate or sustained effort has been made to contend against it. Indeed, I might even proceed one step further, and observe that your statements, taken strictly as they stand, do not so much as show a consciousness of its existence, far less of its grave and formidable character. You have under your charge and responsibility many thousand convicts formed into probation parties, or living together at Government depôts. It is only with extreme rarity that you advert in your despatches to the moral condition of these men. You have discussed the economical questions connected with their maintenance or their coercion, and you have even entered into argument, though in a manner too little penetrating, upon their offences against the laws. But into the inner world of their mental, moral, and spiritual state, either you have not made it a part of your duty to examine, or else—which for the present issue is, I apprehend, conclusive—you have not placed Her Majesty's Government in possession of the results; and I need scarcely point out to you that this is the region in which reformatory efforts are to operate, and that it is a region very distinct from that of offences actually brought under the cognisance of the law."

This despatch was accompanied by a letter of the same date from Mr Gladstone marked "Secret." It was addressed to Sir Eardley Wilmot in these terms:—

"I have now to discharge a duty still more painful and delicate than that of addressing you in a public despatch to communicate to you your recall from the administration of affairs in Van Diemen's Land. Adverting to the fact that this recall rests upon the allegation of a failure on your part with respect to special and peculiar duties only, which attach to the care of a penal colony, but not to that of colonies in general, you may feel some surprise at the circumstance that I have made no allusion to the possibility of your employment during the remainder of the ordinary term of six years. I should have felt authorised to express a willingness to consider any favourable opportunity which might offer itself for such employment, had it not been for the circumstance that certain rumours have reached me from a variety of quarters relating to your private life, to the nature of which it is perhaps unnecessary that I should at present particularly allude. Had these rumours been slight, and without presumptions of credibility, I might warrantably and gladly have passed them by. Had they, on the other hand, taken the form of charges or of information supported by the names of the parties tendering it, it would have been my absolute duty, independently of any other reason for interference with your tenure of office, to refer the matter to you, and at once to call upon you for your exculpation. But they occupy an intermediate position. Presuming that I have been justified in refraining from bringing them under your notice up to the present time, I feel that it would be impossible to recommend your resumption of active duties under the Crown in any other colony until they are satisfactorily disposed of. To found proceedings upon them against a person holding office appeared to me a very questionable matter, but I think it quite unquestionable that they must be taken into view when re-appointment is the matter at issue. I know not what your views and wishes on that subject may be. I should not have entered wantonly and needlessly on such a topic as that to which I now refer. My reason for doing so, without waiting for any request from you for re-employment, is that I think that some favourable intimation on that head would have been your due had no obstacle intervened, and I have therefore found myself bound to account for the omission from my despatch of this day of any such intimation."

Sir Eardley Wilmot, writing from Hobart Town, Van Diemen's Land, on October 5, 1846, thus answered Mr Gladstone's letter of dismissal from the public service:—

"I have this day received by the ship *Java* the original despatch of my recall, dated April 30, No. 104, accompanied by your letter marked "Secret" of the same date. If any-thing could lessen or remove the pain with which I received on September 24 last the duplicate of this despatch, it is your letter marked "Secret" of the same date, because being entirely guiltless of any impropriety or irregularity in my private life, and believing that the 'rumours' to which you allude, invented and circulated by my opponents, and hitherto treated with contempt by me and the whole of this colony, are what have lowered me in your opinion and induced you to pause in offering me employment under the Crown in another colony, I am confident that you will, sooner or later, do me justice, and rescue me from the double loss of my office and my character, thus occasioned by the grossest falsehoods that ever oppressed an English gentleman.

"It is impossible for me to grapple with charges of the nature and extent of which I am ignorant; I can do no more at present in answer to your letter than give a general denial to general imputations. Were the accusations specific, I could meet them at once and show their utter falsehood; but placed in the un-English position of a man charged with unknown acts of impropriety, injurious to his character and destructive to his interests, without any knowledge as to who are his accusers, or as to what are the accusations, I most earnestly and solemnly adjure you to specify immediately the dates, places, persons, and circumstances to which the rumours against my private life apply, that I may be placed in the same position before the public as is the meanest criminal when standing before a jury of his country.

"From my first landing in this colony, the system of detraction and calumny which assailed my two predecessors has been pursued against me. Against them it was confined to this colony, but against me it has been carried on at Melbourne, Sydney, and London, but is treated with contempt here, because known to be false. I can say with pride and with truth that the breath of slander has not prevailed here, but when attempted has been treated with general denial and disgust.

"A paragraph appeared in October 1845, in the *Naval and Military Gazette* of London, purporting to be a letter written from Melbourne, in which it was said that my conduct here was so bad that it was impossible for ladies to visit at Government House. I treated this falsehood with scorn; but unknown to, and unasked by me, the highest in this colony addressed to the editor of the paper in question a letter of denial, and in designating the accusation as a notorious falsehood, vindicated themselves, as well as myself from the foul calumny. This letter I transmitted to Lord Stanley in April last. You could not have received it, therefore, until about this time, but I trust the reading of it will dispel the effects of the 'rumours' to which you allude, and as it is your duty, so I believe it will be your wish, to do me justice.

"But in order that my whole conduct may undergo a thorough and rigid inquiry, I felt it incumbent on me for my own sake, as indeed for the honour of Her Majesty's Government, to lay your letter before the Executive Council, calling upon them to investigate my conduct and report accordingly. Thus far I have addressed you, sir, on what affects my honour and character. I trust you will allow me to say a few words on what deeply affects my interests. I resigned my seat in Parliament for one of the most important counties in England, and for which I had stood three contested elections, and thus injured my fortune in order to sustain constitutional principles. I resigned the Chair of the Quarter-Sessions of the county I represented, to which I had been unanimously elected by the Magistracy, and which I held above twenty years with unblemished character, and I may say with some distinction. I separated myself from my wife and family for six years, to undertake an unasked-for and irksome office in another hemisphere. I incurred great expense in preparing for this duty, which economy, not inconsistent with public and private liberality, has yet not enabled me to meet. And now, after three years of toil and anxiety, at twenty days' notice only, I am relieved of the administration of the affairs of this colony by the arrival of an administrator, deprived of my income, and not only that, but prevented from a return to office under the Crown in another colony until 'rumours against my private life,' of the nature of which I am ignorant, and which I have had no opportunity to answer, are satisfactorily explained.

"To embark for England immediately with your letter of April 30 before me, would be risking the defence of my character, and my return to office, on the same unfounded basis on which I have been deprived of both; for it is clear that in England I could only meet the unauthenticated and anonymous 'rumours of my private life' by my own and personal unauthenticated contradiction; whereas it is in this colony alone that evidence must be found either to prove their truth or prove their falsehood.

"It is my intention, therefore, to wait with patience until I hear again from you, believing that when you receive the public demonstrations in my favour, which I shall transmit to you, and the report of the Executive Council, you will at once restore me to the favour of Her Majesty's Government, and that I shall receive from you an appointment under the Crown in another colony, where my services may be useful, and to which I can proceed direct, without encountering the long and harassing voyage to England."

The Chief Justice of the colony, the Colonial Secretary, the Colonial Treasurer, the Colonial Auditor, the Attorney-General, the Solicitor-General, the Crown Solicitor, the Surveyor-General, the Master of the Supreme Court, the Chief Police Magistrate, and the Collector of Customs promptly and spontaneously signed a declaration describing the accusation against Sir Eardley Wilmot as a "cruel slander," and an allegation that was "totally and most notoriously false." Ever since Sir Eardley assumed the Government down to that moment, "we and our families, the families of the other Government officers, and of the principal inhabitants of the colony, have had the honour (for so we account it) of being frequent visitors at Government House." This declaration was supplemented by a report signed by Colonel Cumberland, the officer commanding the Imperial troops at the time in Van Diemen's Land, on behalf of the Executive Council, certifying in the most explicit terms that as far as their observations had gone during the private and official intercourse which they had personally had with him since his arrival in the colony, nothing whatever had transpired that would justify such an allegation against the private life of Sir Eardley Wilmot. Furthermore, a repudiation in the following terms was signed by all the leading citizens of the metropolis and its vicinity, and addressed to the superseded Governor:—

"We, the undersigned inhabitants of Van Diemen's Land, having heard that your recall has been influenced by reports injurious to your moral character, deem it to be a duty we owe to truth and justice to express our unqualified contradiction of those reports, and we feel the more imperatively called upon to do so, from the fact of many of us having differed in opinion upon various measures of your Government. Upon the occasion of your retirement into private life, we beg to assure you that you carry with you our best wishes for your future welfare."

These proofs of his innocence of the offence alleged against him in Mr Gladstone's "secret," letter, were transmitted by Sir Eardley on October 30, 1846, to Earl Grey, who had in the meantime become the Minister for Colonial Affairs, and were forwarded by His Lordship to Mr Gladstone. In the accompanying letter, Sir Eardley wrote:—

"The victim of the most extraordinary conspiracy that ever succeeded in defaming the character of a public servant, and subjected to the condemnation of a Minister of the Crown, founded on anonymous information and unauthenticated representations, I appeal confidently to your Lordship for that justice which the meanest criminal has a right to at the hands of his country. I truly say that the whole of this colony demands it as well as myself, and trusting that Her Majesty's Government will voluntarily and immediately redeem the pledge of reinstating me in office under the Crown in some other colony without that delay which my situation here would make most inconvenient, I wait here with patience and in privacy for that satisfaction which Mr Gladstone himself admitted was my due when the representations against my character were satisfactorily explained."

Mr Gladstone's last letter to Sir Eardley Wilmot is a remarkable specimen of the right honourable gentleman's supreme skill in retiring from an untenable and impossible position in the midst of a dusty cloud of verbiage of his own creation. Writing from Hagley, Stourbridge, on March 9, 1847, Mr Gladstone said :—

"I have received from Lord Grey a copy of your letter of October 5, addressed to me as Secretary of State, in which you adjure me to specify immediately the dates, places, persons, and circumstances to which the rumours against your private life, forming the occasion of my letter marked 'Secret,' and dated April 30, 1846, apply. The persons who made known to me the existence of such rumours did not profess to support their credit by any statements of particulars of the kind to which you refer, but to found them upon general notoriety. It is not, therefore, in my power to convey to you what I have not received. Those, however, who appeal to notoriety afford, by that appeal, the means of putting their allegations to the test. In your letter of October 30 to Earl Grey, of which his Lordship has likewise been so good as to send me a copy, you transmit a resolution expressing, in terms necessarily vague, but sufficient for their purpose, the most unqualified contradiction of those reports injurious to your moral character, which had been the subject of my communication to you. The framers of the document evidently understood their general nature, and you acquaint Lord Grey that it is signed by all the leading and influential inhabitants of the capital of the colony and its neighbourhood with a few exceptions, which exceptions may be explained on political grounds, and including members of council, magistrates, merchants, and clergy of all denominations; and, further, that the resolution would be transmitted by the next ship for England.

"I lament, so far as the case before me is concerned, that I am no longer in a condition to try the issue, which, in the execution of a public duty, I was the instrument of raising. It will not rest with me, as you are aware, to say whether the resolution described by you, when it appears, will be sufficient to neutralise charges purporting to convey matter of public notoriety. I must say, however, that had I continued to hold the Seals of the Colonial Office, I should have thought a public attestation of this kind, if so signed as to correspond with your description, an appropriate and sufficient answer to accusations which, as they did not specify particulars, could not be open to the ordinary methods of confutation. From such accusations you would be entitled under such circumstances to full acquittal; and it is scarcely necessary for me to say with how much avidity I should have been prepared to recognise a just occasion of withdrawing the reference I had made—a reference which caused me the deepest pain, and which nothing but the most imperative considerations would have extracted from me. The effect which a confutation by public and general testimony of the accusations against you would have had upon my estimate of your claim to a continuance of public employment is, I think, sufficiently described in my secret letter.

"I observe it is stated in the resolution that the parties signing it had heard that your recall had been influenced by reports bearing upon your private character. It is right that I should entirely disavow having been moved by any such considerations in the advice which I thought it my duty to give. Your recall arose exclusively out of the causes detailed in my public despatch. If I discharged a repulsive duty in referring to matters of private life and obligation when I addressed you in April last as Secretary of State, it does far more of violence to my feelings to recur to the subject now, when I also am in a station altogether private, and yet find myself addressing, on matters of the utmost delicacy and entirely beyond my cognizance, one whose years and station I am bound unfeignedly to respect, and over whom in no particular can I claim any superiority. Permit me to express the hope that the office I have had to discharge, repugnant alike to your feelings and my own, has not been rendered additionally and needlessly offensive to you by any wanton obtrusiveness or inconsiderate language on my part."

Sir Eardley Wilmot was not destined to enjoy the poor satisfaction of reading this inferential apology and implied exculpation from the ex-Minister who had wrought his downfall on no stronger or more trustworthy testimony than the malignant gossip of a handful of personal and political enemies. The superseded and cruelly-wronged Governor was in his grave, done to death by slanderous tongues, when Mr Gladstone's qualified acquittal reached Hobart. His funeral in that city was made the occasion of a great and striking demonstration of public sympathy, all classes and creeds joining in tributes of respect to his memory, and in expressions of reprobation at the disgraceful means that were successfully employed to encompass his ruin. Several of the public journals expressed their sentiments in what was, under the circumstances, pardonably strong and heated language. The *Colonial Times*, for example, declared that Sir Eardley Wilmot had been murdered, that his assassins had obtained the consummation of their hopes, that the annals of English history did not record so accursed a transaction, that it would have been more manly and humane on the part of Mr Gladstone to have shot the late Governor, and that the latter had fallen a victim to the dagger of the slanderous assassin. It was subsequently proved conclusively that there was not the slightest foundation for the anonymous charges levelled against the personal character and private life of Sir Eardley Wilmot—irresponsible and unsupported charges on which Mr Gladstone so hastily, inconsiderately, and incomprehensibly acted. These charges were eventually traced to a couple of discontented officials, an archdeacon of the Church of England, and one of the heads of the Convict Department. That being so, it is somewhat difficult to understand Mr Gladstone's statement, in his secret letter to Sir Eardley, that the rumours in question had reached him from "a variety of quarters." It is significant that one of the first actions of Sir Eardley Wilmot's successor was the dismissal of the archdeacon in question from the post of Superintendent of Convict Chaplains.

On his deathbed, Sir Eardley asserted that he had received no directions or instructions from Mr Gladstone on the matters mentioned in the despatch of his recall.

"If," he said, "such instructions had been ordered by the House of Commons to be printed and produced, the answer would have been—*nil*. Thus the Minister would have been condemned. To save himself, therefore, I am treated like Admiral Byng. In addition to this, the anonymous calumnies against my private character were allowed to have weight. I think that nothing but Mr Gladstone giving ear to those atrocious falsehoods could have induced the doing to me what never was done to any Governor before.

"I have sent the necessary papers to Lord Grey, Lord Lansdowne, Lord John Russell, and the Duke of Wellington. I have petitioned the Queen, and, if necessary, I shall go to the Imperial Parliament. I do not think they will allow an old member of their body, whom they know and respect, to suffer the grievous wrong inflicted upon him by Mr Gladstone."

The *Hobart Town Courier*, one of the leading journals of the colony, and a political opponent of Sir Eardley's, declared that if Mr Gladstone's communications had been published before the late Governor's death, they would have rescued the name of Sir Eardley from much reproach, and converted political enemies into personal friends.

"Few would be found," said the *Courier*, "to commend the mockery of justice that consigned him to dismissal and disgrace on rumours so confessedly vague, and on charges which the Minister failed to substantiate. Mr Gladstone could not 'convey what he had not received.'"

On March 26, 1847, Lord Stanley brought the case of Sir Eardley Wilmot under the notice of the House of Lords, and mentioned that, during the time he held office as Colonial Secretary in 1845, reports had reached him affecting the private character of Sir Eardley, similar to those that had been sent to Mr Gladstone, but he could never get beyond the vaguest allegations, and whenever he attempted to touch upon particulars, the answer was that no particulars were required, inasmuch as the fact was notorious all over Van Diemen's Land. But when these imputations were published in a London journal, and in that shape returned to the colony, they were immediately met by the spontaneous declaration of all the principal persons in Van Diemen's Land that what was stated in England to be a notorious fact was in Van Diemen's Land a notorious falsehood.

"I express no opinion," said Lord Stanley, "as to the truth or the falsehood of those charges; but when an officer of the Crown at a great distance is assailed by charges in which no facts can be proved, when he remains on the spot to meet every inquiry, and submits to the most rigid scrutiny among the society where it was stated his conduct was a matter of universal notoriety, and when from that society the allegations made receive a positive and peremptory denial, and when he has been told that these rumours, unless met, would for ever prevent him from being employed by the Crown, I think it due to that officer that these statements should be put before the public, accompanied by the refutation of the charges most unfavourable to his character."

The matter was mentioned in the House of Commons on June 7 by Mr Spencer, who read letters from Dr Nixon, the local Anglican bishop, Dr Willson, the Catholic Prelate of the Colony, and the Colonial Treasurer, all testifying to the propriety of Sir Eardley Wilmot's conduct, and to the fact that the calumnious rumours were not credited by any respectable persons in the colony. Lord Brooke and Mr Dugdale, Sir Eardley's former colleagues in the representation of Warwickshire, bore testimony to his character as Member of Parliament and Chairman of Quarter-Sessions. Sir Robert Peel declared his belief that the charges were utterly unfounded, but pointed out that his right hon. friend, Mr Gladstone, was placed in a peculiar and painful position, three persons of unexceptionable character having informed him that the private life of Sir Eardley was, in their opinion, incompatible with the proper discharge of his duty as a public officer. One of the informants was at that moment in England, and had been asked to sanction the use of his name, but had declined to do so. Lord John Russell affirmed that all the charges alleged against Sir Eardley's private life had been swept to the winds. A protracted discussion ensued, in the course of which Sir James Graham pointed out that Mr Gladstone's "secret" letter to Sir Eardley was strictly private, and meant only in kindness for the recipient's information. Mr Hawes, the Under-Secretary for the Colonies, added that the only record of Mr Gladstone's "secret" letter known to the Colonial Office was the despatch by Sir Eardley Wilmot himself, in which it was incorporated. Mr Roebuck characteristically improved the occasion with a dissertation on irresponsible colonial administration. Here was a Governor in a distant colony dismissed on calumnious, false, and unsupported charges, whispered against him in England. That was only one illustration. Sir Eardley was not a solitary victim. Hundreds were pining away, the victims of colonial misrule.

On the following Tuesday, Mr Horsman and Mr Beckham Escott pressed for the names of the informants. Mr Hawes adhered to the statement that in the Colonial Office there was no official record of the names, and he was therefore unable to supply the desired information. Sir James Graham, however, stated that the informants were three in number. One had been in the service of the Crown, but was so no longer, and had refused to allow the use of his name. Mr Gladstone's letter, however, rested on the information of two other gentlemen, one occupying a high station in the colony, and the other a public servant. Their names had been communicated to the present Sir Eardley Wilmot, who would probably himself require an explanation. Sir James added that he did not feel warranted in publicly mentioning their names, because it would leave the persons in question exposed for twelve months to the obloquy under which they would lie, on the presumption that they had given false information.

Mr Gladstone was not in a position to take part in these debates and defend his conduct in connection with the recall of Sir Eardley Wilmot, as he had temporarily ceased to be a Member of the House of Commons. It was the interval between the severance of his parliamentary relations with the borough of Newark and his return for the University of Oxford. But although out of Parliament for the moment, Mr Gladstone was not the man to remain silent under the storm of censure and abuse with which he was assailed, both in the British and Colonial Press, when the tragic death of Sir Eardley Wilmot, and the circumstances that had led up to it, became known. A pamphlet of sixteen pages was promptly published in London, under the title of "The Case of Sir Eardley Wilmot, Considered in a Letter to a Friend, by Stafford H. Northcote, Esq." This young gentleman of twenty-eight, the nominal writer of the pamphlet, was at the time Mr Gladstone's private secretary. As Sir Stafford Northcote, subsequently Earl of Iddesleigh, he became in after years a distinguished statesman himself, and the leader of the Conservative party in the House of Commons.* The justification for the publication of the pamphlet is thus alleged in the prefatory note :—

"It is with great regret that I find myself compelled, in the following pages, to bring before the public the faults of the late Sir Eardley Wilmot as a Colonial Governor. This necessity has been imposed upon me by those, who, not content with clearing his character, have thought fit, most gratuitously, and, as I think, most foolishly, to blacken that of Mr Gladstone, by asserting that the grounds of Sir Eardley's recall were not those publicly assigned and justified by Mr Gladstone, but others, which he not only never assigned, but always denied to have influenced him."

The pamphlet opens with an expression of sorrow that an impression unfavourable to Mr Gladstone should still prevail in the minds of some persons who were apparently but imperfectly acquainted with the facts. The reader is then assured that Mr Gladstone did not recall Sir Eardley Wilmot on account of the rumours affecting his private character, but on account of his having given general dissatisfaction by his mode of transacting public business, and more particularly on account of his having shown himself utterly incompetent to administer a very important and very difficult system of convict discipline. Replying to the allegation that Mr Gladstone thought he was acting on one ground, when in reality he was proceeding on the other, the writer enters

---

* Mr Andrew Lang was apparently unaware of the existence of this pamphlet. It is not mentioned in his "Life, Letters, and Diaries of Sir Stafford Northcote."

into an interesting little essay on Mr Gladstone's mental characteristics :—

"In support of this hypothesis, people talk in a vague way about the peculiar constitution of Mr Gladstone's mind, a rather favourite topic with those who desire to accuse him of something which they dare not openly allege against one who is so singularly and conspicuously placed beyond the reach of slander, by the known purity and simplicity of his life. It is worth while, in the present instance, to inquire what that peculiarity in Mr Gladstone's mind is, which is supposed to have led him to mix up two motives together, and to act upon them as if they were one, and without consciousness that they are more than one. Mr Gladstone is usually, I believe, charged with two faults — hair-splitting and mystification. His mind is pre-eminently logical; in the eyes of many it is logical to a fault. This leads him to make subtle distinctions, and because he goes on distinguishing where others are unable or will not take the trouble to follow, he is accused of hair-splitting. Most people are content with a rough division; two or three courses appear to them to exhaust all the modes of action possible; Mr Gladstone is more minute in his inquiries, and asks whether these courses are not themselves capable of subdivision. Where legitimate distinction ends and hair-splitting begins, and whether he oversteps the boundary between them, I do not now inquire, but I believe the peculiarity which I have noticed is one of the characteristics of his mind. But, if this be the case, he is the very last person in the world to jumble up two or three premisses together, and draw a conclusion from the lump without discovering what he is about—the very last person who will fall into the error of supposing that two bad reasons make one good one—the very last person to say, 'Sir Eardley is a bad Governor, but not bad enough to be recalled for that; and he is said to be a bad man, but there is not evidence to recall him upon for that; still, upon the whole, there is a case against him, so let him be recalled.'"

Passing on to the second fault alleged against Mr Gladstone —the difficulty of discerning his real and actual meaning through the dense verbal clouds of his own creation—his private secretary observes :—

"Mr Gladstone's alleged tendency to hair-splitting will not, as we have already seen, bear out the theory that he deceived himself; will, then, that theory stand upon his supposed propensity to mystification? I think not. I am not now about to do battle for Mr Gladstone's style; whether that is elegant or inelegant, grammatical or ungrammatical, has as little to do with the present question as the legibility or illegibility of his handwriting. The real question is whether the despatch to Sir Eardley Wilmot states the grounds upon which he was recalled with sufficient clearness to enable a plain man to understand them, and whether he would understand them to be such as they are now represented to have been. Much as the language of the despatch has been found fault with, I will venture to risk the issue on the passage containing that obnoxious phrase which has become almost a bye-word."

The passage thus emphasised by Sir Stafford Northcote has already been quoted. The obnoxious phrase was the one in which Mr Gladstone had censured Sir Eardley Wilmot for not having made it his duty to inquire "into the inner world of the mental, moral, and spiritual state" of the convicts under his jurisdiction. A number of the leading organs of English opinion had subjected this singular expression to severe criticism, and had placed upon it the interpretation that Mr Gladstone had complained because Sir Eardley "would not write cant."

An ingenious but hardly convincing or successful attempt is then made to show that Mr Gladstone's "secret" despatch to Sir Eardley was not what its language denoted—an abrupt dismissal from the public service in consequence of vague, unspecified, unexamined, and unsubstantiated charges reflecting on his personal character—but something in the nature of a private or friendly communication from one gentleman to another :—

"Next, as to the blasting of Sir Eardley's character, I freely grant, nay, I am forward to assert that, since Mr Gladstone was not in possession of information upon which to found a distinct charge, he would have been wholly unjustifiable had he taken any step upon the information he actually had, which could in the slightest degree prejudice Sir Eardley's reputation in the eyes of the public. But he took no such step; absolutely none. The public had no more reason to think badly of Sir Eardley's moral character after the 30th April 1846, than they had before; and, if Sir Eardley himself had not brought the matter forward, they never, to the end of time, would have known, for aught Mr Gladstone had done, that his morality had been called in question. Neither did Mr Gladstone prejudice him within the walls of the Colonial Office. How can that be, I imagine I hear you say, when he wrote him a secret despatch on this very subject? I can only reply, if you choose to call every letter that a Secretary of State writes, a 'despatch,' I cannot find fault with you, but I must just remark that there is more mystification and more sophistry in the use that has been made of this one word in this case than Mr Gladstone was ever charged with in the whole course of his life. There are such things as despatches marked 'secret,' which, nevertheless, are recorded in the Colonial Office; and from the misuse of the word, it has been supposed that the document in question was one of these. It was no such thing. The so-called 'secret despatch' was neither more nor less than a private letter; as purely a private letter as a note of invitation to dinner is a private letter. It was never recorded in the Colonial Office; existing clerks and succeeding secretaries knew no more of it than they knew of Mr Gladstone's letters to his father or his brothers; it was a private communication between man and man, in which the one who had heard rumours prejudicial to the reputation of the other, informed him of the existence of those rumours, of their vague and indefinite character, and of the injuriousness of their effects. The letter told Sir Eardley exactly how matters stood, and left him at liberty to act as he might think advisable. He might, had he so pleased, have put it behind the fire, and nobody would have been the wiser; but he had the option of using the information it contained for the purpose of clearing his character, and of that option he availed himself. Undoubtedly, Mr Gladstone would have shown more of the wisdom of this world had he availed himself of the advantages of his position to stop Sir Eardley's promotion without assigning a reason. True, his conscience might have reproached him for dealing cruelly with a helpless and possibly a calumniated man; but I suppose his present assailants would have been perfectly satisfied with such a course."

At page 14 of the pamphlet there is a significant statement, which amounts to a virtual admission, that Mr Gladstone was deceived by his informants, or at least that he attached an exaggerated importance and an undue weight to the estimate of Sir Eardley Wilmot's character, formed in that nebulous school for scandal called "general notoriety." By the pen of his private secretary, Mr Gladstone thus reveals the flimsy foundation on which the charges against Sir Eardley Wilmot rested, and passes a vote of censure upon himself for having lent a willing ear to the intangible and irresponsible gossip originated by the Lady Sneerwells, the Mrs Candours, and the Sir Benjamin Backbites of a remote and clique-infested colony :—

"Persons in this country, who now appear among the defenders of the late Governor, knew that his character was impugned, and were silent. Persons of the highest station in the colony, who also come forward, now that the tide of opinion sets in Sir Eardley's favour, to declare that they can, of their own knowledge, pronounce those charges to have been false, knew that they were made, and gave confirmation to them by their manner of speaking and writing of him."

After that amazing admission, nothing more remains to be said. It cuts the ground completely from under Mr Gladstone's feet, and shows how dangerous and delusive a thing it is to accept "general notoriety" as trustworthy evidence. How Mr Gladstone could have so summarily and arbitrarily dismissed a Colonial Governor twenty years his senior, an irreproachable and respected English gentleman, and an erstwhile colleague of his own for years in the House of Commons, on charges that were not supported by a solitary shred of legal evidence, and had no avowed basis beyond a "general notoriety" that was dissipated into congenial space the moment it was approached, to use a familiar phrase of his own, passes the wit of man.

Mr James Fenton, in the ninth chapter of his "History of Tasmania," points out that Sir Eardley Wilmot came to the colony at a period of exceptional difficulty. On the one hand, the free population, impatient for the management of their own affairs, were stirred by violent political agitation; while, on the other hand, the control and employment of a daily increasing multitude of criminals, despatched from the old country, were constantly becoming more difficult in consequence of the rapid and abrupt changes of system produced by the varying whims and caprices of the Colonial Office. Under these circumstances, no Governor could administer the duties of his post with satisfaction either to the colonial public or to himself, and still less so to the authorities of Downing Street, who attributed the evils of the penal system to defective management in the colony, rather than to the imperfections of the system itself.

Owing to the breaking-up of the penal settlement at Norfolk Island, and the cessation of transportation to New South Wales, Van Diemen's Land became at this time the great centre of convictism. The probation system—perhaps the worst plan of convict discipline ever devised—was in active operation all over the island. Gangs of those probationers were stationed in every town and village, filling the free settlers with dismay and alarm. To Lord Stanley, says Mr Fenton, belongs the odium of initiating this abominable system of congregating together masses of criminals, whose vices flourished in the congenial atmosphere which surrounded them. The Governor, in his despatches to Lord Stanley, depicted its social effects. He pointed out that the country was inundated with unemployed prisoners, who must either starve or steal; that a yearly-increasing pauper population would swell the catalogue of crime and increase the public expense in every form; that the number out of employment was fearfully great, and that land—cleared, fenced, and in cultivation, with houses and buildings—might be bought at the upset price of waste land, in consequence of the lamentable condition of the colony and the general feeling of insecurity. Never was a British colony in such a deplorable position. The maintenance of police and prisons had plunged the country into a debt of £100,000, which was rapidly increasing, on account of the almost entire cessation of land sales, hitherto the chief source of revenue. In 1841 the upset price of Crown lands was 12s. per acre, and 79,140 acres were sold; in 1847 the price was raised to £1, and only 3701 acres were sold.

With a decreasing revenue and an increasing debt, it would have taxed the powers of a more gifted statesman than Sir Eardley Wilmot to have satisfactorily managed the complicated affairs of Van Diemen's Land. No course was open to him but further taxation, and this brought him into violent collision with the independent members of his Legislative Council, who strenuously objected to the colony being saddled with the expense of maintaining this huge and odious convict system—an expense that in ordinary fairness and justice ought to have been borne by the Imperial Exchequer. The Governor's position, adds Mr Fenton, was a most unenviable one. He was tied hand and foot by Downing Street. He was expected to rule the colony with wisdom, while he was perplexed and hampered on all sides. The revenue was altogether inadequate to the needs of efficient government, and all channels of increase seemed to be closed. In his endeavours to obey Imperial orders, Sir Eardley came into unpleasant conflict with the colonists. If some of his proceedings were hasty and ill-judged, the situation he was called upon to face demands a lenient interpretation of acts which were forced upon him in a dilemma almost unparalleled in the history of colonisation. Dealing with the circumstances of Sir Eardley Wilmot's sudden recall by Mr Gladstone, Mr Fenton writes :—

"In Mr Gladstone's long political career, he never committed an act of greater injustice than in this instance. He accompanied the official announcement of recall with a private letter, stating that Sir Eardley was not removed on account of any errors committed in his official capacity, but that rumours reflecting upon his moral character had reached the Colonial Office, the nature of which would shut out His Excellency from further employment. A more cruel assault upon the character of a gentleman holding the dignified office of representative of Royalty can hardly be conceived. He was condemned on the baseless information of vague rumour, and denied the liberty of defence. The colonists were astounded when the matter became known. Those who differed from the Governor on public questions, now united with his friends to support him under such a cruel wrong. They regarded him as a deeply-injured man, whose kind-hearted affability and freedom of address were magnified into an impurity of motive by some thinker of evil. Even the Bishop of Tasmania, whose official intercourse with the Governor was not cordial, generously bore testimony in His Excellency's favour. The Chief-Justice and 250 leading members of the community, in an address to His Excellency, repelled the accusation; all whose local observation made them the best judges of personal character, exonerated the Governor, and extended to him their deepest sympathy. But it is easier to inflict a wound than to heal it; the stab was too deep to be cured. Sir Eardley Wilmot retired into private life, intending to remain for a time in the colony, but he died on the third day of February 1847, eight days after the arrival of his successor, Sir William Denison. The inhabitants were shocked at the news. The circumstances connected with his retirement had aroused the sympathies of all, and the indignation of many; and those feelings were intensified when the melancholy fact was announced that he had fallen a victim to the wound so rashly inflicted by Mr Gladstone. Although the late Governor was well stricken in years, it was not the waste of physical power, nor the cares and anxieties of an exceedingly unthankful position in the public service, that had snapped the thread of life: it was the unwarrantable charge and unjust dismissal that had broken his heart."

The Rev. John West, an earlier and far more voluminous historian of Tasmania than Mr Fenton, described the circumstances of Sir Eardley Wilmot's recall in these terms:—

"Mr Gladstone, who had received the seals of office, conveyed to Wilmot the notice of his removal. The despatch is a singular example of its author's mental habits. While he complained that the Governor's statements were obscure, he gave his own views in odd and scarcely intelligible terms. Thus, the Governor had adverted to the moral condition of the convicts 'in a manner too little penetrating,' and he had not made it a point of his duty 'to examine the inner world of their mental, moral, and spiritual state.' These whimsical terms of reprobation excited universal astonishment. The English Press, with some truth and bitterness, described such demands as an encouragement of hypocrisy and religious pretence. No wise or good man will discredit religious teaching, but all such will look with suspicion, and even disgust, on the statistics of prison piety—generally false and designing in proportion as it is loud and ostentatious."

Mr West adds that the

"Preposterous imputations upon Sir Eardley Wilmot's private character melted away the moment they were touched. Mr Gladstone was condemned for entertaining them. He seems more worthy of censure for his indefinite method of stating their nature and the authority on which they rested. The moral character of a Governor is of moment to a colony, and a just consideration in his appointment, but when assailed, it should certainly have all the protection of a full and open inquiry."

Sir John Franklin, the illustrious and ill-fated Arctic navigator, who was the immediate predecessor of Sir Eardley Wilmot in the Governorship of Van Diemen's Land, had his career in the colony brought to a similarly abrupt and unaccountable termination by what his latest biographer, Mr H. D. Traill, very properly characterises as "a despatch of uncompromising, not to say brutal, severity" from Lord Stanley, the Colonial Secretary of the day. Sir John Franklin had only done what every self-respecting Governor would have done under similar circumstances—suspended from office an insolent and openly mutinous subordinate—but for this necessary action he was not only cruelly censured by Lord Stanley, but also subjected to a personal indignity of the most embarrassing and humiliating character. His appointed successor in the Governorship actually arrived four days before he himself received official notice of his recall. Sir Eardley Wilmot had to remain outside Government House for a fortnight, while Sir John Franklin was busily engaged in packing up. The mere mention of these facts is sufficient to show how far we have advanced, and how marvellously the methods, manners, and customs of Downing Street have changed for the better during the last half century. Writing of the strange and sad experiences of Sir Eardley Wilmot and Sir John Franklin as Colonial Governors, seems at first sight like recalling the despotic ideas and high-handed ways of five centuries ago—not what happened only fifty years ago in the reign of Queen Victoria. No Colonial Secretary would now dream of treating a Colonial Governor as Mr Gladstone treated Sir Eardley Wilmot, or as Lord Stanley behaved towards Sir John Franklin. In Parliamentary, no less than in administrative affairs, the vastly improved sense of justice and propriety is equally manifest. It is certain that no House of Commons would now tolerate the bitter and venomous diatribes with which Mr Disraeli assailed Sir Robert Peel in the forties, neither would any Parliament of a leading British colony sanction the vitriolic speeches and barbed lampoons with which Robert Lowe, at the other end of the earth, was simultaneously hounding his earliest Australian friend, host, and patron—Governor Sir George Gipps—into his grave.

One further singular circumstance in the relations between Mr Gladstone and Sir Eardley Wilmot may be briefly referred to. Amongst the prisoners in Van Diemen's Land at this time were three of the leaders of the Chartist agitation—John Frost, Zephaniah Williams, and William Jones. At the head of 20,000 men, they had marched into Newport, and come into collision with the military. A number of lives were lost during the encounter, and the leaders were placed on their trial. Frost, Williams, and Jones were found guilty of high treason in having levied war against the Queen, and sentenced to be hanged, drawn, and quartered at a special assize held in Monmouth. On appeal, a technical point in their favour was argued so successfully by their counsel (afterwards Barons Pollock and Fitzroy Kelly), that the fifteen judges disagreed, and the death penalty was thereupon commuted to transportation for life. As prisoners in Van Diemen's Land, the conduct of the three Chartist leaders was exemplary in every respect, and Zephaniah Williams, on one occasion, distinguished himself by rushing into a burning lunatic asylum and rescuing a number of the inmates at the peril of his own life. This brave action was officially brought to the notice of Mr Gladstone by Sir Eardley Wilmot, who recommended a remission or mitigation of sentence by way of recognition and reward. But Mr Gladstone declined to endorse this reasonable recommendation. He was at that time still a Conservative, and possibly he did not foresee that, in the years to come, he would be eloquently advocating and energetically passing into law, those identical Radical and Reforming principles for the promotion and propagation of which Frost, Williams, Jones, and their fellow Chartists struggled, laboured, agitated, and endured long years of bitter exile and imprisonment.

CHAPTER XIV

MAJOR DE WINTON: OLDEST LIVING GLADSTONIAN

FORTUNATELY the officer who was appointed to the command of the first military detachment sent to the new settlement formed at Port Curtis by Colonel Barney, and to whose duty it fell to hoist the British flag on the spot where the town of Gladstone now stands, still survives in our midst. He was then Lieutenant de Winton of the 99th; he is now Major de Winton, a genial and gracious veteran, a familiar and respected figure in London military and philanthropic circles, a former editor of the *United Service Magazine*, and for many years a member of the governing body of the Junior United Service Club. His very interesting reminiscences of service in various parts of the world are now in course of publication in the regimental periodical, *The Nines*.

Major de Winton was gazetted as Ensign of the 99th in July 1841.

"A finer Line Regiment," he writes, "never wore Her Majesty's uniform than the 99th when they marched into Chatham in 1841. These were the pre-railway days, when the words 'route' and 'march' had more literal significance than now. At the time of the arrival of the 99th, the Chatham Barracks were exceptionally crowded, and for some time the officers' mess was at 'The Sun,' the well-known coaching-house, kept by Winch. Good old 'Sun'! Who of those quartered in Chatham in the forties does not remember the supper laid out for the passengers by the Dover mail; the egg-flip, a speciality of the house; the parting glass of that alluring compound exchanged with the traveller, seen often for the first time and for the last, while the expostulating guard, hardly appeased by the proferred glass, declares that he will never be able to make up the time in the next stage. As if it were yesterday, I remember the mid-day coach drawing up at 'The Sun,' and depositing me with kit and traps. A captain of the corps gave me a friendly greeting, and proferred his services to accompany me to the barracks to report myself to the Colonel. How lasting are first impressions! That kindly greeting, the introductions to those who became to me brother officers indeed, will never be effaced from my memory."

The Chatham of Major de Winton's early days, viewed from the standpoints of sobriety and morality, was a very different place to the well-ordered Chatham of to-day.

"Imagine a number of young fellows, just released from the strict discipline of school, suddenly severed from the controlling influences of family associations, and in many instances supplied with money with injudicious liberality, launched amidst the temptations and the demoralising associations of a garrison town, and we can readily realise the result—dissipation, debauchery, and utter ruin of not a few. The scenes I have witnessed would, if described in detail, be derided by the novelist. I have known twelve dozen of wine sent after mess to a subaltern's room, and have seen the morning's sun revealing prostrate forms in hopeless intoxication, amidst a wreck of furniture and broken bottles. There were low public-houses, which a lax police suffered to be open until all hours, or, what was worse, though nominally closed during the prohibited hours, open to all possessed of the watchword and the golden key, where orgies indescribable were enacted. Large indeed must have been the number of young men, the pride of their parents, with bright prospects before them, who succumbed to the horrible fascinations which allured those who desired—ill-omened expression—to see life."

Sheerness was the next place in which Major de Winton was quartered, and there, too, the apostle of temperance and the social reformer might have found plenty of material to work upon.

"In those days, the excellent institutions called Sailors' Homes were unknown, and the sailor landing with a pocket full of money fell an easy, though it must be admitted, a not unwilling prey to the sirens of the sea-ports. Among the too many licensed houses of entertainment, was one known as the 'Never,' from a current belief that it had never been closed, day or night, since it was first opened, at a period in the remote past."

In April, 1843, Major de Winton was ordered to take up duty as an officer of the military guard on the convict-ship *Constant*, bound for Van Diemen's Land, or Tasmania, as it is now called. The Surgeon-Superintendent of the vessel, Mr J. S. Hampton, became in after years Governor of Western Australia. Describing the voyage, the Major observes :—

"Contrary winds drove us out of our course, and we sighted the island of Fernando de Noronha, the Brazilian convict settlement, which has been described as the convicts' Eden. Whether it was that the fame of this settlement had reached the ears of our convicts, and a desire had seized them to put it to practical test, I know not; but at this time we discovered a plot to take the ship, the plan of which, to put it mildly, did not include the landing of the officers and guard on the terrestrial paradise then in view. The ringleaders of the plot were flogged, isolated, and put in heavy irons; and, needless to say, our vigilance was thenceforth redoubled. I have often thought that, with systematic combination, the taking of a ship by convicts might in those days have been achieved without very much difficulty. The old flint muskets were to the last degree unreliable, and as for the cutlasses with which the sentries were armed, they were little better than pieces of hoop-iron."

After a passage of 110 days, the *Constant* arrived at Hobart, the Tasmanian metropolis, and landed her prisoners. The Governor of the colony at the time was the renowned Sir John Franklin.

"He was about leaving for England, having already projected the Arctic voyage in which he and his intrepid companions perished, martyrs to scientific research, in the regions of eternal ice."

From Hobart Major de Winton proceeded to Sydney, and joined the Australian headquarters of his regiment.

"Although transportation to New South Wales had ceased, there were a considerable number of convicts still serving their time on the public works, and our regiment was to a large extent scattered in detachments in various localities, either as guards over stockades or as contingent aids to the civil power. Many of the officers held quasi-civil appointments, receiving for these extra pay from the Colonial Government. In the early days of the colonies administrative offices fell to military officers, and rightly so, as their training caused them to exact discipline amongst those over whom they were set, and their magisterial decisions were, from habit, framed on the lines of military courts, wherein equity and law are harmoniously blended. Colonial history bears testimony to the equitable rule of military Governors, and in penal settlements the rule of the military officer, strict as it often was, was preferred to that of the civilian by the prisoners themselves, as they realised that the former had no subtle aims to serve or sordid ends to gain."

The soldier's life at an outlying station in the early days of Australian colonisation is thus depicted by Major de Winton:—

"Military duties were nominal, of recreation there was little. There would be two or three shanties, called hotels, where colonial beer, a vile and adulterated compound, and colonial rum, a fiery liquor yclept 'Old Stringy,' were vended; whither the draymen and stockmen resorted, and where the bullock-drivers put up on their way down to the coast with the wool clip of the season, and on their way back to the station with stores. On their way down they had their wages sometimes for twelve months in the form of an order by the squatter on his Sydney agent, and it was no uncommon thing for the bullock-driver to hand this order to the landlord with the request to 'sweat this down five pounds.' Then the host would collect all the available loafers, the bullock-driver would stand treat, take a glass or two with every new-comer, and soon succumb to the effects of the villainous liquor. After forty-eight hours of mingled intoxication and slumber, the landlord would tell him that he had been there a week, and had gone beyond his margin of cash. The driver would then yoke up his bullocks once more, and, after a parting glass all round, resume his journey to the coast. These so-called 'hotels' were the centre of attraction in every small settlement, and as wages were high, stockmen and other visitors were always ready to stand treat, notably to the soldier, who was popular and regarded as *bon camarade.*"

Major de Winton's colonial experience has furnished him with a budget of amusing anecdotes. Here is a humorous incident of the Maori wars in New Zealand :—

"From time to time conferences were held with so-called friendly chiefs, though the direction in which their friendship tended was not always ascertainable. At one of those conferences, Colonel ―――― presiding, a friendly chief, interrogated through the medium of the interpreter by the Colonel on a point which he deemed of much moment, uttered some words which seemed to convey derision or disapprobation, and rising, took up his spear, threw his rug around him, and with haughty mien left the conference. Turning to the interpreter, the Colonel asked him what the chief had said.

"'Oh, nothing,' replied the interpreter; 'he seemed put out and was talking nonsense.'

"*The Colonel:* 'I insist on knowing what he said. It is for me to judge of the relevance to the subject, and as this chief has been represented to me as one whose opinions have great weight in the councils of the friendly tribes, I attach much importance to his views.'

"*The Interpreter:* 'I assure you, sir, there was nothing in what he said; in fact, he spoke so indistinctly that I hardly caught his words.'

"*The Colonel:* 'Mr ――――, as a sworn interpreter attached to Her Majesty's forces, you are amenable to the Articles of War, and I must warn you that any dereliction from your duty may be attended with very serious consequences to yourself. The chief spoke distinctly, and I insist upon his words being faithfully interpreted. Mr ―――― (to one of the officers), take down the interpreter's exact words, in order that they may be faithfully recorded on the minutes of this meeting.'

"*The Interpreter:* 'Very well, sir, if you will have it, the chief says you are an old ass.'"

Attempts to impose the habits and customs of civilisation upon aboriginal races are not unfrequently disastrous. They are also occasionally comical, as the following anecdote serves to show :—

"A settler about to be married, invited his mother and female relatives to visit the new house he had built. A number of blacks were employed about the place, and, as these were always primitively attired, or in other words, not clothed at all, he was much exercised on the subject in view of the early arrival of his guests. In his perplexity he could think of no covering but sheets of newspapers, and on the appointed day he clothed his dusky band in the sheets of the *Sydney Morning Herald,* one at the back and one in front with a strip of bark for a girdle. It unluckily happened to be a very windy day, and as the boat conveying the ladies approached, the blacks were seen engaged in frantic efforts to keep down their improvised literary petticoats. The scene was irresistibly ludicrous."

Major de Winton was at headquarters in Sydney when Robert Lowe reached the summit of his colonial fame in that city. On the day that he was returned for Sydney as the leader and orator of the popular anti-transportation party, the troops were confined to barracks and the barrack-gates closed. Standing on the coping-stone of the officers' quarters, the Major was an eye-witness of the surging and cheering crowd that unyoked the horses and drew their newly-elected member in triumph through the streets of the metropolis— the first and only occasion during his long political career in both hemispheres on which Robert Lowe was the object and central figure of such a popular demonstration. In after years, when he was being mobbed and hooted in Whitehall, that day on which he was the idol of the Sydney populace must have frequently flashed on his recollection.

Coming to the circumstances and incidents of his connection with Mr Gladstone's new colony on the shores of Port Curtis, Major de Winton remarks :—

"Consequent upon the cessation of transportation and loss of Government expenditure, there was for a long time a dearth of labour, and a general depression in New South Wales; but firm in their trust that the beautiful land of their adoption would, when freed from the stigma attaching to a penal colony, attract from the old country both capital and labour, the colonists bore with fortitude their trials and privations. Meantime, at home, the cessation of transportation to New South Wales—the whilom principal dumping ground for the criminals of the United Kingdom—was being felt, and the attention of the Imperial Government was turned to the selection of a spot whereon to establish a new penal settlement. Port Curtis was fixed upon. Lying several degrees north of the most northerly settlement of New South Wales, it was deemed that no exception could be taken to the establishment of a penal colony in a region so remote. In 1847, instructions to occupy a suitable site in the neighbourhood of Port Curtis, and to make arrangements for the reception of convicts, reached Sydney; and officers, civil and military, were appointed to form the *cadre* of government of the new colony. Colonel Barney, R.E., was appointed Superintendent. The military force consisted of a detachment of the 99th Regiment: Captain Day in command; Lieutenant de Winton, subaltern. Two ships, the *Lord Auckland* and the *Thomas Lowry*, were taken up for the conveyance of the party. The *Lord Auckland* took Colonel Barney, the civil staff, Captain Day, a portion of the military, some artizans and mechanics. The wives and families of several of the officers accompanied them, as it was then thought that the new colony would be the future home of those appointed to the chief offices. The *Lord Auckland* was the first to sail; the *Thomas Lowry*, with the remainder of the military and stores, leaving about a fortnight later. When lying in harbour, the *Bramble*, Lieutenant Youl, R.N., commander, arrived, and as she had been surveying on the North Australian coast, our captain went on board to gain information respecting the harbour of Port Curtis—at that time only roughly charted. I accompanied him, and I have a lively recollection of the visit. The *Bramble* swarmed with cockroaches, and with these we had literally to contend at the breakfast to which Youl had kindly invited us.

"The medical officer of the expedition having gone in the *Lord Auckland*, in view of eventualities I applied for a doctor for our party, and just before sailing, an assistant colonial surgeon came on board, having been hunted up at an evening party. He was in evening dress, with black hat; his sole *impedimenta*, a little black bag and a case of instruments. He was a charming fellow — an Irishman — and at once adapted himself to the situation, his first act being to *razee* his tall hat, divest it of its felt, and convert it into a head-covering more suitable for tropical wear. Curious is memory; of the incidents of the voyage—and some more important there must have been —this is the only one I can now recall.

"When we made Port Curtis, guided by the information obtained from Lieutenant Youl, we kept the south shore. We had seen the *Lord Auckland* lying at the north side of the harbour, and learnt later that she had grounded on a bank not then charted, and that her passengers had been put ashore on Facing Island, where they had encamped. Hardly had we let go the anchor, when a boat with two men put off from the shore, and the men informed us that they had been sent from Facing Island to sink for water on the mainland, but were in deadly fear of the natives, whom they had seen assembling in great numbers near where they were at work. I said I would send a sergeant and a few men for their protection. But on their representation of the very large number of the natives, and their hostile attitude, I thought it better to land in greater force. So hastily getting together some tents, a cask of water, some ship biscuits, and beef, I put off with twenty men, and took military possession of the spot, where is now situated the town named after Mr Gladstone. Night had fallen when we had got tents pitched, and, as the Americans say, 'fairly fixed up,' and having posted sentries, tired out, I lay down, the ground for a bed, a travelling valise for a pillow, and so to sleep. I was awoke by a commotion and a voice saying, 'Call the officer.' Rushing out, I found that a shower of spears had descended among us. All were quickly on the alert, and we could see dusky forms moving amongst the trees in the neighbourhood of our camp. Judging it possible that we might be attacked in force, I ordered a few shots to be fired, upon which there was a stampede, and we were not that night further disturbed. In the morning I disembarked all the men, telling off some to pitch tents, and others to clear away the trees and bush around, as we had brought saws and hatchets from the ship. This work, and scouring the bush in light infantry order, within a distance of a mile or so from the camp, filled up our first day's occupation. The object of scouring the bush was to show the blacks that we were in some force. Occasionally, we saw dusky figures; but I would not allow any firing. Catching sight of a man, Paddy Long, raising his musket to fire at a black, I shouted to him to drop it, and told him that for the first blackfellow he shot in cold blood, I would shoot him.

"Now, Paddy Long was a very good fellow, who would not, as the saying is, 'harm a fly'; but his conception, doubtless, was that we were out on a shooting party, and, indeed, a raid on the blacks was, in my time, by squatters often so conceived; and in cases where the squatters' cattle have been speared, it is difficult at times to draw an ethical line, especially in districts where Her Majesty's writ does not run. We preach the law of right; but the older natural doctrine of might has always prevailed, so long as brute, animal or human, is stronger than his fellow. It is the old story of the invasion of Canaan by the Hebrews. A desire to spread the benefits of civilisation may count for something; and the argument that the earth, as a whole, is the heritage of the human race, and is to be occupied in such a way as is most for the advantage of the human race, is a forcible one. Still, it must be admitted that without the stimulus of gain, progress would be slow, and thus we may rejoice that the appetite for gain exists in sufficient strength for the purpose. Reflections such as these did not occur to me at the time. Indeed, my chief concern was that I had neglected my obvious and primary duty, viz. to report myself in person to my commanding officer. The condition precedent was, however, where to find him. So hailing the *Thomas Lowry*, I asked them to send a boat. While waiting, I observed a boat approaching from the east, and as it neared, I made out Captain Day in the stern sheets; and right glad was I when, on receiving my reports, he expressed his approval of my proceedings, and of the spot selected for our encampment. From Captain Day I learnt the particulars of the going ashore of the *Lord Auckland*, and that the whole party were now encamped on the east, or sea side, of Facing Island.

"Some days later I paid a visit to the island; young Henry Day, who was afterwards in the 99th, having come over with an invitation. The distance from my encampment to the spot on which we landed on Facing Island, in the harbour, or west side, was about six miles, and we had to make our way through a mile or so of bush to reach the encampment. In going through the bush I had experience of the spiders' webs, the cordage of which is so strong as to lift off the traveller's hat. I found the *Lord Auckland* party comfortably encamped on a high ground overlooking the sea. They were all in the best of health and spirits, and so far as the situation admitted, certainly had made the best of it. I spent with the party a most enjoyable evening, got a shake-down in a tent, and left early the next morning for my detachment, and found all well.

"The only diversion for the men was fishing. Near the encampment was good fishing ground, and this fact was probably responsible for the desire of the blacks to expel us from the spot. Bathing was dangerous on account of the sharks. Life was somewhat monotonous, and as our rations were limited to the regulation ones of salt beef, salt pork, and biscuits, and these latter not wholly unconscious of worm and weevil, what are called 'the pleasures of the table,' were not for us. Dwellers in the Australian bush are wont to curse the mosquitoes, but they are quite pleasant fellows compared to the sand-flies, which here swarmed after sundown. Oft have I left my bed at night, and with a double gauze covering my face, and hands inserted in pockets, walked for hours on the beach, and finally thrown myself on the sand exhausted by the vigil compelled by the sand-flies.

"For some time we had heard nothing of the natives, when one day I was told that some were seen on the other side of the flat, at the south side of our encampment. I determined to interview them, and, if possible, to establish friendly relations. I was accompanied by the sergeant only. As we approached, they made signs that we should send back the dog which was following us. This we did. Then, that I should lay down the stick I carried. This done, two or three approached us, and by signs invited us to accompany them to the bush. This we did, but halted when we had advanced a little way. Our companions were then joined by others, and they pulled grass, and laid it down, motioning us to be seated. We sat down in a circle, the sergeant, myself, and I think half a dozen blacks. These were all men of fine physique, about six feet high, perfectly naked. They were apparently quite friendly, and as they were evidently much interested in our clothing, I divested myself of a coloured necktie I was wearing, and gave it to him who appeared to be a chief. Giving a red pocket-handkerchief to another, the others made signs to possess other articles; but as we did not wish to return to camp *in puris naturalibus*, we had to limit our gifts. One of the blacks left us for a few minutes, and on his return brought what I took to be the shin bone of a kangaroo. He made signs of eating, and I endeavoured to convey to him, by pointing to the sun, that we would on the following day, at the same hour, bring something to eat. On sitting down, we were careful to sit facing the bush, and the sergeant now told me that he saw several natives armed with spears among the trees a short distance off. On this, I thought it prudent to close our visit. This had to be done with circumspection, without hurry or evidence of suspicion or alarm, and withal, without turning our backs on our assumed friends. Suffice it to say, we effected our retreat in safety, from a position at no time free from risk, and at one time fraught with peril.

"Writing from experience gathered in different parts of Australia, I am inclined to demur to the opinion widely held that the Australian black is incapable of civilisation. That he is receptive of instruction where his interests are immediately concerned, is indubitable; and it is hardly realisable that the constructor of the boomerang is incapable of acquiring knowledge. The blacks with us, who had never seen a white man, projected their spears by the aid of spear sticks, which gave a powerful aid to propulsion; and used slings which carried stones a considerable distance. As I write, there lies before me a spear-head constructed from a portion of a soda-water bottle, serrated at the sides, and notched on both surfaces. It would be capable of inflicting a terrible wound. The ingenuity which must have been brought to bear in this case could certainly be utilised under more favourable conditions.

"Our expedition was a pioneer one; our mission to locate the future settlement; and ships were to follow from Sydney with free workmen and time-unexpired convicts, to construct roads and buildings. We had only been some weeks at Port Curtis, when a small steamer arrived with orders for the return of the party. The *Lord Auckland* being disabled, a portion of the party embarked in the *Thomas Lowry*, amongst them Mrs Barney, and others of the ladies.

"During the return voyage to Sydney an unpleasant incident occurred. Our captain was an excellent sailor, but on occasion he was inclined to partake too freely of a brown brandy of exceptional quality. Enforced inaction during the time his ship lay in Port Curtis probably aggravated his failing, and an attack of *delirium tremens* developed a few days after we left Port Curtis. There was nothing for it but to confine him to his cabin. The chief officer, on whom the command now devolved, was a young man without experience of Australian waters; and making the land he asked me to go aloft, and see if I could recognise a headland. This I readily did at Nobby Island, at the entrance of Newcastle Harbour, about eighty miles from Sydney, and in due course we made Sydney Heads, when the pilot took charge.

"Colonel Barney, Captain Day, and the remainder of the party remained for some months in North Australia, and on their return, put into Brisbane, where I was then quartered. And I learnt that before they left, they planted on Facing Island, and on the mainland, pumpkins and other seeds, and left live stock for the benefit of those who should come after them. Gladstone is now a city, and Port Curtis ranks as a port only second to that of Sydney, admitted to be the finest in the known commercial world."

Major de Winton retains one interesting memento of the foundation of Gladstone in the following communication :—

Port Curtis,
March 18, 1847.

Lieutenant de Winton,
Commanding Detachment 99th.

Sir,—The natives have been heard this morning, close to where I am discharging timber for Her Majesty's Government in the creek. For the protection of the timber and the lives of those landing, I have the honour to request you will send a small detachment on board the cutter.

I have the honour to be,
Sir,
Your obedient Servant,
J. S. Whitely.

The back of this letter is thus endorsed :—

"In compliance with this letter I have ordered one corporal and three men to proceed immediately on board the cutter mentioned.

"G. J. DE WINTON,
"*Lieutenant, 99th Regiment.*"

CHAPTER XV

THE GLADSTONE OF TO-DAY

RESUMING the regular course of events in the history of the Gladstone colony, the first incident deserving of record was the speedy revival and rapid recovery of the place after the very serious blow to its orderly progress and prosperity, inflicted by the great gold rush. That blow was of a twofold character. Not only was the town of Gladstone emptied of nearly all its able-bodied inhabitants, but during the closing weeks of the rush, a new town and a formidable rival sprang into existence, at the head of the navigation of the Fitzroy River, about ninety miles to the north. This new town, Rockhampton, although possessing none of the natural advantages with which Gladstone had been so liberally endowed, nevertheless went ahead at a much more rapid rate, and it has ever since bulked so largely in the eyes of the outer world, as to throw the older and more historic settlement somewhat in the shade. But Gladstone, although prostrated for a season by the slings and arrows of outrageous fortune, was too favourably circumstanced to remain recumbent and depressed for any length of time, and, as a matter of fact, the year following the collapse of the great gold rush found the little town once more upon its legs and ready to start upon a fresh career. A number of the old inhabitants had returned in the penitential mood of the prodigal son; sturdy young recruits, impressed by the attractions and probable future importance of the place, commenced to come in; trade and commerce began to revive; ships and steamers were again seen in the beautiful and commodious harbour, and Gladstone entered on a career of progress and prosperity that has never since been interrupted, and which now bids fair to be crowned with the full fruition of its early hopes and aspirations.

It is only fair to add that, whilst Gladstone as a town received a rude and serious shock from the great gold rush, the district generally may be said to have benefited on the whole by the unprecedented incursion of invading diggers from the south. The intimate connection between the rush to Port Curtis and the subsequent settlement and prosperous development of the district, is clearly established by Mr Booth.* He points out that among the thousands who came to search for gold, there were many who looked beyond the failure of the immediate object of their quest. Affairs in the southern colonies at the time were not particularly bright or promising. Speculation and over-trading had been accompanied or followed by disaster, and many of those who had joined in the rush felt that their energies must find vent and employment in other directions than the colonies they had left. The natural riches of the new land—the lack of gold notwithstanding—were too palpable to be overlooked. The old settlers were few and far between, but they had prospered, and therefore a considerable number of the newcomers made up their minds to enter into that prosperity. Many of them were entirely destitute of means, and few indeed were possessed of sufficient money to enable them to settle in a country where horses, cattle, and sheep constituted the chief classes of property. But they had "colonial experience"—a valuable commodity when properly applied. After a desultory sort of survey—sufficiently minute, however, to take in all the requisite features of the new country —numbers of this class of adventurers returned to the South, where they told the story of the new land around Port Curtis, with the result that soon sheep and cattle stations were being taken up in all directions. Stock was carried to the new settlements by every possible means. The mere spending of the money requisite to carry out the plans of

---

* "Australia Illustrated," by Edwin Carton Booth, vol. ii. p. 167.

the day was a pleasant operation. Those who had borrowed the means to make a fresh start in life were, perhaps, the happiest of all; but the "new chums," who had brought money with them, also enjoyed a merry time. It was a joyous life, seeking pastures new by the banks of beautiful rivers, on the pleasant plains, and the still more pleasant hill-sides. Many travelled from Victoria and New South Wales overland, driving their sheep and cattle before them to stock their new stations in the North. Numbers who had made money in business and grown rich in the southern cities also took up new country in the North, being desirous of enrolling themselves in the colonial aristocratic caste of the "squatters." As settlement increased, townships assumed an importance, and prospered beyond the most sanguine dreams of their first inhabitants. Cotton soon began to be cultivated on a considerable scale, and another profitable investment was found in the growth and manufacture of sugar.

Mr E. C. Booth gives an excellent picture of the Gladstone of twenty years ago in his "Australia Illustrated." * He describes it as a settlement that is sure to grow. He recommends English emigrants who, while desirous of making new homes in the great south land, still wish to retain the pleasing characteristics of the English country-town of the old type, to settle in Gladstone, which, he adds, deserves to be a cathedral city, if only because of its intense respectability.

In 1859 the town came prominently before the public, both in the home and colonial press, in connection with the question of the capital of the newly-created colony of Queensland. The choice was practically limited to two candidates—Brisbane and Gladstone. It was undeniable that Gladstone, by reason of its central position, its superb and capacious harbour, its promising future, its interesting personal and historical associations, and the variegated resources of the surrounding district, had the weight of argument on sits ide, and presented

---

* Vol. ii. p. 202.

superior claims to metropolitan distinction. But vested interests and seniority of foundation operated in favour of Brisbane, and secured the prize.

Sir George Fergusson Bowen, the first Governor of Queensland, visited Gladstone shortly after his arrival in the colony, and received an address of welcome from its citizens. In the course of his reply, the Governor remarked:—"The beauty of the scenery around your town, and the excellence of its harbour—almost unrivalled on the eastern coasts of Australia — render it worthy of the eloquent statesman whose name it bears, and who first projected a settlement on the shores of Port Curtis."

Writing to the Duke of Newcastle on December 4, 1860, Sir George Bowen described Port Curtis as probably the best harbour, after that of Sydney, on the eastern coast of Australia. The Government of New South Wales had founded on its shores a township which had been named Gladstone, and had become the outlet of the adjacent pastoral counties of Pelham and Clinton. The excellence of the harbour, the salubrity of the climate, and the beauty of the surrounding scenery, combined to render Gladstone an eligible site for a flourishing town; but the river Fitzroy, further north, afforded a more ready access to the interior of the colony, and consequently the settlement of Rockhampton on its banks had advanced more rapidly than Gladstone.

On November 18, 1865, Sir George Bowen wrote a very interesting letter to Mr Gladstone, giving an account of his second vice-regal visit to the town that had grown up on the site of the intended capital of the colony of North Australia.

"You will probably feel some interest," wrote Sir George, "in the condition and progress of the beautifully situated town in Queensland of which you are the godfather. I venture, therefore, to enclose a copy of the addresses presented to me on my recent official tour of inspection to the northern districts of this colony, including an address from the Mayor of Gladstone, and another from the miners on the neighbouring goldfields. You will see

that in my reply to the Mayor of your town, I quoted from a
speech recently delivered by you at Liverpool. The present
Mayor of Gladstone is proud of eing also a Lancashire man. I
have just returned from a cruise of 2000 miles, all in the
waters of Queensland. I was received with great cordiality at
every seaport, especially by the Gladstonians, and also by the
diggers on the goldfields in the vicinity, who invited me to a
public banquet given in a large tent in the centre of the diggings.
The dinner, wines, and speeches were all equally good. You are,
doubtless, aware that Australian gold-mining has now become a
regular pursuit, without the recklessness and turbulence of former
years. The deputation of the mining body, who had been elected
by their fellows to act as my hosts, were all evidently men of
sense and education. I am confident that you will also learn with
interest that the Queensland Parliament, on my recommendation,
has adopted those Acts which you have recently passed through
the Imperial Parliament for the improvement and the extension
of the Government Savings Banks, and for the granting annuities
and life assurances on the security of the public revenue, and for
ameliorating in other ways the condition of the working classes.
You will see from the enclosed copy of my prorogation speech that
I alluded to this subject in closing the session for 1865. From
the concluding paragraph of the same speech you will learn the
wonderfully rapid, but solid progress of Queensland during the six
years of my administration."

Gladstone was formally incorporated on February 1, 1863,
and has ever since been governed in all its local concerns
by its own Mayor and Board of Aldermen. Ample and
prudent provision was made at the time for the probabilities
of future growth and expansion. With commendable sagacity and foresight, and a prophetic inkling of what the
requirements of the city of Gladstone were likely to be
before the close of the nineteenth century, the municipal
boundaries were so arranged as to enclose an area of eight
and a half square miles. The Gladstone of to-day is a
bright, busy, and beautifully-situated town, occupying for
the most part an extensive sloping terrace near the mouth
of the River Boyne, and commanding a glorious prospect

of the blue waters of Port Curtis, dotted with numerous richly-grassed islands, one of which, by the way—Curtis Island—was the scene of the early married life of one of the most popular of contemporary Anglo-Australian novelists, Mrs Campbell Praed. Mr Praed, a relative of Winthorp Mackworth Praed, the poet who won the Chancellor's prize medal at Cambridge, in 1823, for the best poem on Australia, was an Australian squatter, and Curtis Island constituted one of his runs. The station homestead, looking over the lovely creamy beach and across the sun-lit waters of the harbour to Gladstone, was his favourite residence. The background of the town is supplied by a succession of picturesque ranges with the crowning peak of Mount Stanley, from the summit of which one of the finest scenic panoramas in the Southern Hemisphere is to be viewed. Dense forests of valuable timber are to be discerned in various directions, smiling grain fields and thriving orchards afford frequent glimpses of peaceful content and steady industry, and looking over the town beneath and the harbour beyond, the white-capped waves of the Pacific may be traced for many a mile, while the musical murmur of the billows, as they strike the sounding shore, falls pleasingly on the ear.

Ever since its foundation, the exportation of cattle and horses has been one of the leading industries of Gladstone. A return prepared by Mr Henry Friend, senior, the stock inspector and oldest identity of Gladstone, shows that during the past thirty years there have been exported from Gladstone to Great Britain, India, New Caledonia, New Zealand, Melbourne, Sydney, and Batavia, cattle, horses, and sheep, to an aggregate value exceeding a quarter of a million. With the completion of railway communication to all parts of the interior, this trade must necessarily experience a very appreciable development. A commencement has already been made with the direct shipment of live stock from Gladstone to England, but whether this is destined to become a permanent and profitable industry will depend upon the amount of success attained in surmounting the difficulties and drawbacks incidental to the long sea voyage of 12,000 miles.

The Hon. Henry Stuart Littleton, son of Lord Hatherton, speaking from an experience of many years as a residential Queensland squatter, recently gave it as his opinion that, if suitable boats were specially built for this trade so as to obviate the rolling, the loss in transit would be extremely small, and the live cattle trade between Gladstone and England could be made a success. A demand for Australian live cattle has lately sprung up in South Africa, and as the Cape is only half the distance to England, Gladstone is not unlikely to find a new and profitable customer in that quarter.

Mr J. Y. Foote, for many years manager of the Gladstone branch of the Australian Joint Stock Bank, wrote a few months ago :—

"I am of opinion that Gladstone is the finest natural port of Australia, fully equal to Sydney Harbour, so far as commercial utility for shipping is concerned. For shipment of horses and cattle to India and Europe, it possesses advantages far before any other Australian port. As a recent instance, a steamer of 5500 tons entered the harbour, moored alongside the Government jetty, and in 36 hours proceeded to India with 600 horses, shipped on board from Gladstone. Brisbane to the south, and Rockhampton to the north, have hitherto been formidable rivals, by reason of their railways into the interior, but now that the Government has undertaken the extension of the Main Trunk Line to Gladstone, virtually making that city the northern terminus, I consider no part of Australia likely to make quicker strides towards a phenomenal progress than Gladstone."

Notwithstanding its unfortunate early experiences in the matter of the pursuit and discovery of the precious metal, Gladstone has the distinction of being the first goldfield gazetted by the Government of Queensland. Or, to be strictly correct, one of its environs, Calliope, is the oldest goldfield in the colony, and its auriferous resources are not yet exhausted.

The latest report of the Mining Department of Queensland, containing information brought down to the end of 1895, states the yield for the year from all the lines on the Gladstone goldfields at 8246 tons of stone, which produced 7179 ounces of gold, of the total value of £25,119. In addition to these results of crushings of auriferous stone, alluvial gold to the amount of 1474 ounces was found in the vicinity of Gladstone during the same period. It is alleged, on the authority of the Mining Department, that "alluvial deposits are widely scattered over the Gladstone district, and they should give employment to a number of men for years to come in anything like normal seasons." The number of miners on the Gladstone fields at the end of 1895 was reported to be 1137 whites and sixty-six Chinese. Of the former, it is officially recorded that they are "as a rule married men, settled down, and adverse to leading a nomadic life," this contented disposition being credited to two favouring circumstances—the exceptional healthiness of the climate, and the proximity of the fields to the principal centres of population. It is suggested in the report that the dredging of the river Boyne in the Gladstone district would reveal rich discoveries, having regard to the large area of gold-bearing country traversed by that stream and its tributaries.

A few miles to the west of Gladstone excellent coal has been discovered and worked, and the report of the Assistant Government Geologist leaves little room to doubt that the seams are of the most valuable and permanent character. Another field of mineral activity is thus referred to in the report of the Department:—

"There are a number of manganese mines in the Gladstone district, but a limited market operates against their development. The one situated at Auckland Hill, not very distant from the town, exported about 300 tons of ore, principally for the use of the chlorination works of the Mount Morgan mine."

There is a large auriferous belt in the Raglan district

in the immediate neighbourhood of Gladstone, and nuggets of considerable size and value have been discovered there from time to time, but this, in common with most of the fields in the locality, demands systematic development and the assistance of outside capital.

The cultivation of the sugar-cane is now extensively carried on in the Gladstone district. Farmers find a very satisfactory profit in cultivating comparatively small areas, and bringing the produce to a central mill. Dairy farming is also an important industry, the country around Gladstone being remarkable for its rich grass lands.

Socially, the town of Gladstone is well supplied with the institutions and agencies that are characteristic of the progressive colonial centre. The Anglicans, Catholics, and Presbyterians have erected commodious churches for the accommodation of their respective adherents. The Gladstone Hospital is an admirably conducted institution, and deservedly occupies a noble site. The School of Arts, with its library and reading-room, furnishes the colonial equivalent to the polytechnic palaces of the old land. For the Gladstonians who are less inclined to reading, study, and self-education, the Musical and Dramatic Club, the Racing Club, the Cricket Club, and various other organisations devoted to recreation and sport, are available. The Pastoral Society of Gladstone is a strong and influential body, thoroughly representative of the staple industry of the district. A number of friendly and benefit societies have flourishing branches or lodges in Gladstone, and the Queensland Government is represented in the town by a resident magistrate, a goldfields warden, a collector of customs, postal, telegraphic, and various other officials. The increasing demand for hotel accommodation has contributed some superior structures to the town, and preparations for further improvement and expansion in this direction are in progress. There is considerable coaching activity in the streets of Gladstone, vehicles running regularly to and fro between the town and the various goldfields within a radius of sixty miles. The harbour is well supplied with piers and jetties, the principal one, named the Victoria Pier by Governor Sir Anthony Musgrave, providing twenty-six feet of water at the lowest tide. The leading local newspaper is the *Gladstone Observer*, a well-conducted and enterprising journal, that has for many years ably advocated and represented the interests of what it described in its prospectus with pardonable pride as "the premier port of the colony of Queensland." It recently issued a special edition of 50,000 copies, avowedly to "advertise the capabilities and resources of Gladstone, and present outsiders with a faithful picture of what the district is like. Merchants attract trade and build up gigantic businesses by advertising their wares, and we believe many Australian towns would likewise be built up, if their inhabitants adopted a similar method of bringing their locality under the public ken. The practice has often been resorted to in America with wonderful success, many of the large American cities being monuments of the enterprise of capitalists who selected the sites and placed the advantages of settlement so clearly before the public, that towns sprang into being with astonishing rapidity. We are not vain enough to imagine that a single effort will have so magical an effect on Gladstone, but it is palpable that an issue of 50,000 copies of a newspaper, distributed amongst the leading business men and capitalists of Australia, must attract a certain amount of attention to this locality." As a reason for making this special effort to bring Gladstone into prominence, the *Observer* pointed out that when railway communication with the South and the West was completed, Gladstone would be sure to develop into a very important shipping and commercial centre. Then "the magnificent harbour of Port Curtis will be connected by rail with every important coastal town in Australia, and Gladstone will speedily take its position, not only as the port of Central Queensland, but as the most important maritime town in the colony, for its harbour is excelled only by Port Jackson on the Australian seaboard." In proof of this assertion, the report of Mr W. D. Nisbet, the Government Engineer for Harbours and Rivers, is quoted.

"As regards the anchorage in the harbour, I was especially struck with its extent, apparent permanence, and security in all winds. I find it possesses an area of at least 3000 acres, with a depth of five fathoms and upwards at low water, after allowing a good deep-water channel up through the centre. This would accommodate 500 of the largest class of vessels riding with double anchors as usually moored in harbours, or 200 to 250 moored to allow the full swing of the cable, as in open roadsteads. There may be said, therefore, to be no practical limit to the accommodation the harbour will afford for vessels of the very largest class.

"Owing to its accessibility at all times, and excellent deep-water berthage, I consider it the most eligible calling-place on that part of the coast for large mail and other steamers not going up to Rockhampton, and requiring rapid despatch. The harbour is capable of affording the utmost convenience for landing and discharging passengers and cargo, putting coals, stores, and provisions on board, and, if need be, for effecting repairs; and it appears to me that, with proper arrangements, the requirements of such vessels may be met with the greatest certainty and regularity."

The chief reason why Gladstone had not progressed in proportion to the extent of its great natural advantages, is traced by the *Observer* writer to the absence of facilities for land transit, but the railways in course of construction will, he says, "put a new face on the old order of things. The district is largely peopled with land selectors; Gladstone is also surrounded with numerous cattle stations; there is no place in Australia where fruit is so easily grown and available for export on so large a scale; there is, in fact, ample scope for development in many directions, and that development must take place when we are placed in direct railway communication with the southern capitals."

The leading merchants and exporters of cattle in Gladstone are the Messrs H. & J. Friend, sons of the original founder of the business, the Mr Henry Friend, senior, already alluded to. This latter gentleman is the patriarch of Gladstone, and a very old and respected colonist. He sailed from Southampton with his wife and two children in July, 1854; landed in Sydney on November 7; experienced some of the vicissitudes of fortune on the Turon goldfield; and came to Gladstone towards the close of 1855, to assist in the construction of a reservoir, working as a labourer at 10s. a day. When the reservoir was completed, he made up his mind to settle down in Gladstone, and started business as a store-keeper on a modest scale. With each succeeding year the business became more and more prosperous, until eventually the present extensive stores and large wharfage accommodation had to be provided, chiefly in order to cope with the ever increasing consignments of wool sent down to Gladstone from the squatters' stations, for export to Europe and America.

Another old resident is Mr William Kirkpatrick, whose acquaintance with Gladstone covers a period of close on half a century.

"When I first arrived in Gladstone," he writes me, "there was but one house in the place worthy of the name. It was built of saplings and bark, on the rise above the cattle-yards. Mr R. E. Palmer was building a store on the ridge where the present Court-House stands. Sir Maurice O'Connell, the Government Resident, subsequently purchased the building from Mr Palmer, and converted it into a Court-House. When I first came to Gladstone, the only fresh water available was at what was then called the Police Creek, whence it was brought to the little town by drays. A young man was killed off one of those water-drays, and was buried at Barney Point, where his tombstone may still be seen. It bears the inscription:—'Underneath this stone are deposited the remains of Thomas Miller Stratford Riddell, eldest son of the Acting Colonial Secretary of New South Wales, and Mrs Riddell. He was born at Sydney on January 22, 1832, and died at Port Curtis on September 16, 1854, aged 22 years.' Lieutenant Lestrange, of H.M.S. *Torch*, who was killed by the blacks, was also buried at Barney Point by the side of Mr Riddell's son.

"Colonel Barney first landed on Facing Island, and afterwards established his headquarters at Barney Point; but he did not remain long, and when he returned to Sydney, he said no white people could live at Port Curtis. The party, headed by Sir Maurice O'Connell, also landed at Barney Point in March, 1854, and shortly afterwards Governor Sir Charles Fitzroy visited the settlement in the *Torch* man-of-war. On Christmas Day, 1855, the blacks killed all hands on Mount Larcombe, destroyed the stores, and drove away all the sheep. In the same year we had a visit from a geologist named Stutchbury, and two assistants. He was sent out by the Royal Geological Society of England to report on the minerals of Australia. He discovered gold at the back of the town of Gladstone. That was the first gold found in this part of the country, but the news was kept very quiet at the time. Sir Maurice O'Connell did not wish it to be made public. Towards the end of 1857, a party was formed in Gladstone to prospect for gold in the neighbourhood of Gracemere Station. Old Chapple found golden quartz at the back of Dungreo on the Don water-shed, and then came the great rush from all parts to Port Curtis.

"When the first shearing took place on Marian Vale Station, the blacks rushed the place, speared one of the partners in the neck, and killed one of the shearers. Next year they killed two shepherds on the same station.

"The surveyor who laid out the town of Gladstone was Mr M'Cabe. Early in Sir Maurice O'Connell's time the settlement ran short of provisions, and we had to live on rice for six weeks, until the New South Wales Government sent H.M.S. *Torch* with a cargo of flour to our relief. The *Albion*, Captain Hardy, arrived at Gladstone shortly afterwards with a general cargo, and then there was no further danger of famine."

Another old resident of Gladstone writes :—

"Colonel Barney's visit was short and somewhat inglorious. Sir Maurice O'Connell acted as Government Resident until separation came, and the new colony of Queensland was created. The country in those days was wild and infested by wild blacks or 'myalls,' as they were called. I think one of the most exciting incidents of Sir Maurice's administration was the murder of all hands, with the single exception of a black boy, on Mount Larcombe Station by the myalls. It was a thrilling incident, but perhaps not more so than many other outrages that occurred in the pioneering days of what was then called the Northern

Territory. Not the least important feature of Sir Maurice O'Connell's administration was the survey of the squatters' runs in the Port Curtis district. There is a tradition that Sir Maurice had a very knowing horse called Jerry. Sir Maurice used to fix his starting-point and allow Jerry to measure the distance, one hour's journey being reckoned at four miles. So regular and reliable was Jerry, that he was never known to be a hundred yards out in the four miles, and as a mile or two of country did not matter much in those days, no difficulties arose from this rough-and-ready mode of surveying and fixing the boundary lines of the squatters' stations."

Addressing the members of the Royal Colonial Institute on April 12, 1881, Mr Thomas Archer recalled his impressions and experiences of the Gladstone district in the early forties. The population in those old times, he said, consisted of a few squatters or pastoral tenants of the Crown, their scattered servants, about a dozen store-keepers and publicans, and half a dozen Government officials. Those were the times when the squatter ranged at will over the face of the land, turning into profit for the community, and occasionally for himself, vast tracts of country that had lain waste and desolate since creation, and would, but for him, have probably continued so for a long time to come, for it was an axiom in the history of Australian settlement that in the interior the squatter or pastoralist must precede the settler or agriculturalist. The reasons for this were not far to seek. Agricultural produce was so bulky and heavy in proportion to its value that it could not be grown profitably when it had to be sent over long and often difficult roads to market. Where there was no population on or near the place of production to consume it, and no railways or navigable rivers to carry the produce to market, the cost of carriage must inevitably prove fatal to any chance of profitable farming; and these conditions unfortunately obtained in the far interior of Australia. The principal articles produced on a grazing station were, on the contrary, comparatively easily brought to market. Wool could be compressed into small bulk in proportion to its value and weight, and was easily handled and carried; while beef, mutton, hides, and tallow had the advantage of walking to market on their own legs at a comparatively trifling cost to the producer. In those early times the squatter was his own explorer, his own surveyor, his own road and bridge maker, his own carrier, and too often, his own shepherd, cook, bullock-driver, and laundress.

Transportation had suddenly ceased; immigration was in its infancy; labour was scarce, dear, and bad; consequently, no kind of employment, save one, was considered *infra dig*. The blight of gentility had not then spread over the surface of society like a canker, destroying everything like manly independence. The only exception to this liberal code was keeping a public-house. The line had to be drawn somewhere, and it was drawn there. If a gentleman stooped to this degrading occupation, he was ruthlessly sent to Coventry.

Many an Eton or Harrow schoolboy and University man had to strip off his coat, turn up his sleeves, and submit to the most servile but salutary labours, realising that he who would have a faithful, interested, and attached servant should serve himself. Much good the lesson did them. In those times there was no paternal Government to open the way for the squatter, to direct his steps through the wilderness, and to tax him. Crown Lands Commissioners reigned over districts as large as three or four English counties, and a £10 license-fee, with an almost nominal assessment, was all the direct taxation to which he was liable. But all that was now changed, and cultivation, civilisation, taxes, matrimony, and intense respectability reigned supreme in regions where they were but little known in the good old days.

Mr Archer added this interesting reference to his relations with the blacks when he was a pioneer settler in the Gladstone country:—

"The simple truth is that Providence has not furnished the blacks with natural capacity to understand anything except what appeals to their senses. In all that does so they are quite equal to most races in intelligence, but go beyond that, attempt to explain to them any subject that requires an effort of the reflective faculties to understand, and they are totally incapable of making it. I say all this in sorrow, for I like the natives, and esteem them for their many good qualities. Few have had more opportunities for knowing them intimately, for in my youthful days I was thrown much amongst them in a country that was then the remote interior, and contained many blacks and very few whites. I have journeyed with them, camped with them, partaken of their fare when very little else was to be had, and at one time I spoke one of their numerous dialects with tolerable fluency. During the whole of my residence in the colonies I have seen much of them, and I am not conscious of the least lurking prejudice against them; but truth is great, and impels me to say what I have said in answer to those who allege that we are robbing of their country and exterminating an interesting and improvable race, and not doing enough for their civilisation and conversion. Sir, I say that these charges are unjust. It cannot be intended that that vast expanse of glorious country should be for ever reserved to the uses of a few scattered wanderers, while in the old countries men are treading each other into the mire for want of space."

Gladstone has latterly been receiving many flattering attentions from the gentlemen of the Press, and there is hardly one of the illustrated Australian weeklies which has not given a page of engravings, accompanied by a descriptive article on the charming little city by the shores of Port Curtis. Mr F. W. Ward, the editor of the *Brisbane Courier*, who recently went on a journalistic cruise along the coast of Queensland, was particularly struck by the number of Gladstonian friends and prophets he encountered. "On the ships," he remarks, "one is sure to meet Queenslanders who are enthusiastic about the future of Gladstone." A second journalistic observer predicts that "the next decade will be sure to witness marvellous changes in the Port Curtis district." A representative of the *Queenslander*, who recently visited Gladstone, describes it as the most charming seaport on the whole coast of the colony.

"Possessed of a harbour," he writes, "which has only one rival in all Australia, and which has the most valuable requisites for the development of a great shipping trade, with tens of thousands of acres of rich grass lands, with vast timber resources, with mineral areas which are just beginning to be placed under the pressure of prosperous development, and with soil prolific of grains, grasses, and fruits, it is a marvellous puzzle why Gladstone has not long since risen to the dignity of a large commercial, manufacturing, and seaport city. That nature has intended it to be such I am convinced, and the artificial barriers which have retarded its progress and the proper development of its magnificent possibilities, must some day be swept aside and destroyed. Gladstone is looking wistfully and hopefully forward to the time when it will be connected by rail with the South, and when from mast-tops in the harbour the flags of many nations will be flying. The shipping of the Queensland coast is yet in its infancy, and Gladstone harbour presents a prospective commercial prominence that some day will develop enormously, and attain an international as well as a colonial eminence."

Extensive frozen-meat works have lately been erected in Gladstone; a local company has been formed to develop this rapidly-growing industry; and Gladstone is already one of the chief centres of the trade.

CHAPTER XVI

MR GLADSTONE'S TRUE PRINCIPLES OF COLONISATION

FROM the mass of speeches, pronouncements, and writings of Mr Gladstone on colonial affairs, I select one utterance for separate and particular notice, inasmuch as it is the most striking and suggestive, the most elaborate and eloquent, the most comprehensive and closely reasoned of all his addresses on the relations between the Mother Country and her daughter lands beyond the seas. It is his speech on the second reading of the New Zealand Government Bill in the House of Commons on May 21, 1852. On that occasion, Mr Gladstone formulated what he conceived to be the true principles of colonisation. New Zealand was a colony in which Mr Gladstone would naturally feel a warm personal interest. His relative by marriage, Lord Lyttleton, was one of the founders of the New Zealand province of Canterbury, and amongst the "Canterbury Pilgrims" (as they are known in local history) or pioneer settlers, were several of Mr Gladstone's early friends and acquaintances. Moreover, the first Anglican Bishop of New Zealand, Dr George Augustus Selwyn, was Mr Gladstone's closest companion at Eton, and an intimate friend in later life. Mr Gladstone maintained a correspondence with his old friends amongst the "Canterbury Pilgrims," notably the Hon. J. E. Fitzgerald, who became the first Premier of New Zealand. The reading of a remarkable letter from this gentleman constituted a dramatic episode in the speech of Mr Gladstone on the second reading of the Home Rule Bill of 1893.

At the outset of his speech on the New Zealand Government Bill forty-five years ago, Mr Gladstone said he was not aware of a single case of a colony dealt with by recent legislation, in which a just, and what he might call for the sake of precision, a normal relation between the colony and the Mother Country had been arrived at. By the term "normal relation" he did not mean a relation founded upon the speculations of philosophers or economists alone, but he meant a relation which had been developed in the world of actual life, and which, with regard to its leading outlines and all its essential features, was the old relation that in former times—although it was the custom to ridicule those times as having been comparatively unenlightened—subsisted between the Mother Country and the North American colonies.

The prevalent conception of a colony, as it appeared to him, was this:—It was regarded as something which had its centre of life in an executive government; the establishment of a colony was viewed as something which was to take effect by legislative enactments, or by the executive power of the Crown, or by the funds of the people of England. This administrative establishment, according to the present colonial system, was the root and trunk around which, by degrees, a population was to grow, under which, by degrees, that population was, according to a modern and in this case most unhappy phrase, to be trained for freedom, and to which, in course of time, some modicum of free institutions was to be granted. That he thought was a true description of the manner in which, and of the idea under which, the foundation of the modern British colonies had been ordinarily conducted. Now, he conceived that a fundamental difference prevailed between the colonial policy pursued during recent years and the policy pursued in the other departments of the State. In the Home Department, the financial arrangements of the country, the Foreign Office, certain leading principles were continuously carried out, and upon those leading principles there was a general concurrence of opinion, so that, for example, no person ever seriously proposed to alter the fundamental principles upon which the foreign policy of the country had been conducted by a long succession of Ministers. But that which he thought required still more and more to be presented to the mind of the House and of the people of England, until it became with them a living and a practical conviction, was this proposition, that in the policy they had pursued in the foundation of colonies—he spoke of free and planted colonies, not military posts or colonies whose social relations were disturbed by questions of race—they had proceeded on principles fundamentally wrong; and that the Acts introduced and passed by the Imperial Parliament for the purpose of raising, by slow and reluctant degrees, the structure of freedom in those colonies, were not so much recognitions of a right principle, as modifications, qualifications, and restraints imposed upon a wrong principle.

Now, what was this right principle of colonisation to which he referred? It might, in his view, be enunciated in one word, or at least one phrase, to which he would presently come. Their ancestors, 200 years ago, when they proceeded to found colonies, did not do it by coming down to the House of Commons with an estimate prepared, and asking so many thousands a year for a Governor, a Judge, an Assistant-Judge, a Colonial Secretary, and a large apparatus of minor officers. What they did was this: they collected together a body of free men destined to found a free State in another hemisphere upon principles of freedom analogous to those of the parent State, which should grow up by a principle of increase intrinsic to itself, and, enjoying that freedom under the shelter against foreign aggression from civilised powers which the Imperial power of England was to afford them, should in process of time propagate the language, manners, institutions, and religion of the English nation in distant quarters of the globe. But it was not on artificial support from home that these colonies leaned, and the consequence was that they advanced with a rapidity which, considering the undeveloped state of communications and of commerce at the time, was little less than miraculous. That was the consequence to them, and the consequence to the Mother Country was this—the home exchequer was never

troubled with pecuniary charges for their maintenance.
On the contrary, they were ever ready to assist England
in time of war, and instead of being called on to send
regiments, service companies, and he knew not what besides,
to maintain the domestic police of those colonies and keep
the peace for them against unruly members of their own
communities, or against savage tribes upon their borders,
such was their admiration of freedom and such their profitable use of it, that not only did they not ask for regiments
and service companies, or petition for means to keep the
peace, but they held it as a grievance if England attempted
to impose upon them her little standing armies, and they
considered that, having been educated in English habits
and ideas, they were perfectly competent to follow out
for themselves the paths in which those habits and ideas
conducted them.

Such was the then state of things. Departing from
that scheme of policy in later days, they had implanted
a principle, if not of absolute, yet of comparative feebleness, in their distant settlements. They had brought upon
themselves enormous expense, and, by depriving their
distant colonies of the fulness of political freedom,
they had deprived them of the greatest attraction that
could possibly be held out to the best part of the population to emigrate, because Englishmen did not love to
emigrate to countries where they could not enjoy the
political franchises which they enjoyed at home, and where
the regulation of their interests would be committed to
the hands of a Government, which, however mild and
equitable, must still be called in principle, despotic. Whatever might be said as to despotism—and he was not disposed to take an over-severe view of it where it was
adapted to the habits and social condition of a country
—yet, as regards free-born Englishmen, such a system was
most monstrous and irrational, and the consequence had
been that there was a subject of complaint present and
familiar to them all, namely, the great difficulty in getting
the superior classes of the community to emigrate, for the

high-minded, well-educated men, who would have been themselves the centres of a valuable social influence, had been reluctant to leave the shores of England, because they were unwilling to forfeit the advantages of a state of high civilisation and to incur a certain deprivation of the great bulk of their political liberties. And thus their modern colonists, instead of remaining as in former times, in continuous and hereditary possession of their liberties after quitting the Mother Country; instead of keeping and handing them on as the regular and unquestioned heritage of their children in another hemisphere, went out to Australia or New Zealand to be deprived of those liberties, and then, perhaps, after fifteen, twenty, or thirty years' waiting, to have a portion given back to them with great and magnificent language about the liberality of the Imperial Parliament in conceding free institutions. During all that time, they were condemned to hear the whole of the miserable jargon about training them for free institutions, and fitting them for the privileges thus conferred; whereas, in point of fact, so far from thus training and fitting them, every year during which they were kept out of the possession and the familiar use of such institutions, and retained under the administration of a despotic Government, rendered them less fit for free institutions, and the consequence was that when free institutions were at length introduced, great embarrassments ensued, liberty came as a novelty, its working was something strange and unknown, attended with hazard, uncertainty, and excitement, and thus inconvenient or disastrous consequences were brought about, which might have been avoided by following that which in this case no one need be ashamed of holding up to commendation as the wisdom of their ancestors, and walking in the path they had struck out for the guidance of future generations. Let the people sent out to colonise a distant land take root unmolested in their new ground as the seed of a future community, as the natural and living centre around which population was to grow; and instead of training them for free institutions, let it be remembered that the best training they could have was the training they had already received before quitting the shores of England, and while they were still British citizens. Let them carry their freedom with them even as they carried their agricultural implements, or anything else necessary to establish them in their new abodes. So let them hold it for themselves, and so let them transmit it to their children. That was the true secret of subduing the difficulties of colonisation.

In propagating these opinions, he did not rest upon the speculations of philosophers and economists. He rested upon the facts of history. The system which he recommended, and which he was convinced would gain ground from year to year in the feelings and convictions of the country, was the very same system in the main as that on which the whole of the great and wonderful operation in colonising North America was conducted—the system which Edmund Burke studied, examined, and comprehended from top to bottom, and which he described in his great speech on American taxation, when he warned the Imperial Parliament against the erroneous and destructive consequences of attempting to establish administrative power over their distant dependencies, or to extract from them some miserable and contemptible pecuniary benefit, instead of seeing that the great interest and purpose of England in colonising was the multiplication of her race; that her policy was to trust to the multiplication of her race for the propagation of her institutions; and that whatever course of legislation tended most to the rapid expansion of population and power in her colonies, necessarily tended most to enhance the reflected benefits that she was to derive from their foundation. That sound colonial policy reached its climax in what might be called Tory times, although they were times immediately preceding the invention of the now familiar political designations. In 1662 the Charter of Rhode Island was granted. It was the most remarkable of all the early charters for its enlarged and liberal spirit, yet in its general character it was akin to the rest of the charters under which the infant settlements of New England throve and prospered. At the present day it was considered a monstrous idea that colonies should have free local jurisdiction for local purposes. It was not considered safe to allow colonies to pass, at their own discretion, a law relating to the making of a road, the deepening of a harbour, or any local purpose; so that an Act of this kind, after passing a colonial legislature—nay, even after receiving the Governor's assent, was not secure from reversal, but was still, as it were, in a state of suspended existence for two years and upwards. It was remitted to England, considered in England, and again sent to the colonies; and thus, until the news was received there, its fate was uncertain. In point of fact, a period of nearly three years might elapse in the distant colonies between their final decision on local questions—the only criterion of fitness in this case that was worth a moment's attention—and their final knowledge whether the decision was to take effect. That was the state in which they were placed, and the way in which their affairs were managed. He should like to know what the feelings, temper, and humour of the English people at home would be if this were the mode of dealing with laws passed by them on subjects which they understood—say, for instance, an Act for the construction of a Great Western railroad or other similar purpose—if such an Act, passed on their own knowledge of the circumstances and exigencies of the case, were to be transmitted to another quarter of the world, and there kept by somebody in an office for two years, while some person or persons unknown were deliberating upon its fate. Yet that was the system under which, in this age of freedom and enlightenment, they were content that their colonies should subsist.

The old idea of a colony might be represented, as he had said at the beginning of his remarks, by a single phrase—it was in fact the idea of a municipal corporation. Now, it would be useful to consider the sense attached to that phrase. In the departure from it was to be found the key of the alteration of their colonial policy from the old model.

They did not treat their municipalities with the same system of misplaced absolutism that they applied to their colonies. They placed their municipalities under the restraint of the general law of the land, but for purposes properly local, they were endowed with absolute freedom. The by-laws of Liverpool or of Manchester—places counting their population by hundreds on hundreds of thousands—were not sent to the Secretary for the Home Department to be kept for two years, that he might consider whether they were to be carried into effect or not, but they went into operation at once. Would it be possible for them, by any strain of imagination, to realise to themselves what the condition of such municipalities would be if that were not so? Such a system would seem to them fitter for Turkey than for England. The colonial system of their ancestors was well considered, and was founded on the dictates of political justice. The colonies were subjected on the one hand to the general restraints of the law of England, and again, according to the language of their charters, they were to have their laws as near as might be agreeable to the laws of England, whilst in other respects they were, for all practical purposes, absolutely and entirely free. Furthermore, he would say that the degenerate and degrading ideas they now had of retaining the substance of colonial patronage partly, and still more the name, in the home country, for the supposed benefit of Ministers, or influence of the Crown, were totally foreign to the notions of their ancestors six generations ago. The colonies at that time, on the general basis of municipal corporations, were the possessors of their own soil; they were for all purposes of police, except that of conflict with civilised powers, the defenders of their own frontiers; they were the bearers of their own charges; they were the electors of their own officers; and they were the makers of their own laws. Every one of those salutary principles had been reversed within the last seventy years. They now retained at home the management of, and property in, colonial lands. They had magnificent sums figuring on their estimates for the ordinary expenses of Colonial

Governments, instead of allowing these governments to bear their own expenses. Instead of allowing the colonies to judge what were the measures best adapted to secure their peaceful relations with the aboriginal tribes, they were told: "You must not meddle with the relations between yourselves and the natives; that is a matter for the Imperial Parliament." A Minister sitting in Downing Street determined how the local relations between the inhabitants of a colony and the aboriginal tribes were to be settled in every point, down to the minutest detail. Nay, even their strictly internal police, Imperial troops were often called upon to maintain. The idea of their electing their own officers was regarded as revolutionary in the extreme—if not invading the Royal supremacy, it was something almost as bad, dismembering the Empire; and, as to making their own laws upon local affairs, without home interference or control, that was really an innovation so opposed to all ideas of Imperial policy, that he thought his hon. friend, the Member for Southwark (Sir William Molesworth) was the first man in the House bold enough to propose it. Thus, in fact, the principles on which colonial administration was once conducted had been precisely reversed. The colonies had come to be looked upon as being, not municipalities endowed with local freedom, but petty States. If the fundamental idea of their forefathers had been adhered to—that colonies were municipal bodies founded within the shadow and cincture of the Imperial power of England; that, having imposed on them such positive restraints as were thought necessary, they were left free in everything else—all those principles, instead of having been reversed, would have survived in full vigour, millions would have been saved to the Imperial Exchequer, and something far more important would have been done by planting societies more worthy by far of the source from which they sprang; for no man could read the history of the great American Revolution without seeing that, 100 years ago, the colonies, such as they then were, with the institutions they then possessed, and the political relations in which they then stood to the

Mother Country, bred and reared men of mental stature and power, such as far surpassed anything that colonial life was now commonly considered to be capable of producing.

The Charter of Rhode Island was, on the whole, the best and most perfect exhibition of the ancient maxims of colonisation. Its constitution consisted of three orders—a Governor, a body of assistants, and a body of freemen. The freemen, as it was anticipated in the Charter that they would become numerous, were to meet by representation; and thus, in these elected freemen, with the distinct order of assistants, a principle was laid down—the principle of the double chamber for legislation—which had stood the storm of the American Revolution and the strain of all subsequent political vicissitudes, and which at present subsisted with undiminished vigour in every single State of the American Union. But, further, while the first Governor was named in the Charter, and was to hold office for a year, his successors were to be appointed by the free voice of the colonists; and, doubtless, to many it would appear astonishing that that power should have been conceded in 1662, when not merely the warmth, but the fever of Royalism was at its height in England. They were not only to elect their own Government, but to make their own laws, subject to no other restraint in the world, except that, as far as circumstances would permit, such laws should not be contrarious but agreeable to the laws of England. They were to appoint their own officers and judges; they were to constitute their own courts of justice; they were to arm, embody, and march their own force for self-defence, and appoint its commanders; they were to be the possessors of their own soil, and, lastly, they were to be the bearers of their own charges. It might be asked what security was taken for their good behaviour to others? The security taken, whether perfect or not, was certainly as perfect as any more recent policy had furnished. It was provided that in the event of their offending any Prince or Power in alliance with the Crown of England, they should either be bound to make restitution to the satisfaction of the Crown, or else, in the words of the Charter, they "shall be put out of the allegiance and protection." Now, two centuries had passed, and had produced many changes in the character of mankind, and he would not say that in all points which might now be in debate, the Rhode Island Charter ought to be implicitly and blindly imitated; but this he would say, that, looking to the constitutions given of late years to the colonies, the Acts they had passed, the difficulties that had followed, the millions paid from the Imperial Exchequer for the suppression of insurrections and for the maintenance of wars with savages, the worrying processes to which colonists had been subjected, the complaints on all sides of the deteriorated tone of society in many of the dependencies, the reluctance, once universal, and still somewhat prevalent, of educated and superior men to cast their lot and make their home in the colonies—noticing all this, and remembering that 200 years ago, a system conceived in another spirit was carried out by their forefathers, they surely could not draw the comparison—he should rather say the contrast—without a blush upon their faces.

Having thus reviewed the general aspects of colonial policy, Mr Gladstone proceeded to address himself to the particular Bill before the House for the better government of New Zealand. On the whole, the Bill was, in his opinion, creditable to Her Majesty's Government, not because it went back to the system generally represented by the Rhode Island Charter, but because it indicated a real intention to approximate to that system, and conceded a larger measure of freedom than had hitherto been given under Parliamentary enactment to any of the colonies. His hon. friend, the Member for Southwark, had complained of the Bill as recognising too much the political existence of the local settlements, and had suggested that it should be left to the central legislature to create local political authorities, according to the dictates of expediency. On the contrary, he must say, notwithstanding his respect for the authority of Sir William Molesworth, and general concurrence in the views of his hon. friend on colonial policy, that he thought the recognition of these local settlements one of the most excellent features of the Bill. One of the characteristics of modern legislation, as far as the colonies were concerned, had been its arbitrary character. They, in the Imperial Parliament, had endeavoured to draw lines for themselves instead of following those which nature and subsisting circumstances had marked out for them. It was, in his opinion, a mistake to suppose that a large amount of population was required to constitute a self-governing political society. The right hon. gentleman, the Secretary for the Colonies, had said—here are six settlements, the inhabitants of which are united by proximity to one another, by common pursuits and relations, in a great degree by common ideas, and a common industry and trade, but generally separated from one another by wide intervals of space. Well, there was—if he might so call it—the social unit, and the right hon. gentleman had recognised it, and had departed from the modern traditions of colonial policy by granting a considerable share of political power to those small communities, working independently one of the other. In this arrangement he was glad to find a protest against those attempts to centralise by law where there was no sufficient attraction to a natural centre, which could only produce weakness and dissatisfaction. When he considered how well an opposite system had worked in North America, when he considered how much of the character of the Union, and its stability, depended on the strict division into States, and the rigid maintenance of their separate authority and jurisdiction, he did not hesitate to say that the recognition of these small communities in New Zealand, which were to have a substantive political existence of their own, while, at the same time, they were associated together for other more general purposes, was, in his view, one of the fundamental merits of the Bill, and promised, nay, constituted a real advance in the spirit of British colonial policy.

He came now to the passing of laws, and he observed with satisfaction that the right hon. gentleman had introduced the thin end of the wedge, although it was a very thin end indeed, to relax, and finally, as he hoped, to break up the present system. It was now for the first time proposed by a Minister that Bills might be passed by a Colonial Legislature, and might finally pass into law without being subject to what was termed the veto at home. The district legislatures of New Zealand were to be empowered to make laws upon all subjects, with certain specified exceptions. These Acts were to be liable to veto only from the Governor of New Zealand, and although an unduly prolonged period of time was assigned him for the exercise of that power, yet in principle the concession was important, for, if that officer should not think fit, these measures would never be heard of in Downing Street as subjects for deliberation at all. Now, this was a matter in which much care and consideration were requisite, and the ground had to be carefully measured and ascertained before going to the extreme length which on general principles might be thought desirable; but, keeping those principles in view, he thanked the right hon. gentleman for the qualified recognition of them by the provisions of the Bill.

Another valuable feature of the measure was the arrangement proposed with regard to the composition of the smaller or district legislatures. Here, again, the right hon. gentleman had had the courage to burst the bonds of another most mischievous modern superstition—he meant the superstition which prescribed that a certain number of nominees should be introduced into the legislative constitutions of the colonies, in order to maintain what was called the just influence of the Crown. The right hon. gentleman had provided that in the district legislatures there should be only one house or chamber. This he so far regretted, that he would have preferred a plan based upon the old distribution into the two orders of assistants and freemen, but as there was to be only one chamber, he was heartily glad that there were to be no nominees in it. No Crown influence was to be cherished by such spurious means; election, and election only, was to prevail; and the Secretary of State had delivered himself and them from the idea, which had sat upon them in former times like a nightmare, that a colonial constitution could not work without an infusion of nominated members—a device that, so far as he could perceive, had no purpose except that of sowing and perpetuating dissension.

The right hon. gentleman had, moreover, made another step in advance, a step much in accordance with the old spirit by which the first British colonies were guided, in proposing to hand over, with certain restrictions, the control of their own land to the colonists. Now, this he took to be no small merit in the Bill, especially when he reminded the House that two years previously, when they were invited to legislate for New South Wales, it was in vain that some Members urged upon the Government and upon Parliament the necessity and the equity of doing the same thing. The Bill gave to the colonists of New Zealand that right of dealing with their own lands which was refused in 1850 to the more mature and powerful colony of New South Wales, and, although the boon was clogged with objectionable conditions, yet by it the right hon. gentleman showed that in principle he was willing to assent to the demand made by the colonists in regard to this weighty particular.

Mr Gladstone then proceeded to discuss a variety of details of the Bill, once more citing the example and authority of the United States, which he described as "the great source of experimental instruction, so far as the colonies are concerned." Against the proposal to make the Upper House or Legislative Council of the Central Parliament of New Zealand a body of nominees, Mr Gladstone entered an earnest and eloquent protest. In this important particular, he said, the plan of the present Colonial Secretary differed, and he must say greatly degenerated, from the plan of Lord Grey. Having had the misfortune frequently to differ from that noble lord on questions of colonial policy, it was with the greatest pleasure that he acknowledged the excellence of his plan in this particular respect. Lord Grey's intention was that the Legislative Council should be composed of persons elected by the district legislatures. It was quite plain whence he had derived that hint. It was from the United States of America, and, in going to the constitution of the United States to draw hints and suggestions for the improvement of modern colonial institutions, Lord Grey had resorted to the very best fountain of instruction founded upon experience. If there was one thing in the constitution of the United States which more than others entitled the great authors of that astonishing work to the gratitude of their countrymen, and to fame as wide and lasting as the world, it was the system which they had devised for the election of the Senate, which, proceeding on the principle of providing for the election of Senators from separate States, each considered as a unit and all as equal, established a check on the power of mere numbers or pure popular election. In practice it had been found most difficult to work the system of nominated legislative councils in the colonies, and, as regards political principle and opinion, it was the party favourable to stability which was endeavouring to get rid of those nominated bodies, and to substitute elective councils in their place. The real truth was that they had here another of those vulgar superstitions, which it was necessary to protest against from year to year, until they became effectually and utterly exploded—the superstition which induced men to believe that it was right to have a body of legislators in the colonies appointed by the Crown for the purpose of checking the free action of popular sympathies. If it were true that the home country had a set of interests distinct from the interests of the colony in respect to its local affairs, the Imperial Parliament would be acting on a sound and right principle in making provision for the separate and independent maintenance of those interests. But it was not so. The Mother Country had no conceivable interest apart from those of the colonies. What served their purpose best served its purpose best. The notion of setting up a body of men by nomination who were to be representatives of the interests of the home country, which were no interests at all, was a most gross and serious error, not merely one of those idle errors that lay by in the lumber-room and did no good and no harm, but an error full of practical mischief, and tending to keep up that intermeddling in the local concerns of the colonies, which was so prolific of weakness to the Mother Country, and of vexation to her colonial children.

Another point to which he must refer had relation to the New Zealand Company. An hon. member had spoken of the disinterested conduct of that Company, and he did not at all question that patriotic motives had governed the gentlemen who formed its directorate. But he must confess that for colonial purposes, when companies of this nature got beyond the purely commercial business of bringing the capital of the old country into contact with the soil of the new, he looked upon them with ineradicable jealousy. So long ago as the time of Adam Smith, they had acquired the ill repute of being the greatest obstacles to the well-being of colonies. They had one most unfortunate instance of this in the case of the Hudson's Bay Company, which spread a death-like shade over a large region of North America. He objected altogether to the management at home of the local affairs of colonies such as they now had in view, but if they were to have government from home, let it be the Queen's Government, let it be the Government on that Treasury bench, the Government they could face and interrogate, with which they could argue, and whose errors they could expose and condemn; but as to companies of this kind, which fell into the hands of irresponsible individuals, into which necessarily a narrow spirit crept, and a spirit that gradually became more and more narrow, he certainly looked upon them with the greatest jealousy when once they got beyond that which he had ventured to characterise as their proper sphere. No doubt there might be exceptions, and the New Zealand Company might be one of these. He certainly did not mean to draw a comparison between it and the Hudson's

Bay Company, but he maintained that too much of territorial power and of political relation had belonged to it.

The right hon. gentleman, the Secretary of State, had thought fit, following the traditions of his department in this particular instance, that the settlers in New Zealand, composed of Englishmen and natives as intelligent as Britons at home—that each one of the six districts of the colony should be governed by a Superintendent, who was not to be elected, but who was to be nominated by the Governor of New Zealand, and that this functionary should have provided for him, by the parental care of the Home Government, a salary of £500 per annum. Now, he would respectfully suggest that if they could get rid both of the nomination and the salary, it would be a great improvement in the Bill. From what source was it that political appointments derived their attractiveness and honour? He had the distinction of sitting in an assembly of 600 gentlemen who gave their laborious services to the country without fee or reward. They had, again, in the service of the State a great multitude of salaried offices; yet no man could say that these salaried offices, many of them bringing distinction as well as emolument, were coveted more than a seat in the House of Commons. Why was such a seat, with the heavy burden of duties attached to it, so coveted? Because every seat in the House of Commons was a mark of the confidence of a portion of their fellow-countrymen. That confidence stood instead of money, and it did the work of money better than money itself could do. If these New Zealand communities were allowed to choose out from among themselves those whom they believed to be the best men, it would be found, without undertaking to provide a salary of £500 a year, that the office would become the object of honourable competition. It would be, in addition, he ventured to predict, the means of making the colony attractive in a degree far greater than at present, and of drawing from England to New Zealand men of a different class, men of a higher class than could ever be got to go in numbers to any of the colonies until the colonies were stamped with the same broad, and deep, and indelible character of freedom, which had been marked upon all their home institutions.

Sir John Pakington, the Secretary of State for the Colonies, followed Mr Gladstone in the debate, and referred to the eloquence and ability of his speech, adding that he had listened to it with the greatest pleasure. At a subsequent stage, Sir John described Mr Gladstone's speech as "an essay upon our colonial system."

CHAPTER XVII

MR GLADSTONE AND THE COLONIES

THE maiden speech of Mr Gladstone in the House of Commons, delivered on May 17, 1833, was on a colonial subject. It was, in point of fact, a reply to an attack made on Mr Gladstone's father by Lord Howick, who had recently relinquished the post of Under-Secretary for the Colonies, in connection with the treatment of the slaves on the Gladstone estate in Demerara. "The noble Lord," said Mr Gladstone, "has attempted to impugn the character of the gentleman acting as manager of my father's estates, and in making this selection, he has certainly been most unfortunate, for there is not an individual in the colony more proverbial for humanity and the kind treatment of his slaves than Mr Maclean. That gentleman has acted in judicial capacities and has during his long residence been appointed to very important trusts. I hold in my hand two letters from Mr Maclean, in which that gentleman speaks in the kindest terms of the people under his charge; describes their state of happiness, content, and healthiness; and recommends certain additional comforts, which, he says, the slaves well deserve."

Mr Gladstone returned to the charge on June 3, and entered into a still more elaborate defence of the management of his father's sugar plantations in Demerara, but without convincing Lord Howick, who rose immediately afterwards, and said that he "saw nothing in the statements of the hon. member who had just sat down that would shake his former arguments. In Demerara there was a great temptation to exact an undue quantity of labour, and the slaves were fast perishing."

As Under-Secretary for the Colonies, Mr Gladstone introduced on March 19, 1835, a Bill of a very beneficent character for the improvement of the conditions under which emigrants were carried from England to new homes beyond the seas. He expressed a hope that there would be no opposition to the measure, as humanity and good feeling required some legislative enactment on the subject of emigration. The question involved was one of no small importance to the community. It was not necessary for him to impress upon the House that anything which affected the comfort of the thousands of emigrants who quitted their shores every year was worthy of their attention, especially when it was borne in mind that the class in question was the poorest in their midst. The provisions of his Bill were comparatively few, and he would give a brief outline of them to the House. In the first place, it was found that under the existing system, the emigrants, during the voyage and on their arrival, were subjected to a variety of restrictions and expenses which, as they were generally persons possessed of but small means, were in most cases destructive of their future prospects. That was one of the abuses which his Bill proposed to remedy. The next provision of the Bill would make it compulsory on owners and masters of vessels to retain emigrants, if the latter so desired, for forty-eight hours on board after the arrival of the ship. The reason for this provision was to be found in the expense and inconvenience which these poor people experienced on being thrust out like the beasts of the field into a strange place, without lodging or shelter. It was, therefore, most desirable that they should have the privilege of remaining on board the vessel for a period after their arrival. The Bill also proposed to limit the number of passengers on emigrant ships, and to increase the quantity of the food. It provided that every ship carrying upwards of one hundred passengers should have a surgeon on board, and that every craft carrying under that number should have a medicine chest. Next, the master would be responsible for the contracts entered into with emigrants by the accredited agents of owners, because much misery had recently resulted from a non-fulfilment of contracts by agents in some of the out-ports. It was but justice to these poor people that the owners should be responsible for the acts of their agents, and the master was the individual most accessible in a distant port, or even at home. It was finally proposed to make the penalties inflicted by the Bill recoverable by summary process, before two magistrates, either in England or any of the British colonies. The Bill passed into law before the close of the session without encountering much opposition.

The first speech of Mr Gladstone on a colonial subject, fully reported in *Hansard*, is one he delivered on March 8, 1837, in relation to the then disturbed condition of Lower Canada. At the outset of this speech, he took up the position that all colonies were to be regarded as children of the Mother Country. The most noteworthy passage in this speech was Mr Gladstone's statement that he did not think the separation of the colonies from the Mother Country was at all times, and under all circumstances, to be regarded with apprehension; but no one could look at the condition of Lower Canada at that moment, and not perceive that it was surrounded by difficulties which would make a separation from the Mother Country anything but advantageous to itself.

On the following December 22, there was another debate on the affairs of Canada, in the course of which Mr Gladstone acknowledged that he was not terrified at the prospect of separation. He did not think that the prosperity of England was dependent upon her connection with Canada. He was aware that there was an interchange of good offices and commercial advantages, but if any one were to look at the balance of the account, he would undoubtedly find that in point of commercial advantage, England gave more than she received. But that was not the question. The question was, whether in a country where no practical oppression had been proved to exist, where person and property had been secure, and would continue to be so but for the machinations of popular agitators, where the law was duly administered, where the taxes were mild or none at all, they were, for the sake and on the ground of speculative and organic changes which promised no advantage to the colonies, and which must prove utterly destructive of the analogy and the harmony which had existed between the Mother Country and the Canadians, to be terrified from maintaining that which they believed to be just on the first manifestation of the spirit of insurrection.

Mr Gladstone again intervened in a debate on Canadian affairs, which took place on January 23, 1838, in connection with the Papineau revolt. After discussing in detail the alleged grievances of the insurgent colonists, and demonstrating, as he thought, the hollowness of their pretences, Mr Gladstone alluded to a statement that was calculated to create an impression favourable to the justice of the rebel cause, viz. that the United States were prosperous and flourishing as an independent community, while the energies of Canada were crippled, her commerce fettered, and the development of her resources retarded by her connection with Great Britain. They were told of the rapid progress of the American colonies of Britain when emancipated from her sway, as compared with the slow rate of their advances before. He, indeed, believed that there was no more remarkable example in history of speedy advancement in all that constituted the greatness of a nation than was furnished by the career of the American colonies of Great Britain, now forming the United States. As one remarkable instance of their prosperity, he might mention that the duties collected at Philadelphia advanced in fifty years from £25,000 to £500,000. But the foundations of the power and grandeur to which these colonies had attained, were laid by the fostering care of Great Britain during the term of her dominion, and it was under British protection that their infant resources had been allowed to expand. The benefits which they had received from the rule of the parent State were thus described by Edmund Burke in his celebrated speech on American taxation:—

"Their monopolist happened to be one of the richest men in the world. By his immense capital, primarily employed not for their benefit but his own, they were enabled to proceed with their fisheries, their agriculture, their ship-building, and their trade, too, within the limits, in such a manner as got far the start of the slow languid operations of unassisted nature. This capital was a hot bed to them. Nothing in the history of mankind is like their progress. For my part, I never cast an eye on their flourishing commerce, and their cultivated and commodious life, but they seem to me rather ancient nations grown to perfection through a long series of fortunate events and a train of successful industry, accumulating wealth in many centuries, than the colonies of yesterday, than a set of miserable outcasts a few years ago, not so much sent as thrown out on the bleak and barren shore of a desolate wilderness, 3000 miles from all civilised intercourse."

Surely it stood to reason, Mr Gladstone proceeded, that in the infancy of a country it was far better that it should be connected with an old nation where capital existed in abundance, where the habits of men had been matured by the influence of long-established civilisation, and the resources of social life had been fully called into action, than that it should be left to itself to struggle unaided with the difficulties inseparable from an early stage of society. Such had been the case of Canada, and what was the real rate of her progress which had been represented as so slow? If compared with the United States, its advance in prosperity was found to be even more rapid. In 1775 the population of Canada was but 60,000. It now amounted to 600,000, having been multiplied tenfold since that year. At the commencement of the American war, the population of the United States was 2,500,000, and it now amounted to 15,000,000, having increased sixfold. How did these facts agree with the statements of the advocates of the insurgents, who attempted to persuade the world that Canada had made no progress, and had derived no benefits from its connection with the Mother Country?

On July 10, 1838, Mr Gladstone rose to call attention to a petition he had presented from the inhabitants of Albany in the Cape Colony. Albany had been founded as a frontier post for the protection of the colony against the predatory incursions of the Kaffir tribes. The tract of country inhabited by these advanced colonists had received additions from time to time, and was denominated the ceded territory. It was peopled by British subjects of an honest and industrious character, who had conveyed thither their skill and capital during the administration of Lord Charles Somerset, and had remained there on the faith of receiving protection and support from the British Government. The colonists complained that faith had not been kept with them, and made various representations of the losses they had sustained from being in immediate contact with a barbarous enemy. These representations had been neglected by the Home Government, and the interests of the colonists had been sacrificed, so much so that the ceded territory had been entirely given up to the Kaffirs, who now mingled with the farmers to the great prejudice and injury of the quiet and peaceable subjects of Great Britain. Feuds and contests were of frequent occurrence, sometimes attended by bloodshed and consequences of the most lamentable character. The feeling of insecurity thus generated amongst the colonists caused many of them, and particularly the Dutch Boers, to emigrate. The resources of the colony were thus left without employment, and a great part of the land remained uncultivated. Agricultural produce had greatly risen in price, and in the case of the great staple of corn and meal, to the extent of 300 per cent. Fatal collisions with the natives were of constant occurrence. The Dutch Boers, disheartened by their misfortunes, had withdrawn from the colony into the desert, and placed themselves beyond the pale of society. Such was the precarious and unsafe position of the eastern portion of the South African territories of Great Britain, the evils attending which it was the bounden duty of Parliament to remove. Mr Gladstone, therefore, concluded by moving an address to Her Majesty, praying for the appointment of a commission of inquiry to investigate on the spot the past and present state of the relations of the colonists in the eastern part of the Cape of Good Hope with the Kaffir tribes, together with the best means of preventing a recurrence of the recent emigration of the population beyond the frontier.

Sir George Grey, on behalf of the Government, opposed the motion on the ground that an adequate inquiry had already been instituted, and steps taken to tranquillise the country. The troubles referred to had been largely due to the aggression of British subjects upon the aboriginal inhabitants, and their endeavours to extend their territory for selfish and interested purposes. The pretext for these enlargements of territory from year to year had been the presumed necessity of increasing the security and safety of the colonists by placing an intermediate territory between them and the Kaffir tribes. The result was aggression on the part of the colonists, often causeless and unprovoked, and on the part of the aborigines irruption and massacre. Bloodshed had followed this attempt at acquiring that to which the aggressors had no right, but measures had been taken by the Colonial Government to put a stop to such sanguinary conflicts.

On a division, Mr Gladstone's motion was defeated by a majority of nine.

One of the most important speeches of Mr Gladstone on colonial policy in general, and Canadian affairs in particular, was delivered in the House of Commons on May 29, 1840. He declared that the problem of the relations between the North American provinces and the Mother Country was one of the most difficult and delicate ever submitted to any legislature, because the question they would have to determine in a thousand various forms, and which would continually recur upon them, was this—in what manner, and how long, should they maintain a connection between societies which, though still politically one, yet were not socially one, but of which the original elements differed in many most important particulars? No one could look at the colonial laws respecting succession and the distribution of property, the habits and employments of the colonists, their feelings with regard to aristocracy, and the principles entertained respecting national religion throughout the North American provinces, and fail to see that there were great differences, original and inherent, in the elements out of which society was composed. These differences must render exceedingly difficult the regulation and the maintenance of the union between a country essentially aristocratic in its feelings and principles, as he believed England to be, and countries in which some of the elements of society certainly seemed to tend towards democracy as their final consummation and development. It seemed to him that the maintenance of the connection between the Mother Country and the colonies should be regarded rather as a matter of duty than one of advantage. He could understand much better the doctrine that there was a duty incumbent on Great Britain with respect to the colonies, than the doctrine of those who said that, upon the mere balance of advantages, or as a case of political necessity, the connection should be maintained. So long as they retained the colonies as receptacles for their surplus population, they remained under a strict obligation to provide for those who left their shores at least what semblance they could of British institutions, and a home as nearly as might be like that which the emigrants had left, and to which the emigrants, when they became colonists, continued to retain a fond attachment. Upon that ground, he would always be glad to see the Imperial Parliament inclined to make large sacrifices for the purpose of maintaining the colonies as long as the union with the Mother Country was approved of by the people of those colonies. But he conceived that nothing could be more ridiculous, nothing could be more mischievous, than to suppose that Great Britain had anything to gain by maintaining that union in opposition to the deliberate and permanent conviction of the people of the colonies themselves. Therefore he thought that it should be a cardinal principle of Imperial policy to regard the union between Great Britain and Canada as dependent upon the free will of both parties. He also thought it of great importance that it should become thoroughly known and understood by the loyal people of British North America that the Mother Country looked to them as fellow-labourers in the work of maintaining the present connection, that they must not leave Parliament in the position of a mere Imperial authority, imposing by force the yoke of British connection on a reluctant population, but that they must be active and cordial co-operators, understanding that it was their part to contribute at least as much to the perpetuation of the union as the Imperial Parliament could do on its part. It would be a great problem for the statesmanship of the future, when those growing societies would have attained to such a degree of maturity as to be truly fit for self-government, to fix upon the period when the connection with the parent State should be severed. Meanwhile, preserving a temperate and conciliatory policy, with united action in Parliament, establishing in particular a liberal system of government, making non-interference the rule and interference the exception, they should maintain at the same time with a firm hand the supremacy of the British Legislature, and its right to assert that supremacy, recognising the necessity of having an executive unity throughout all portions of the Empire, and consequently repudiating, as one of the shallowest of all possible delusions, the doctrine of responsible government as connected with the perpetuation of the union.

On April 27, 1841, Mr Gladstone took a prominent part in the inauguration of the Colonial Bishoprics Fund, at a numerously attended meeting, convened by the Archbishop of Canterbury, in Willis's Rooms. To Mr Gladstone, who spoke immediately after Archdeacon Manning (the destined Cardinal of the future), was entrusted the resolution:—
"That a fund be raised towards providing for the endowment of bishoprics in such of the foreign possessions of Great Britain as shall be determined upon by the Archbishops and Bishops of the United Church of England and Ireland." The proceedings of the day, he said, clearly proved that the members of the Church of England were prepared

and ready to move forward, under the united guidance of their rulers, with heart, wishes, and property in the undertaking on which they had embarked. It might be regarded by some as a principle that the increase of the colonies added to the wealth of the colonists, and that out of that increased wealth, they were bound to provide for their own spiritual necessities. But that was a fallacy which could not be too widely contradicted. The point to be taken into consideration was this. Persons went to a new colony having everything to gain, and it was a matter of years ere those who had emigrated were placed by their exertions in a position to bear any expenses beyond those which the absolute necessities of their families demanded. It was to provide for this intermediate period between their first settlement and the day when they reached a condition of comparative affluence which would enable them to contribute to the support of the Church, that the object of the present movement was directed. He would ask what was to become of their fellow-countrymen, whilst in that intermediate state, if something were not done for them? If the meeting desired to provide for the spiritual welfare of those of their fellow-countrymen who, from circumstances, were induced or compelled to resort to a colony, let all present come forward and aid the undertaking which was now presented to their support. Mr Gladstone emphasised the pecuniary advantages which Great Britain had derived from her colonies, and strongly urged that people at home were bound, out of their abundance, to do something to supply the spiritual wants of their countrymen beyond the seas, who had contributed so largely to the temporal benefits of the old country. At the close of the meeting, a subscription list, amounting to £23,000, was read. It included £2000 from Her Majesty the Queen Dowager; £10,000 from the Society for Promoting Christian Knowledge; £5000 from the Society for the Propagation of the Gospel; and £1000 from John Gladstone and Sons.

After the lapse of fifty years, during the greater part of which period he had held the office of treasurer, Mr Gladstone was happily spared to join in the celebration of the jubilee of the Colonial Bishoprics Fund, at another crowded meeting in St James's Hall, on the afternoon of June 19, 1891. He moved the first resolution, recognising the remarkable success which had attended the extension of the episcopate in the colonies of the Empire and the missions of the Anglican Church throughout the world. At the outset of a very striking and eloquent speech, he referred to the likelihood that he was the only person present that day who was also present at the inaugural meeting of the Fund in April, 1841. He certainly thought he was the only man—he would not say the only man living, but the only person living and also available for the occasion—who took part in the proceedings of that memorable meeting. This was a delicate allusion to Cardinal Manning, who had also survived the semi-century, but whose secession from the Church of England in the interim had effectually disqualified him from standing by the side of Mr Gladstone at the jubilee meeting, as he had done at the inaugural gathering in Willis's Rooms. Nevertheless, Mr Gladstone embraced the opportunity to pay a glowing tribute to the power and influence which the Archdeacon Manning of that early period had exercised over the minds and hearts of the assembled Churchmen in Willis's Rooms. He described Archdeacon Manning's speech on that occasion as sending a thrill of exaltation through the whole assembly, delivered as it was by a man of eminence, of known devotion to his work in his own sense, and one whose whole mind and heart were then given to the service of the Church of England. In a most striking and powerful speech, Archdeacon Manning delineated the condition of the English Church in the Colonial Empire of England. He pointed out upon how vast, how gigantic a scale Englishmen were occupying the waste places of the earth, and then he pointed to the scanty evidence which had been given of any care evinced by the Church of England for the propagation of the Gospel in those vast countries. He contrasted the meagreness and feebleness of their spiritual efforts with the wonderful, undying, untiring energies of the commercial powers and the spirit of emigration. He said the Church of England had now to make her choice between the temporal and the spiritual. She had to determine whether she would be the beast of burden, or whether she would be the evangelist of the world. That was a noble appeal and a noble challenge. The force of it was felt. It was taken up and duly answered, and Mr Gladstone added a hope that it would be answered again. If there were grounds for answering it then, when everything was in hope and expectation, much more were there grounds for enlisting in the same service now, when they had before them results which were not only satisfactory, but in their scale and nature, wonderful. He was there that day as an historical landmark. The fifty years which had elapsed since the meeting held under the auspices of Archbishop Howley and Bishop Blomfield, had produced events of the deepest interest, some of them calamitous, others happy and blessed, in their consequences to the Church of England and to the general cause of religion. In 1841 the colonial bishoprics were ten in number; in 1891 they numbered eighty-two. He would venture to say that if the most sanguine man among those who attended the meeting of April, 1841, had been asked to carry his glance forward fifty years into futurity, and form an estimate of what might, on reasonable grounds, be then achieved, he would not have thought of basing his calculations upon any result even nearly, even remotely approaching that which, by the blessing of God, had been actually attained. The Church at home had experienced within those fifty years an immense elevation, and no small part of that elevation was due to the heroic enthusiasm which attended the first efforts at the foundation of the Colonial Episcopate. Names such as those of Bishop Selwyn, Bishop Patteson, Bishop M'Kenzie, Bishop Armstrong, and Bishop Field were names than which none brighter were to be found in the annals of the Church of England or of the Church of Christ at large. Mr Gladstone then proceeded to illustrate in detail one of the great lessons which he conceived to be taught by the event of the day, and that was the vast resources unfolded in the principles of voluntary action within the Christian Church.

Mr Gladstone, addressing the House of Commons on March 22, 1850, on the Australian Colonies Government Bill, and arguing in favour of the creation of an elective Upper House in New South Wales, instead of a Chamber of Crown nominees, said what in his heart he desired to see was the closest possible imitation in our colonies of our own institutions at home. That was the principle which he had at heart. But they could only effect that object through the medium of the inclination of the colonists. To attempt to create a Crown influence—a British influence—to rally a British party, and to make attachment to Britain a watchword in political strife, instead of being, as it ought to be, the common quality of all Her Majesty's subjects in the colonies and at home; let them attempt to do this, and their policy would recoil upon themselves, and the consequence would be that the national movement of the popular mind in colonial communities would be allied to something of distaste for the introduction or the continuance of British institutions altogether.

In the course of the same speech, Mr Gladstone avowedly contemplated the eventual separation of the colonies from the Mother Country, and their erection into independent States. The school of political thought, which identified itself with this theory, and which came to be colloquially known as the Manchester School, was at that time an active and influential force in English public life, but it has been practically extinguished by the rapid rise and the remarkable development of the Imperialistic ideal and the cementing principle of National unity during the past twenty-five years. Mr Gladstone asked the House of Commons to remember the lessons taught by the American Revolution. They should look to the time which might arise when the colonies would assert, he hoped with every regard and affection to the Mother Country, that they were then suited by Providence for the management of their own affairs. Difficulties might attend the crisis, and modern history did not furnish them with instances of a mother country allowing her colonies to declare themselves independent. He was not very sanguine for the future, but when these new States came to be launched into the world, it was of the greatest importance that they should have amongst themselves the elements of good institutions. In the United States, foolish and wicked as in other respects the conduct of this country might have been, England founded good institutions, and the people were now rewarded with the results.

Mr Gladstone on this occasion was one of a minority of 147 that voted against the principle of nomineeism.

At an earlier stage of the discussion on this Bill, Mr Gladstone said he did not like the idea of gathering together a fixed body of gentlemen, who were to be placed in the face of the elected members—not distinguished persons placed there because they were the most distinguished characters in the colony, or who had received nomination as the reward of efficient public service. There was none of the grace or dignity attaching to their position which attached to appointments to the House of Lords, where they had the most eminent men of their professions, great warriors, and those who had distinguished themselves in their various lines of life. On the contrary, they were put there by the influence of the Crown to check and control the actions of the elected members of the popular assembly. The appointment of these men involved a fundamental and a vital error. It proceeded upon the supposition that the Crown had something to defend, which the popular assembly was likely to attack; it proceeded upon the supposition that the Crown had a set of interests in the colony opposed to those of the colonists, which tended to the creation of a sect or party in the colony. He did not deny that the gentlemen so nominated were sincerely loyal, but in his opinion it was most dangerous to do anything that might tend to create a feeling of sect or party in the colony. They should endeavour to make the whole colony one British party. The best course to pursue, in order to obtain that desirable end, would be to leave the colonists to themselves—leave them to the management of their own affairs, show nothing like a feeling of jealousy or distrust of them, nor endeavour to press upon them institutions which appeared to show that this country had separate interests and separate objects in view, for which it was thought necessary to appoint special means of defence.

On the third reading of the Bill, Mr Gladstone made a lengthy speech, in the course of which he pronounced strongly against the retention of the Imperial veto on colonial legislation. This right of veto still exists in theory, and Governors are instructed to reserve for the Queen's pleasure any colonial legislation that seems to them to be in direct antagonism to Imperial interests and Imperial precedents, but it has practically fallen into desuetude during recent years so far as the great self-governing colonies are concerned. At the time Mr Gladstone spoke, it was in full strength and in general operation. He said that up to a recent period he had been deluded with the idea of the utility of the veto, but subsequent reflection had satisfied him that it ought not to be retained. It was the reason why they had at present the whole responsibility of the internal Government of the colonies, and were burdened with the whole extravagant expenditure which flowed from that responsibility—an expenditure which would never be diminished until more rational ideas were entertained of freeing themselves from responsibility in colonial affairs, and he feared it would be long before rational ideas were adopted on this head, if they allowed the present opportunity to pass of giving their fellow-subjects, who were admitted to be quite prepared for the reception of representative institutions, the right of managing their own local affairs. What was the reason for maintaining the Imperial veto on the laws of the colonies? Had it the advantage of securing a uniform system of law throughout the Empire? No such thing, because laws had been passed in several British colonies, which were in many cases at variance with the British law. But if it did not secure uniformity, what did it do? It made law for a considerable period uncertain, thus detracting from the authority of the colonial legislatures, because often a period elapsed of from twelve to eighteen months, and even of two years, between the passing of a law and the obtaining the sanction of the Crown. Until that sanction was obtained, no man could tell whether it was law or not. Surely that was an evil of a very serious kind. Further, it had the effect of lowering the colonial tone, for it was adverse to the cherishing of habits of freedom and self-dependence. There were in all colonies many citizens, the most valuable often for wealth and intelligence, who were at all times too ready to withdraw from public affairs, and that was a tendency which the measure before the House would foster and encourage, because those individuals who were fond of their personal ease would abstain from interfering in the management of colonial affairs when they knew that the Imperial authorities would revise the proceedings of their local legislature, and they therefore trusted to the Imperial Parliament to prevent any flagrant measure from passing. The rights of freemen could never be separated from the responsibilities of freemen, and the rights of freemen could never be taken away without taking their responsibilities also. They would never have had that masculine tone in the American colonies, which actually grew up there, if this system of legislation had prevailed in the seventeenth century. Let them give the colonies those benefits in reality which they professed to give, and let the colonists take the responsibility of framing the details of their own laws.

Mr Gladstone's matured opinions in later life are not unfrequently in sharp contrast to the recorded sentiments of his earlier Parliamentary period. His ideas on colonial independence underwent a complete transformation, as is evidenced in the following extract from a speech delivered at Leeds on October 8, 1881 :—

"But, gentlemen, while I accord to our political opponents the full credit of a conscientious desire to maintain the glory of this Empire, I will say that if there is to be a controversy upon the subject, if we are called to descend into the arena and to argue the matter here or elsewhere, I say it is Liberal and not Conservative policy which has made England respected and England strong. Why, gentlemen, if the old Tory policy of governing the colonies in Downing Street had been maintained, where would those colonies now have been? They would have been by this time groups of independent States. But Liberal policy freely granted to the colonists, in spite of Tory censure, the very same rights that we claim for ourselves in the management of our affairs, and the consequence is, that the inhabitants of those colonies are closely and cordially attached to the name and the Throne of this country, and that, perhaps, if a day of difficulty and danger should arise—which God forbid—from their affection we may obtain assistance and advantage that compulsion never would have wrung from them, and may find that all portions of the British Empire have one common heart, beating with one common pulsation, and equally devoted to the honour and the interests of their common country."

At the present time it would be considered strange, incongruous, and possibly unconstitutional if a British colony avowedly had a paid political agent sitting in the House of Commons and representing its interests, but during the fourth and fifth decades of the century, the fact of the Hon. Francis Scott, Member for Berwickshire, acting in that capacity for New South Wales, does not seem to have excited any particular comment or surprise. On April 16, 1849, Mr Scott initiated a long debate on colonial administration by moving:—

"That a select committee be appointed to enquire into the political and financial relations between Great Britain and her dependencies, with a view to reduce the charges on the British Treasury, and to enlarge the functions of the Colonial Legislatures."

In the course of his opening speech, Mr Scott made an incidental reference to Mr Gladstone's North Australian colony. A great subject of grievance, he said, and a great evil of their present colonial system, was the constantly changing policy in Downing Street. During the previous four years there had been four new Secretaries and four fresh Under-Secretaries in the Colonial Office. Latterly they had seen still greater changes in the office. The colonies not only changed their chief ruler every year or eighteen months, but that master changed his own mind every six weeks, and the orders sent to the colonies were revoked by himself before they could come into operation. For instance, the despatch affecting the social condition of Canada was sent out and revoked within a month. The constitution for New Zealand was sent out and revoked within a year. He would not further allude to the settlement established in North Australia, beyond observing that the Imperial Treasury had been saddled with £15,000 for that vagary. Transportation to Van Diemen's Land was adopted, then abandoned, then resumed, again abandoned, and since resumed in an altered form. A constitution which proved a misfit was sent out to New South Wales, and was now reported to have been only a sample, a pattern not meant for wear, and only sent out as a joke. He might add another of the same sort, which was sent out to the Cape, and which was equally as bad a fit, and of as little comfort to the intended wearer. He remembered hearing of Earl Grey sending shoes to the negroes and razors to men who had no beards; but this was worse, and such cup-and-ball practice, such battledore-and-shuttlecock play was but poor fun for the unfortunate colonies.

Mr Hawes, the Under-Secretary for the Colonies, made an elaborate speech in reply to Mr Scott, concluding by asking the question: Did they mean to surrender any portion of their Colonial Empire? If not, they must pay the price of maintaining that Empire. If they had colonies scattered over the globe, with their merchants and great mercantile interests in them, it was absolutely necessary to protect them. It was necessary that they should maintain the police of the seas. If they attempted materially to reduce their naval force, they would find their trade exposed to danger, and instead of being, as at present, carried on with perfect security and at a minimum risk to all parts of the globe, the risk would be appreciably increased. In a word, if they would have a colonial empire, they must protect it.

If they were prepared to say that the colonies must henceforth protect themselves, then, he would ask, what remained to attach these colonies to the Mother Country? He believed that the Colonial Empire had conferred great benefits upon the Mother Country, and he never wished to see that Empire impaired. The colonists were their fellow-subjects, united to them by the ties of blood and affection; they shared a noble inheritance, of which both were equally proud, and he hoped the day would never come when, from mere mercenary considerations, the Imperial Parliament would consent to weaken and diminish that Empire which their forefathers had won and bequeathed to them to be maintained with honour, justice, and liberality for the mutual benefit of the Mother Country and the colonies.

Mr Gladstone was the next speaker. He agreed with Mr Hawes that no good would arise from granting a committee to enquire into a subject so extensive and complicated. As one who desired to see the attention of the home country brought to bear with an increasing degree of interest on colonial subjects, he was unwilling to assent to a description of enquiry which would not lead to any searching investigation or to any practical result. He also agreed with Mr Hawes that much of the unpopularity which had come upon the Colonial Department attached to it, not on account of any views, or principles, or notions of its own which it had carried into execution, but on account of its having been the organ of Parliament and of the general views of the country. The public mind had been insufficiently exercised, and but partially enlightened on colonial policy. He furthermore agreed with Mr Hawes that no consideration of money ought to induce the House to sever the connection subsisting between any one of the colonies and the Mother Country, but there was a still more important consideration than that of money. It was how to give the greatest and most effective development to their colonial institutions. He thoroughly believed that a sound colonial policy had no tendency to separate the colonies from the Mother Country. Yet he did not think that the expenditure of large sums from the Imperial Treasury tended to strengthen or perpetuate the connection, and he did not hesitate to say that it was a mistake to propose the maintenance of the connection as the one and the sole end which ought to be kept in view. The work and function which Providence had assigned to Great Britain in laying the foundation of mighty States in different quarters of the world, was what ought to be kept steadily in view. Those infant communities ought to be cherished and fostered on principles that were sound and pure—on the principle of self-government—and if they did that, he was convinced that the political connection would subsist as long as it was good for either that it should subsist; and when it ceased, he hoped that the connection, instead of being severed in the midst of bloodshed, as was the case with the United States, would cease, by reason of the natural and acknowledged growth of those communities into States perfectly fitted for self-government and independence, and that, after the termination of the political connection, a community of feeling would still subsist in a similarity of laws and institutions, and in a close union of affection. This would be infinitely more valuable than any political connection with England.

Mr Gladstone then proceeded to enter a resolute protest against a doctrine enunciated by Mr Hawes, that the Imperial Parliament had no right to act upon any question which the legislature of a self-governing colony was engaged in discussing. He held that freedom was the principle on which their colonial policy ought to be founded, but, at the same time, that freedom should be confined to local affairs. Imperial questions it could not, and ought not to touch. With respect to local questions, he would yield to no man in the breadth with which he would assert that, in the fair and free working of a representative constitution, local questions must be left to its sole and entire disposal. But, in questions of Imperial concern, he claimed for himself, and for every Member of the Imperial Parliament, the right to raise his voice, either in the way of objection, inquiry, or discussion of whatever kind, with regard to any colonial proceeding in which he might conceive the interests of the Empire or the honour of the Crown to be involved.

Mr Gladstone admitted that it was a matter of great difficulty to introduce responsible government into the colonies, but he would like to raise the question whether it was a true or a fallacious principle that it was necessary to elevate the colonies to a certain height before they were considered fit for free institutions? He understood Mr Hawes to lay down the doctrine that free institutions would be given to the colonies as soon as they were fit for them, and to assert that most of the colonies were not yet fit for self-government. Setting aside the military posts, the colonies where there was a dominant race, and the colonies which were dependent upon the annual votes of the House of Commons, he could not understand why the other colonies, and especially the Anglo-Saxon colonies, should not be ready for the possession of free institutions, whether their population was large or small. He believed the principle of colonial self-government to possess an elastic force which, though small at present, would expand with the future necessities of the Empire. Had this principle been acted upon in the past, they would have escaped many of the difficulties by which they were environed. He held that they must disembarrass themselves of the fallacious notion that a colony was to be reared and fostered by a Government in Downing Street, that a colony must be raised to the extent of a population of 40,000 or 50,000, like Newfoundland, before it was fit for free institutions. That was the point on which the old colonial policy differed from the new. In founding the New England colonies, the Mother Country did not have the benefit of experience, but before twenty or thirty years had passed, most of these colonies had local self-government. They had it in its entirety when their population was only a few thousands —in some instances only a few hundreds—struggling on a bleak and wintry coast with all the difficulties of Nature, and with but a small hope of attaining that eminence which they had since attained. He did not say that the principle went to the same extent in all, but there were more than one in which even the office of Governor was elective, and in which colonial laws took effect without being submitted to the home country. The main question was, whether colonies should be governed by, and among themselves, or whether they should be governed by a Power separated from them by mighty oceans, not identified with them in feeling or in interest, and not possessed of that minute knowledge which would enable it to stimulate their powers into action, and develop the growth of their social and civil institutions.

Amongst the subsequent speakers were Mr Hume, the Member for Montrose, who strongly supported the motion, and complained that the colonies were not made as advantageous to the Mother Country as they might be, in the direction of absorbing the surplus population; Mr T. C. Anstey, the first gentleman from Australasia to secure a seat in the House of Commons, who characterised the Colonial Office as a great public nuisance, a decided mischief, and the common enemy of the colonies; Sir William Molesworth, who declared that war, rebellion, recurrent distress, dissatisfaction, and extravagant expenditure had been the most striking consequences of their present colonial policy; and Colonel Blackall, afterwards the second Governor of Queensland, who advocated the concession of representative government to the colonies, and urged that they should be treated as children of the Mother Country.

On a division, Mr Scott's motion was defeated by a majority of forty-seven.

On the following June 26, there was a second full-dress debate on colonial policy, arising out of a motion of Sir William Molesworth, that an humble address be presented to Her Majesty, praying for the appointment of a Commission of Enquiry into the administration of the colonies. Sir William delivered a powerful, exhaustive, and well-informed speech, occupying no less than thirty-three columns of *Hansard*, and Mr Hume, in seconding the motion, excused his brevity on the substantial and sufficient ground that "the Hon. Baronet had completely exhausted the subject." Mr Hawes, the Under-Secretary for the Colonies, opposed the motion as "perfectly impracticable and illusory." Mr Gladstone supported it in a lengthy speech, and voted with the minority in its favour. He agreed with Mr Hawes that if the object of the motion was to institute a minute enquiry into colonial administration, and into the abuses or grievances of which the colonies might complain, the House would commit a grave error if it were to address Her Majesty on the subject. But if he understood the question aright, the object of Sir William Molesworth was, not to fasten charges on those who administered the Colonies either in England or elsewhere, but to come to some rule and principle as to the future administration of their Colonial Empire. It appeared to him that instead of resting satisfied with leaving the question in the hands of the Government, they ought to consider whether they should not call in some other mode of enquiring into colonial matters, in order to endeavour to perfect their principles and policy. He thought the time had arrived when such an enquiry ought to be instituted, and looking to the scope of the motion, rather than to its particular wording, he must say he thought the time had arrived when they should make the attempt. The Colonial Department had the conduct of correspondence with countries situated in every quarter of the globe, and from the frequent changes of Ministry which took place under the British constitutional system, before a despatch was answered, a new Ministry might be in office. Then there was the further difficulty with which the Colonial Minister had to contend in a greater degree than other departments, that in nine cases out of ten it was impossible for him to draw the attention of Parliament to colonial questions. He said nine out of ten cases, because in the tenth, the attention of Parliament was obtained, on account of party spirit, to certain colonial questions; but, in that case, the consideration of the question was embittered by party spirit. If there were the same facility for drawing the attention of the House to colonial business, which there was with reference to matters connected with the Home Department, then things would be different; and it was this consideration which had brought him to the conclusion that upon the whole it was his duty, although he knew how objectionable commissions generally were, to support the motion. He would show that there were cases in which the labours of such a commission might be of service. In the first place, it would be most useful that a body of well-selected gentlemen should consider what were the general rules that should be followed in the establishment of new colonies. As a case in point, there was the proposal to establish a new settlement in North Australia, and after £15,000 had been expended upon the enterprise, Earl Grey came into office, and, considering that it was not expedient to go on with this settlement, the project was abandoned in consequence. There should be some reform adopted for binding a decision when arrived at, and that would give Parliament a voice in the question.

Another material point demanding consideration and enquiry was whether the system of military defence carried on in the colonies was not needlessly expensive. There was the case of the Cape of Good Hope and the Kaffir war, where a million and a half of money was virtually spent, or the obligation to pay it contracted, before the Imperial Parliament heard a word on the subject. He was sorry to hear the Under-Secretary speak with so much disparagement of the former colonial system before the independence of the United States, for such was the spirit of freedom in the then British colonies in North America, and such the colonists' sense of competency not only to govern but defend themselves, that they were not, as the Under-Secretary said the colonists were now, perpetually besieging the Imperial Parliament with demands for more troops and ships of war, and with complaints when the troops and ships of war were withdrawn; but with them it was a question of jealousy to have to provide for the permanent maintenance of British troops within the colonies, because they held that they were able to protect themselves. The relation between the colonists and the aborigines with respect to boundaries was another proper subject for examination by a commission. In this matter there had been instances of vacillation and change, of capricious change, having no reference to reason, but merely to accidental circumstances, which were most discreditable. Take the case of the Cape. Some years ago a coercive policy was enforced, and it was resolved to effect the repression of the Kaffir tribes with a strong hand. In 1835, philanthropy was at high-water mark, and the Colonial Office was obliged to give in to those who wished to go the greatest length in favour of the aborigines. The consequence was that the stringent system was given up and a great portion of territory abandoned. What was now the case? For some years philanthropy had been at low-water mark, and very short work had been made of the Kaffirs; the policy of territorial aggrandisement had been pursued to an extent exceeding all example, and they had not only undone all they did when they gave up the ceded territory, but they had made enormous additions to it. Upon the whole, he was satisfied that a carefully appointed commission would be a most material aid and assistance in the discharge of the duties of the government of the colonies. He hoped all parties had the same end in view. What they had to look at was the good alike of the Mother Country and her colonies. If they directed their minds steadily to the promotion of the good of the colonies and of the people of the home country in relation thereto, they need not fear for the permanence of the connection. On the contrary, he believed that would be the way to maintain the connection, and to maintain that which he believed to be even more important than the mere political connection, namely, the love of the colonies for the home country and a desire to imitate the laws and institutions of the great country from which they sprang.

Mr Labouchere (afterwards Lord Taunton), the uncle of the Mr Labouchere of to-day, and himself a Colonial Secretary of the early future, followed Mr Gladstone, and declined to support what was practically a vote of censure upon the whole colonial policy of the British Empire. Mr Adderley could see no reason for refusing the commission asked for in the motion. Lord John Russell wound up the debate, and expressed his surprise that a gentleman so conversant with Parliamentary business as Mr Gladstone should entertain the Utopian idea that, by selecting five persons from various quarters of the House, with one to superintend and arbitrate amongst them, some certain and infallible rule of wisdom in colonial matters would be obtained. The best thing the House could do with regard to colonial policy was to enlarge the freedom of the colonies, and give them greater power for governing themselves.

On a division, 89 voted for Sir William Molesworth's motion, and 163 against it.

That now familiar and flourishing organisation in Northumberland Avenue, the Royal Colonial Institute, represents the growth, expansion, and legitimate development of a movement initiated by a few thoughtful and far-seeing colonists, who met at Willis's Rooms on June 26, 1868, and resolved to found a "Colonial Society." The inaugural dinner of the Society was held at the same place on March 10, 1869. Mr Gladstone, then Prime Minister, was present, and responded to the toast of "Her Majesty's Ministers." It was proposed by the chairman, Viscount Bury, M.P., who referred to Mr Gladstone as "the man who, distinguished among all his compeers by his eloquence and by his talents, stands foremost in the councils of our beloved Queen; a man of whom we can all be proud as a citizen of our common country, distant though some portions of that country may be; and though seas may roll between the place in which we are now assembled and the native homes of some who sit around me, yet we all claim with Mr Gladstone a common citizenship and a common allegiance to our Queen." In replying, Mr Gladstone recalled the fact that thirty-four years had passed since he first became a member of the staff of the Colonial Department, and twenty-three since he last held office in that Department. He adverted to those dates, not for the sake of gratifying an antiquarian curiosity, but for a different and worthier purpose. Looking back over those years, no one could fail to be struck with the great change for the better which had in the interval passed over the spirit of their colonial policy. In the days when he was accustomed to wear out with his footsteps the stairs of the Colonial Office, that office was haunted by a disembodied spirit which received a painful distinction under the title of "Mr Mother Country"; and while that description conveyed no inaccurate idea of the narrow traditions that then hung about the conceptions of English statesmen, on the other side of the water—in every British colony—there was a party which, he rejoiced to think, had since been totally extinguished, under the name of the "British Party." He spoke in the hearing of those who remembered the circumstances and the struggles of those times, when many in England were taught to believe that upon the "British Party," which invariably represented an insignificant minority, depended the whole hope of maintaining the connection between England and the colonies; and that if anything were done to offend the "British Party," or to recognise the vast majority of the colonial community as having a claim upon the sympathies and actions of their countrymen at home, such a policy was certain to be fatal to the Colonial Empire. That was a state of things so strange that to recall it now seemed like bringing back from the grave the spirits of the dead, so wholly was it without a representative in the condition of affairs which now existed. He rejoiced to see around that hospitable board the representatives of the entire British family. He rejoiced that a great branch— possibly the greatest branch—of that family was represented among them that evening by one who, though numerically but an individual, yet had in him a heart which beat warmly with the sympathies that belonged to the origin from which he derived his name and the traditions of his country, and who, in a manner inferior to none that had gone before him, was qualified to represent that spirit of brotherhood which ought to unite throughout the world the whole British race. This was a reference to Mr Reverdy Johnson, the then United States Minister in London, whose speech preceded Mr Gladstone's. In conclusion, Mr Gladstone said there was no degree of latitude or of longitude on the surface of the globe which had not offered its contribution to the gathering of that evening, and he rejoiced that the time had come when it was fully recognised that, while the affection between England and her colonies grew stronger and stronger, the nature of the relation between them was also better and better understood—a relation undoubtedly associated with great Imperial interests, but founded upon something higher and deeper than interest, founded upon honour and affection, and having above all for its basis the essential principle of freedom, a departure from which in the policy which governed the conduct of England towards her colonies would at once destroy both the charm and the value of the connection which subsisted between them. He was glad to think that the time had come when those facilities of communication, which now brought into neighbourhood the remotest quarters of the globe, enabled colonists in England to organise a society which would have the hope of quickening, by constant personal intercourse and sympathies, the relationship which ought to unite all the British colonies. Other clubs had in view the maintenance of a relation between friends and classes. The Colonial Society contemplated a nobler object, that of handing down from generation to generation the great and noble tradition of the unity of the British race.

A banquet was held on November 15, 1872, under the auspices of the Royal Colonial Institute, to celebrate the completion of telegraphic communication between England and Australia. The Earl of Kimberley, then Secretary of State for the Colonies, presided, and read the following letter from Mr Gladstone:—

10 DOWNING STREET,
WHITEHALL, *November* 13.

MY DEAR KIMBERLEY,—I write you a line to say how sincerely sorry I am that I am unable to attend the dinner to celebrate the opening of telegraphic communication with Australia. I should have been very glad, had it been possible, to be present on this occasion, when the strong attachment which now binds, as it has ever bound, the Australian colonies to the Mother Country, is cemented by the completion of so important and so useful a work. Well remembering the time when I had the honour of holding the office which you now so worthily fill, and when I was, as I could hardly fail to be, specially interested in the Australian colonies, I need hardly say how agreeable it would have been to me to meet some of those whose names are still fresh in my memory.

Believe me, sincerely yours,

W. E. GLADSTONE.

Taking as his text the words of Lord Beaconsfield on returning to London from the Berlin Conference, in July, 1878: "Gentlemen, we bring you peace, and peace with honour," Mr Gladstone contributed to the *Nineteenth Century* of the following September, a lengthy article on "England's Mission," in which he ventilated his more matured views on the subject of colonial expansion. The sentiment of empire, he wrote, may be called innate in every Briton. If there are exceptions, they are like those of men born blind or lame among us. It is part of our patrimony, born with our birth, dying only with our death, incorporating itself in the first elements of our knowledge, and interwoven with all our habits of mental action upon public affairs. It is a portion of our national stock, which has never been deficient, but which has more than once run to rank excess, and brought us to mischief accordingly—mischief that, for a time, we have weakly thought was ruin. In its normal action, it made for us the American colonies, the grandest monument ever erected by a people of modern times, and second only to the Greek colonisation in the whole history of the world. In its domineering excess, always under the name of British interests and British honour, it lost them by obstinacy and pride. Lord Chatham, who forbade us to tax, Mr Burke who forbade us to legislate for them, would have saved them. But they had to argue for a limitation of English power, and to meet the reproach of the political wise-acres who first blustered on our greatness, and then, when they reaped as they had sown, whined over our calamities. Undoubtedly, the peace of 1782-83, with its adjuncts in exasperated feeling, was a terrible dismemberment. But England was England still, and one of the damning signs of the politics of the school of Lord Beaconsfield is their total blindness to the fact that the central strength of England lies in England. They are the materialists of politics; their faith is in acres and in leagues, in sounding titles and long lists of territories. They forget that the entire future of the British Empire was reared and consolidated by the energies of a people which was (though it is not now) insignificant in numbers, when compared with the leading States of the Continent. Of all the opinions disparaging to England, there is not one which can lower her like that which teaches that the source of strength for this almost measureless body lies in its extremities, and not in the heart which has so long propelled the blood through all its regions, and in the brain which has bound and binds them into one.

In the sphere of personal life most men are misled through the medium of the dominant faculty of their nature. It is round that dominant faculty that folly and flattery are wont to buzz. They play upon vain-glory by exaggerating and commending what it does, and by piquing it on what it sees cause to forbear from doing. It is so with nations. For all of them the supreme want really is, to be warned against the indulgence of the dominant passion. The dominant passion of France was military glory. Twice in this century it has towered beyond what is allowed to man; and twice has paid the tremendous forfeit of opening to the foe the proudest capital in the world. The dominant passion of England is extended empire. It has heretofore been kept in check by the integrity and sagacity of her statesmen, who have not shrunk from teaching her the lessons of self-denial and self-restraint.

But a new race has arisen, and the most essential or the noblest among all the duties of government, the exercise of moral control over ambition and cupidity, has been left to the intermittent and feeble handling of those who do not govern.

With the Liberal Party, the great duty and honour and charge of our transmarine Colonial Empire is to rear up free congenital communities. They receive a minority of our emigrants, of whom the larger number go to the United States; but, in receiving this minority, they enlarge for our outgoing population the field of choice, and by keeping them within the Empire, diminish the shock and severance of change. It is felt at the same time that Great Britain has, against the merely material advantages of such possessions as British North America and the magnificent Australasian group, greatly enlarged her military responsibilities in time of war. Still, whatever be in these respects the just balance of the account, it is felt that the colonial relation involves far higher elements of consideration; that the founding of these free, growing, and vigorous communities has been a specific part of the work providentially assigned to Britain. The day has gone by when she would dream of compelling them by force to remain in political connection with her. But, on the other hand, she would never suffer them to be torn away from her; and would no more grudge the cost of defending them against such a consummation than the father of a family grudges the expense of the food necessary to maintain his children.

Mr Gladstone concluded the colonial section of his essay on "England's Mission" with a modified echo of his early opinions on the eventual destiny of the colonies. "With their opponents (he is referring to the Opposition to Lord Beaconsfield's Government) it is the welfare of these communities which forms the great object of interest and desire; and if the day should ever come, when in their own view that welfare would be best promoted by their administrative emancipation, then, and then only, the Liberal mind of England would at once say, 'Let them flourish to the uttermost; and if their highest welfare requires their severance, we prefer their amicable independence to their constrained subordination.' The substance of the relationship lies, not in despatches from Downing Street, but in the mutual affection, and the moral and social sympathies, which can only flourish between adult communities when they are on both sides free."

CHAPTER XVIII

A COUPLE OF COLONIAL LECTURES

HAVING regard to his surpassing qualifications as a speaker, the vast range of his reading, his personal magnetism, and wonderful powers of exposition and illustration, it is somewhat surprising that Mr Gladstone should have figured so rarely, in his long public life, in the capacity of a lecturer. No doubt, the explanation is that British statesmen of the first rank are more fettered by the unwritten laws of tradition and etiquette than American public men, who take to the lecturing platform like ducks to water. Still, Mr Gladstone has delivered avowed and advertised lectures in his time, although they have been but few and far between.

While on a visit to Hawarden Castle, then in the occupation of his relative, Sir Stephen Glynne, Mr Gladstone delivered a lecture in the boys' schoolroom of the village, on October 12, 1855, taking as his subject, "The Colonial Policy of England." The address was given at the request of a number of working men constituting the committee of the literary institute of the village. Charges of sixpence and a shilling were made for admission, and there was a crowded attendance.

The English artisan or labourer, said Mr Gladstone, in emigrating, looked to the interest of those over whom God had given him control. He saw in the far-off country a better prospect for his family, better remuneration for his own labour, more of the comforts of life within his reach, and he was thus willing to forego the pleasures of the present for the hopes of the future. Such were the men who were leaving the shores of England in such numbers each succeeding year. Many good, pious men advocated colonisation because it gave facilities and opportunities for conveying to the benighted and the ignorant a knowledge of the truths of the Gospel. Such a motive as that every Christian mind must respect, but it was to be feared that few emigrants left the shores of England impelled by such a motive. The most general influence which had operated in leading thousands to the auriferous shores of Australia would be found in the love of gold, a love which had always existed, and which not unfrequently led to bad as well as good results. There was something marvellous in this love of gold. Persons who could not be acted upon in any other way were often found most enthusiastic in the pursuit of the precious ore. The discovery of a gold mine excited the curiosity and the cupidity of thousands, while the discovery of an ironstone mine scarcely attracted attention at all, and yet the one was not more important than the other. An ironstone mine was as useful, and therefore proportionately as valuable. Without ironstone gold would lose much of its worth, because, while gold was only used as a representative of value, ironstone was the value itself, and the value of each was relative to the other. Yet the discovery of ironstone did not tickle people's fancy or desire like gold. Before the discovery of America by Columbus, there was an idea floating in the minds of philosophers that on the other side of the Atlantic there must be a continent of corresponding weight, which acted as a counterpoise, and kept the earth in equilibrium. The Spanish adventurers, who went out and took possession of that new world, found no gold mines, but they got what was infinitely better—a free soil, and room for active operations in commerce and trade. After describing "the follies and fallacies that kept our colonies poor and dependent, and made them a clog and a burden to England instead of a benefit and a blessing," Mr Gladstone enlarged on his favourite text of the wisdom of conceding to the colonies perfect freedom in all that appertained to their domestic concerns. Some, he said, had argued that, if the colonies were allowed to govern themselves, levy and collect their own revenue, they might be tempted to tax articles which were required in the home country as food, and which were now received in English ports almost duty free. The very selfishness of this idea made it ridiculous. As long as British merchants possessed the spirit of enterprise that had rendered them the glory of the country, they need be under no apprehension that the parent State would suffer, even though the colonists should levy taxes upon the articles of merchandise in which they dealt. The British merchant might always be trusted to find the cheapest and best markets, by using which his capital was alone made productive, and the interests of his country subserved. The moral benefits of colonisation arose out of the influence which attached to the spread of the English language, English habits, and English tastes over the distant parts of the world. To have the scions of English families planting themselves in the colonies, rearing their offspring, and extending the area occupied by the sturdy Anglo-Saxon race, was to increase the moral influence of Old England, and maintain, in a natural and legitimate manner, the prestige of her name. Although much diversity of opinion existed amongst all classes of contemporary politicians in reference to the colonies, yet all were inclining towards a more liberal and enlightened policy, and the spirit of prejudice which distinguished the latter end of the last century had given place to views, opinions, and sympathies which augured well for the future. They might hope, therefore, that the experiences of the past would be of use in the present, and that the future policy of England in regard to the colonies would be candid, honest, and wise; for it was only by a liberal and enlightened course of treatment that the parent country could reap the full advantage and benefit of her great territorial dependencies.

On Monday, November 12, 1855, Mr Gladstone delivered a second lecture on "Our Colonies" to the members of the Mechanics' Institute, Chester, and it was fully reported by the gentleman who is now Mr Justin M'Carthy, M.P., but who was then a young man on the staff of the *Northern*

Daily Times. Mr M'Carthy's report was revised by Mr Gladstone, and published with his permission as a pamphlet of twenty-one pages. At the outset, Mr Gladstone declared that he scarcely knew how to select, from the vast redundance which the subject offered, the limited amount of material that must suffice for a single address. The little word "colonies" included in itself ample matter for the most interesting discussion; so vast that even the minor branches of it had given occasion for the most important and interesting treatises in their distinct and separate forms. If, for example, he named such a question as the discovery of gold in Australia, such a question as the laws which governed and regulated emigration, such a question as the history of negro slavery and the means through which it had been brought to an end, such a question as the treatment of the aboriginal tribes inhabiting and bordering upon various British settlements, or, to name only one more, such a question as the great subject of the transportation of British criminals to distant British possessions—each one of these, apart from every other, was not only sufficient to occupy the utmost period which he could possibly ask that night from the indulgence of his hearers, but had been found sufficient to occupy nights upon nights, weeks upon weeks, and months upon months, of the thoughts of the ablest writers, and the discussions of both Houses of Parliament.

Entering on what he designated as "the rudest and the very slightest sketch of a subject so vast in its range," Mr Gladstone proceeded to point out that the great subject of the colonies of the British Empire had now come to constitute a question of the most just and legitimate interest to every Englishman, and amply justified the zeal and favour that were testified by the crowded attendance of that evening. In the middle of the last century the American Colonial Empire of England was, in simple and literal truth, the envy and admiration of the world. It was then thought that nothing had been seen for centuries upon centuries to compare with that Empire. And yet the American population, at the outbreak of the war of independence, amounted to only two millions of souls. What was the state of things now? Why, the single colony of Canada contained a population nearly equal to the whole of the thirteen American colonies of that time. Such was the magnitude and importance to which that Empire had attained. Again, there was scarcely any European language of note or importance which was not spoken in the colonies. The subjects of the Queen in Malta and the Ionian Islands spoke the beautiful languages of Italy and Greece. A considerable portion of the Canadians, the people of the populous island of Mauritius, the people of St Lucia and other West Indian Islands spoke the language of the great French nation. In British Guiana and at the Cape of Good Hope, Dutch was spoken. In the important colony of Trinidad, Spanish was the vernacular tongue. And thus the Queen of England, of an island which once was looked upon as a separated and remote extremity of the habitable globe, possessed an Empire under which were arrayed, not only barbarous tribes who spoke tongues almost innumerable, but communities who spoke the most cultivated, distinguished, and famous languages of highly civilised Europe.

Turning to the question of emigration, Mr Gladstone said it was formerly a matter of remote knowledge and concern, and even twenty or thirty years ago it was regarded only as a means of getting rid of the off-scourings of the population, but now it had become, on the contrary, a matter of close and domestic interest to many of the most intelligent, the best conditioned and most respected families in the country. In the year 1815, the entire number of emigrants who left the shores of England was 2000. In the fifteen years, from 1815 to 1830, the average emigration of England was 20,000. The average for the years between 1830 and 1844 rose from 20,000 to 80,000. During the next ten years it rose to 267,000, and in the year 1852 the sum total reached no less a number than 368,000 people, over 1000 persons thus quitting the shores of England every day to find a home in the British Colonial Empire. It would thus be seen that the increase in the quantity of the emigration was of a most remarkable character. The change in the quality was still more worthy of notice, because for a long time emigration was nothing but the resort of the most necessitous. Now, on the contrary, in a great many cases—many present that evening would be able to bear testimony to instances within their own domestic sphere or private knowledge—it was not the needy and the necessitous, but it was the most adventurous, the most enterprising, the most intelligent man, the most valuable member of society in the sphere in which he moved, who went to seek his fortune in those distant lands.

Mr Gladstone then entered into a minute discussion of the questions—Why was it desirable that England, or any other country, should possess colonies at all? And, assuming that such possession was desirable, in what manner should those colonies be founded and governed? The time was when these were treated as party questions, but he trusted and believed that that time had passed away, that the truths relating to this great subject were beginning to be generally acknowledged, and that the English people were thoroughly united as to the mode of fulfilling one of the highest functions which Providence seemed to have committed to their hands, namely, that of conducting the work of colonisation and peopling a great portion of the habitable globe. The vast colonisation of modern times, which took its course from eastward to westward across the Atlantic, must have been prompted by some powerful motive. What was that motive? It was the love of gold that drew forth from Italy, Spain, France, England, and Portugal those men whose bold and adventurous spirit tracked the stormy Atlantic, and founded successively, amidst dangers and difficulties indescribable, those colonies which had now grown into the great States of Northern and Southern America. They went to America in search of gold. They found no gold; but observe how, by the wise dispensations of Providence, the very delusions of mankind were made to serve their great interests. In North America there was no discovery of the precious metals worth naming, but there was a discovery of a great and powerful country, teeming with all the resources of nature, offering a home to mankind, and the most extended field for the development of human energy and industry in every branch.

Some had said, and more had thought, that colonies were to be founded for the sake of increasing and improving, by their direct contributions, the revenue of the Mother Country, and of this idea there were contemporary instances in the colonies of Spain, and also in some of the colonial possessions of Holland. But that had never been the view with which the work of British colonisation had been carried on. Others, again, had thought that it must be desirable to possess colonies, because colonies constituted a large addition to the territory of the country. Undoubtedly the possession of territory was valuable, provided a proper use was made of it, but it was not desirable for England or any other nation to possess an extent of territory without bounds and without reference to the power of turning it to account. Then, again, people had a notion that for the reputation of the country it was desirable to possess colonies. He did not deny that the possession of colonies did contribute to the just reputation of England, and add to its moral influence, power, and grandeur; but, if it was meant by this doctrine that it was desirable to have colonies in order to make a show in the world, with which there was no substance to correspond, that, they would all agree, was not a good reason for desiring an extension of a colonial empire. It never could be to the interest of England, or any other country, to be taken for more than it was worth. There was, again, a notion more vulgar than any of these, that it was desirable to possess colonies for the sake of the patronage they afforded to the Home Government. Many present were old enough to remember occasions when persons whom it was not convenient or decorous to provide for at home, had received appointments in the colonies. But of such cases he hoped there would be no recurrence.

An idea far more important, and effective to a far greater extent, was the theory that the colonies ought to be maintained for the purpose of establishing an exclusive trade, the whole profit of which should be confined to, and enjoyed by, the Mother Country. That was, in fact, the basis of the modern colonial system of Europe. Now, look at the effect of an idea of such a nature. When colonies were founded upon this principle, the Home Government acted as if the colony could only benefit one other country by its trade. It proceeded upon the false notion which was once at the bottom of the commercial laws of England, and which was still at the bottom of the commercial laws of many other nations; the notion that there could be any other basis whatever for trade except the benefit of both parties concerned; the idea that any trade was possible where all the gains were at one side; the idea, above all, that whatever was gained by one, was taken from the other. That was the great fallacy of the protective system, the system which prevailed still in many countries of Europe, the truth, on the contrary, with respect to trade being that when one man gained the other man must gain also. There was no possible mainspring of trade, except the benefit of both parties engaged in carrying it on.

Mr Gladstone repudiated any and all of those reasons for desiring the possession of colonies. Why, then, were colonies desirable? In his opinion, they were desirable both for the material and for the moral and social results which a wise system of colonisation was calculated to produce. As to the first, the effect of colonisation undoubtedly was to increase the trade and employment of the Mother Country. Take the case of the emigrant going across the Atlantic. Why did he go to America? Because he expected—and in general he was the best judge of his own interests—to get better wages across the Atlantic than he could get at home. If he went across the Atlantic to get better wages, he left in the labour market at home fewer persons than before, and consequently raised the rate of wages at home by carrying himself away from the competition with his fellows. By going to a colony and supplying it with labour, he likewise created a demand for capital there, and by that means created a trade between the colony and the Mother Country. The capital and labour thus employed in the colony raised and exported productions, for which commodities were wanted in return. Of those commodities a very large proportion was usually sought from the parent country, for it was almost always the case that a colony was founded under circumstances where the country to which the settlers went produced the very commodities which were wanted in the country they had left. Therefore, so far as trade and the gain connected with trade were concerned, it was perfectly obvious that the foundation of a colony, where it was the natural and spontaneous result of the circumstances in which a country was placed, was simply a great enlargement of the material resources of that country. There could be no doubt that the possession of colonies like those of England, which were peopled by the spontaneous operation of natural causes, or, in other words, by the free judgment of the people, each man carrying his labour or his capital to the market where he thought he might get the best price for either, was eminently beneficial, not because it created a more profitable trade than other trades, but because it created a perfectly new trade, and a trade which would not otherwise have existed.

The moral and social advantage of colonies was also a very great one. An increase of population was an increase of power, an increase of strength and stability to the State, because it multiplied the number of people living under good laws, and belonging to a country to which it was an honour and an advantage to belong. That was the great moral benefit that attended the foundation of British colonies. Theirs was a country blessed with laws and a constitution that were eminently beneficial to mankind, and that being so, what could be more desirable than that they should have the means of reproducing in different portions of the globe something as like as might be to the country which they honoured and revered. It was, he believed, in a work by Mr Roebuck that the expression was used, that "the object of colonisation is the creation of so many happy Englands." It was the reproduction of the image and likeness of England—the reproduction of a country in which liberty was reconciled with order, in which ancient institutions stood in harmony with popular freedom and a full recognition of popular rights, and in which religion and law had found one of their most favoured homes. And, as it was the destiny of man to live in society under laws and institutions, it was desirable that he should live under good laws and institutions; and it was because Britons were convinced that their constitution was a blessing to them, and would be a blessing to their posterity as it had been to their forefathers, that they were desirous of extending its influence, that it should not be confined within the narrow borders of one little island, but that, if it pleased Providence to create openings for them upon the broad fields of distant continents, they should avail themselves in reason and moderation of those openings to reproduce the copy of those laws and institutions, those habits and national characteristics which had made England so famous as she was.

Mr Gladstone then proceeded to discuss the practical question how colonies should be founded and governed. He eulogised and described in detail the ancient Greek system of colonisation and the "true spirit of British freedom" in which the first American colonies were established and administered. Touching upon the American war of independence, Mr Gladstone said that before England began the system of meddling and peddling in the affairs of her American colonies, the attachment of these colonies to the Mother Country was warm, strong, and affectionate, but when the British colonists in America saw a disposition to deprive them of their time-honoured hereditary privileges, when they saw that Englishmen, so jealous of their own liberties at home, were disposed to stint and narrow the enjoyment of such liberties by their brethren who had crossed the Atlantic, a bitterness of sentiment sprang up, and that bitterness was not the fault of the Americans; it was the unhappy result of the errors of British policy, and of the circumstances of the time. The unhappy consequence of this feeling, aggravated in the course of a long, bloody, and obstinate struggle, was that at the time when American independence was acknowledged, the affections of the Americans towards their mother-land had received a desperate blow. For a long time the name of Englishman was odious, and naturally odious, in America. The name of England was associated with oppression, and those among the Americans who were known to entertain a strong feeling of affection towards her were odious in the eyes of their fellow-countrymen. That temporary estrangement of feeling, which was then almost total, and which even now, notwithstanding the healing influence of time, had necessarily left some traces behind, was a part of the mighty price that England had paid for the error involved in a misconception of the right manner of governing her colonies, the error of attempting to levy taxes upon the people of America. Some people thought that that was not an error of the English people. Let there be no mistake on that head. If there was one thing in history more clear than another, it was that the English nation, at the beginning of the American war, were united almost to a man in the prosecution of that war. All wars, almost without an exception, had been popular in England during the first year, or even during the second and third, but the American war was especially popular in its earlier stages. The military organisation was all on the side of England, but it was not the want of success in the field that defeated England in the American war. It was this—that though they most commonly beat America in the field, they were no nearer than before to the subjugation of the country. They possessed the ground where the camps had been pitched, but they possessed nothing else. The enemy was in the heart of every man, woman, and child, and driving their soldiery out of the field did not establish the power of England in the hearts of a people who were fighting for their freedom. The case of the American war—considering how universally it was now admitted that a great error was committed in beginning and in continuing it—was one upon which Englishmen could look back with great advantage, for all generations and all times, as a most emphatic lesson of caution, circumspection, and moderation.

From 1783 to 1840 the idea was entertained that it was absolutely necessary that the local affairs of the colonies should be directed from a certain spot in the city of London. It was difficult to believe to what an extent this interference with the affairs of their fellow-colonists was carried. In the first place, it was thought that they in England should retain in their own hands, and on no account give the colonists the disposal of the unoccupied lands of the colonies. Then it was thought that, in addition to the taxes raised by the colonists themselves to support the Colonial Government, there should be another set of revenues, called Crown revenues, to provide for the contingency that the people of the colony might be so ignorant and barbarous as to make no provision for the very first necessities of their own Government. The next step was to keep standing armies in the colonies to discharge the functions of police, the consequence of which was enormous expense to the Mother Country, and the greatest mischief to the discipline of the army, the troops being parcelled out here, there, and everywhere in such small bodies that they lost the unity of action which an army acquired by being trained and disciplined in masses. Another mistake in practice was that of requiring the people of the colonies to establish a civil list, a certain range of salaries for Governors, Judges, Secretaries, and other public officers. Did the Home Government suppose that the colonists themselves did not recognise the necessity of law and order? Another faulty rule was the establishment for each colony of a certain tariff of differential duties, the Mother Country thus dictating by means of commercial laws the price to be paid for commodities coming to the colonies from any quarter of the globe. The North American was thus compelled to pay an extra price for West Indian sugar, and he was compensated in turn by making the West Indian pay an additional price for North American wood; so that instead of the commercial interchange being made a blessing or a benefit, it was made an interchange of evils and reciprocal inflictions. Lastly, it was the custom to exercise patronage in the colonies as far as could be safely ventured, and whenever there were people who were not quite presentable at home, whom the English would not quietly endure to see appointed to office in their own country, it was commonly thought they were quite good enough to hold office, often with a handsome salary, in some remote colony.

The general effect of this system of governing the colonies from Downing Street decidedly tended to alienate the hearts of the colonists from the Mother Country. It led to a knot of people in each colony combining together and calling themselves the British Party. They were always extremely loud in their professions of zeal in support of the executive, and they generally had one or more newspapers behind them. The rest of the community were deemed anti-British, and thus the name that ought to have been the dearest of all names to every colonist, became the arbitrary distinction of the few, as opposed to the mass of the community. On the one side was the Governor, with a little body of official persons, and another little body of individuals picked out of the community. These were tugging one way, supported by the power of the British Government, and on the other side was tugging the whole mass of the colonial population. Happily, all that was now changed. The principle was now fully recognised that the local affairs of the free colonies should be fully managed by the colonists themselves. And, in this connection, Mr Gladstone said he wished to discharge a debt of justice. There were some men in England who had undoubtedly proceeded far in advance of their fellow-legislators with regard to colonial affairs. He mentioned them, because, for the most part, they were men with whose political opinions it was his fate, commonly, or very frequently, to differ. Moreover, he thought that as the time of the greatest colonial freedom—the reign of Charles the Second—was eminently a Tory time, it was but fair, and in the spirit of equal justice, to render their due to men of quite a different political connection—some of the Radical Members of the British Parliament. Mr Hume,

Mr Roebuck, and a gentleman whose name had just been added to the list of the departed—Sir William Molesworth—were all of them great benefactors to their country by telling the truth upon the right method of colonial government, at a time when the truth was exceedingly unpopular. Of Sir William Molesworth he would say, that he had the greatest satisfaction in owning the benefit and instruction which, during many years, he had derived from personal communication with that distinguished man on colonial questions, and in acknowledging how much he had learned from the speeches which Sir William had delivered from time to time on subjects of colonial policy in the House of Commons.

In concluding his Chester address, Mr Gladstone said it was now coming to be understood that the affairs of the colonies were best transacted by the colonists themselves, as the affairs of England were best transacted by Englishmen. Upon this understanding they would act more and more, and with still increasing advantage. By all means, let English institutions be founded in the colonies to the utmost extent to which their circumstances were adapted. The main question was, Who was to be the judge of that extension? They at home were not good judges whether laws useful and convenient to England ought to prevail in the colonies or not. The colonists themselves were the best judges of that. Experience had proved that in order to strengthen the connection between the colonies and the Mother Country, and secure the adoption of British institutions in communities beyond the seas, the hated name of force and coercion, exercised by people at a distance over their rising fortunes, should never be invoked. Let the colonies be governed upon the principle of freedom; let them not feel any yoke upon their necks; let them understand that their relations with the old land were relations of affection, and Englishmen would assuredly reap a rich reward in the possession of that affection unbroken and unbounded. Defend them against aggression from without; regulate their foreign relations; but leave them their freedom of judgment. Then it would be hard to say when the day would come on which they would wish to separate from the great name of England. They coveted a share in that name, and in that feeling of theirs would be found the greatest security for the connection. The greatest purchasers of books relating to old English history were the Americans. The Americans who came over to England sought out and visited the scenes where the most remarkable events in British history had occurred, for they could not forget that they were equally the descendants of the men who had made that history. Let the name of England be made more and more an object of desire to the colonies. Their natural disposition was to love and revere it. The present and past year had afforded some proofs of that. Various colonies, some of them lying at the Antipodes, had offered their contributions to assist in supporting the wives and families of British soldiers, the heroes who had fallen in the Crimean war. This was one of the first fruits of the system upon which had been founded during recent years a rational mode of administering the affairs of the colonies without gratuitous interference. There was every encouragement for the extension of that system. There was so much union of feeling among the public and in Parliament with respect to it, that he trusted they might look forward with the utmost confidence to its prevalence and progress. For his part, he should ever thankfully rejoice to have lived in a period when so blessed a change in British colonial policy was brought about—a transition from misfortune and evil, in some cases from madness and crime, back to the rules of justice, reason, nature, and common-sense.

THE END.

INDEX

INDEX

ADELAIDE, 127.
Anstey, T. C., 244.
Archer, Mr Thomas, pioneer squatter, 117, 136, 201, 202.

BALLARAT goldfield, 121.
Barney, Lieutenant-Colonel, selected by Mr Gladstone as Superintendent of North Australia, 9; his military and colonial career, 37; sails from Sydney to found the Gladstone Colony, 39; untoward landing, 40; sworn in as Superintendent, 41; his administration attacked, 44; vindicates his principles and policy, 65; eulogises Port Curtis, 68.
Bigge, J. T., Imperial Commissioner, recommends settlement at Port Curtis, 14.
Blackall, Colonel, 244.
Blacks, fights with, 42, 77, 143, 144, 148, 200.
Booth, E. C., describes gold rush, 124; depicts influx of squatters to Gladstone country, 189.
Bourke, Sir Richard, Governor, advocates new colony in North Australia, 14.
Bowen, Sir George, Governor of Queensland, visits and describes town of Gladstone, 191.
Brisbane, 73, 76, 78, 101, 190, 191, 194.
Bury, Viscount, 248.

CALLIOPE River, named by Sir Charles Fitzroy, 82; district gazetted a goldfield, 194.
Canada, 225, 226, 259.
Chapel, W. C., discovers gold near Gladstone, 94, 95, 96, 98.
Chartist prisoners, 173.
Clarke, Rev. W. B., eminent geologist, 98.
Cooksland, suggested name of Gladstone Colony, 35.
Cowper, Sir Charles, 120.
Curtis, Port, selected as site of Gladstone Colony, 9; its discovery and previous history, 10; visited by Colonel Barney, 38; district opened up by squatters, 85; shipping activity, 97, 103, 107, 108.

DENISON, Sir William, appointed Governor of Van Diemen's Land, 52; despatches war vessel to relief of gold-diggers, 119; his strictures on the Australian digging population, 127.
De Winton, Major, sails for Port Curtis, 40; his military experiences, 175, 176, 177, 178; takes part in formation of Gladstone Colony, 181; hoists British flag on site of present town of Gladstone, 182; establishes friendly relations with the blacks, 184; returns to Sydney, 186.
Disraeli, Benjamin (afterwards Earl of Beaconsfield), 173, 251, 252, 253.

INDEX

EMIGRATION, discussed by Mr Gladstone, 259, 262.

FITZGERALD, Hon. J. E., 205.
Fitzroy, Governor Sir Charles, instructed by Mr Gladstone to form new colony, 23; censured by Earl Grey, 57; defends his proceedings, 58; proclaims increasing importance of Gladstone, 77; installs Sir Maurice O'Connell as Government Resident, 81; foreshadows gold discoveries, 82; predicts a prosperous future for Gladstone, 83.
Flinders, Captain Matthew, discovers Port Curtis, 10.
Foote, J. Y., on advantages of Gladstone Harbour, 194.
Forster, Hon. William, 76.
Franklin, Sir John, Governor of Van Diemen's Land, 151; shamefully treated by Lord Stanley, 172.
Friend, Henry, Gladstone pioneer, 193, 198, 199.
Frost, John, exiled Chartist leader, 173.

GLADSTONE, Right Hon. W. E., early intimate relations with the colonies, 1; becomes Secretary of State for the Colonies, 5; his despatches on the Transportation question, 6; establishes new penal colony of North Australia, 9; drafts its constitution, 23; develops its land policy, 29; defends his action in establishing North Australia, 61; his despatches on the probation system, 151; his recall of Sir Eardley Wilmot, 152; consequential painful controversy, 154, 155, 156, 157, 158, 159; defended by Sir Stafford Northcote, 164; deceived by informants, 167; his treatment of a Chartist exile, 173; receives letter from Sir George Bowen describing town of Gladstone, 191; expounds true principles of colonisation, 205; opposes nominee Upper Houses, 218; eulogises Constitution of United States, 219; criticises Colonial Chartered Companies, 220; on membership of House of Commons, 221; his maiden speech in Parliament, 223; introduces bill to improve emigrant ships, 224, 225; discusses Canadian affairs, 226, 227; presents petition from Cape Colony, 228; analyses relations between colonies and Mother Country, 230, 231; speeches in connection with Colonial Bishoprics' Fund, 232, 233, 234; contemplates eventual separation of the colonies, 235; condemns Imperial veto on colonial legislation, 237; claims Colonial Empire preserved by Liberal Party, 239; advocates extension of colonial self-government, 242, 243; supports inquiry into administration of colonies, 245; discusses abandonment of his North Australian colony, 246; speaks at inauguration of Royal Colonial Institute, 248, 249, 250; denounces Lord Beaconsfield's policy of colonial expansion, 251, 252; enunciates the colonial policy of the Liberal Party, 253; lectures on "The Colonial Policy of England," 255; delivers a second lecture on "Our Colonies," 257; gives reasons why possession of colonies desirable, 262, 263, 264; lessons from the loss of the American colonies, 265; rejoices in blessed transformation of colonial policy in his lifetime, 268, 269.
Gladstone Observer, 197.
Gladstone, town of, successfully established, 2; suggested seat of new bishopric, 3; requisites of site detailed by Mr Gladstone, 30; value of land in, 33; growth and development of, 71; strongly favoured by Sydney Government, 73; made a Government Residency, 74; first sale

of Government land in, 75; its growing importance, 77; visited by Governor Sir Charles Fitzroy, 80; influx of population, 83; alleged extravagant Governmental expenditure, 84; unprecedented rush of gold-diggers to, 93; exodus from the town to the goldfield, 96-103; suggested capital of Queensland, 129; its isolated position, 135; its physical environment, 139; its trading relations, 140; threatened with famine, 141; first local sale of Government lands, 142; demand for Parliamentary representation, 144; its freedom from native outrages, 149; British flag hoisted by Major de Winton, 182; interesting memento of first foundation, 186; revival of the town after the gold rush, 188; invasion of squatters, 189; candidate for capital of Queensland, 190; visited by Governor Sir George Bowen, 191; proclaimed a corporate town, 192; scenery described, 193; goldfields in neighbourhood, 195; local institutions, 196-198.

Gold fever, 100-128.

Graham, Sir James, approves plans of North Australia, 17; discusses Sir Eardley Wilmot's case, 163.

Grey, Earl, orders abandonment of Gladstone Colony, 51; his reasons for this action, 53; censures financial administration of the colony, 57.

Grey, Sir George, 229.

HAWES, Mr B.; on colonial defence, 240, 241.

Hay Brothers, pioneer squatters at Port Curtis, 85.

Herbert, Sir Robert, 74.

Hingston, E. P., his reminiscences of the gold rush, 128.

Hume, Joseph, 244, 267.

Humours of a gold rush, 112, 114, 131.

IMPERIAL veto on colonial legislation, 217, 237, 238.

KIRKPATRICK, W., Gladstone pioneer, his reminiscences, 199, 200.

LABOUCHERE, Mr H. (Lord Taunton), 247.

Lang, Andrew, 164.

Lang, Dr John Dunmore, his views on the Gladstone Colony, 35.

Littleton, Hon. H. S., on Gladstone industries, 194.

Lord Howe's Island, visited by Sir Charles Fitzroy, 82.

Lowe, Robert, Right Hon., leads popular agitation against Mr Gladstone's revival of Transportation, 8; assails Colonel Barney in prose and verse, 47; attacks Governor Sir George Gipps, 173; object of popular ovation in Sydney, 180.

Lyttelton, Lord, outlines constitution of Gladstone Colony, 51; one of the founders of New Zealand, 205.

M'CARTHY, JUSTIN, 257.

Mahon, Lord, attacks Earl Grey for abandoning the Gladstone Colony, 60.

Manning, Cardinal, 231, 233.

Martin, Sir James, 76.

Melbourne, 7, 101, 108, 125, 127, 129, 132.

Mitchell, Sir Thos. Livingstone, 141.

Molesworth, Sir William, 213, 215, 244, 245, 268.

Moran, Cardinal, interesting historical discovery, 3.

Morgan, Mount, 134.

Mort, T. S., 85.

Mossman, Samuel, prophesies metropolitan honours for Gladstone, 129.

NATIVE police, their remarkable qualities, 78.

Newport, Chartist riot at, 173.

New South Wales, evolution of, 22.

Nisbet, W. D., reports on Gladstone Harbour, 197, 198.
Norfolk Island, 16.
North Australia, colony of, Mr Gladstone's most interesting experiment, 2; the theatre of his Transportation policy, 9; discussed by Lord Stanley, 15; approved by Sir James Graham, 17; sanctioned by Lords of Treasury, 21; constituted by Mr Gladstone, 23; established by Colonel Barney, 41; assailed by Robert Lowe, 47; vetoed by Earl Grey, 51; expenses of founding, 57; referred to by Mr Gladstone in Parliament, 246.
Northcote, Sir Stafford (afterwards Earl of Iddesleigh), publishes pamphlet in defence of Mr Gladstone, 164; describes Mr Gladstone's mental characteristics, 165.

O'CONNELL, Sir Maurice, appointed Government Resident at Gladstone, 74; opens up the Port Curtis country, 76; formally installed by Sir Charles Fitzroy, 81; assailed by Sir Henry Parkes, 84; officially reports payable gold in Gladstone district, 93; effects of his despatch, 101; reports progressive increase of gold production, 102; alarmed at enormous influx of diggers, 112, 116; pacifies excited concourse, 123, 132; his correspondence, 135; his difficulties with black police, 137, 138; describes country around Gladstone, 139; discusses plans of Gladstone with Sir T. L. Mitchell, 141; replies to attacks of Sir Henry Parkes, 142; his official expenditure as Government Resident, 143; deprecates reduction of Gladstone defensive force, 144; acts as district mailman, 145; his authoritative account of the gold discovery, 146; reviews his career as Government Resident, 148.

O'Donovan, Denis, 135.
Oxley, John, 11, 13.

PAKINGTON, Sir John, 222.
Parkes, Sir Henry, 72, 83, 84.
Peel, Sir Robert, 162, 173.
Pioneer, adventures of a, 86.
Pioneer settlers, privations of, 42.
Polding, Archbishop, 3, 76.
Praed, Mrs Campbell, 193.
Probation system, 150, 151, 153, 169.

QUEENSLAND, 35, 71.
Queenslander, newspaper, on the future of Gladstone, 203, 204.

ROBERTSON, Sir John, 101.
Rockhampton, 145, 188, 191, 194, 198.
Roebuck, J. A., 163, 263, 268.
Rosebery, Lord, 1.
Royal Colonial Institute, 248, 250.
Russell, Lord John, proposes penal colony in North Australia, 14; defends Sir Eardley Wilmot, 162; advocates enlargement of colonial freedom, 248.

SCOTT, Hon. Francis, criticises formation of Gladstone Colony, 239, 240.
Selwyn, Bishop, Mr Gladstone's early friend, 205, 234.
Separation of colonies, Mr Gladstone's ideas upon, 225, 230, 235, 242, 254.
Sinnett, Frederick, historian of the Gladstone gold rush, 105; his description of the diggings, 112.
Squatters occupy country around Gladstone, 59, 71, 78, 85, 93, 189.
Stanley, Captain Owen, 69.
Stanley, Lord (afterwards Earl of Derby), suggests new penal colony in North Australia, 15; answers objections, 16; eulogises British colonisation, 19; establishes probation system, 150; brings case of Sir Eardley Wilmot before the House of Lords, 161; his inconsiderate treatment of Sir John Franklin, 172

Stutchbury, W., discovers gold near Gladstone, 200.

Sugar cultivation in Gladstone district, 195.

Sydney, returns Robert Lowe, 9; excited by gold discoveries in Gladstone district, 100; raises fund for relief of luckless diggers, 121.

Sydney Morning Herald strongly opposes formation of Gladstone Colony, 45; defends Sir Charles Fitzroy, 59; announces rich discovery of gold in Gladstone district, 94; advocates caution, 96; indicates Gladstone as destined northern metropolis, 97; describes rush of gold-diggers as astounding, 103; moralises on the rush, 120.

TRAILL, H. D., 172.

Transportation justified by Mr Gladstone, 27, 151.

UNIACKE, JOHN, his early description of Port Curtis, 12.

VAN DIEMEN'S LAND, desperate condition of, 6; Mr Gladstone's measures for its relief, 7; steps taken by Lord Stanley, 17; urgency recognised by Lords of Treasury, 21; exceptional difficulties of situation, 168, 169; Chartist leaders exiled to, 173.

Victoria, 129.

WARD, F. W., on future of Gladstone, 203.

Western Australia, expense of penal establishment in, 54.

Williams, Zephaniah, Chartist exile, performs act of bravery, 173.

Wilmot, Sir Eardley, appointed Governor of Van Diemen's Land, 151; recalled by Mr Gladstone, 152; receives "secret" letter from Mr Gladstone, 153; indignant denial of charges in "secret" letter, 154, 155, 156; sympathy of leading officials and colonists, 157; acquitted by Mr Gladstone, 159; his pitiful death, 160; his case discussed in Imperial Parliament, 161, 162, 163; his case reviewed in a pamphlet by Sir Stafford Northcote, 164; opinions of local historian, 168.

www.ingramcontent.com/pod-product-compliance
Lightning Source LLC
Chambersburg PA
CBHW032112230426
43672CB00009B/1708